THE PRIMACY OF SEMIOSIS:
AN ONTOLOGY OF RELATIONS

How do things come to stand for something other than themselves? An understanding of the ontology of relations allows for a compelling account of the action of signs. *The Primacy of Semiosis* is concerned with the ontology of relations and semiosis, the action of signs. Drawing upon the work of Gilles Deleuze, John Deely, and John Poinsot, Paul Bains focuses on the claim that relations are 'external' to their terms, and seeks to give an ontological account of this purported externality of relations.

Bains develops the proposition, first made in 1632 by John Poinsot (John of St Thomas), that, ontologically, signs are relations whose whole being is in *esse ad* ('being-toward'). Furthermore, relations are found to be univocal in their being as relations. This univocity of being is antecedent to the division between '*ens rationis*' and '*ens reale.*' The ontology of relations Bains presents is thus neither mind-dependent nor mind-independent insofar as the rationale of the relation is concerned.

The Primacy of Semiosis provides a semiotic that subverts the opposition between realism and idealism, one in which what have been called 'nature' and 'culture' interpenetrate in an expanding collective of human and non-human. Bains's work promises to be a touchstone for semiotic discussion for years to come.

(Toronto Studies in Semiotics and Communication)

PAUL BAINS is an independent scholar living in Perth, Australia.

PAUL BAINS

The Primacy of Semiosis
An Ontology of Relations

UNIVERSITY OF TORONTO PRESS
Toronto Buffalo London

© University of Toronto Press 2006
Toronto Buffalo London
www.utppublishing.com

Reprinted in paperback 2014

ISBN 978-0-8020-9003-4 (cloth)
ISBN 978-1-4426-2698-0 (paper)

Toronto Studies in Semiotics and Communication
Editors: Marcel Danesi, Umberto Eco, Paul Perron, Peter Schulz, and Roland Posner

---

Library and Archives Canada Cataloguing in Publication

Bains, Paul
   The primacy of semiosis : an ontology of relations / Paul Bains.

(Toronto studies in semiotics and communication)
Includes bibliographical references and index.
ISBN 978-0-8020-9003-4 (bound). – ISBN 978-1-4426-2698-0 (pbk.)

1. Semiotics. 2. Ontology. I. Title. II. Series: Toronto studies in semiotics and communication.

P99.B23 2006   121'.68   C2006-900496-X

University of Toronto Press acknowledges the financial assistance to its publishing program of the Canada Council for the Arts and the Ontario Arts Council.

  Canada Council   Conseil des Arts
for the Arts   du Canada

University of Toronto Press acknowledges the financial support of the Government of Canada through the Canada Book Fund for its publishing activities.

*This book is dedicated to
Lina, Dani, and Manu
for being there.*

Contents

Preface ix

Abbreviations xi

Introduction: The Drama of Relation and Its Characters 3

1 An Even Briefer History of Relations 15
  Terminology 18
  Discussion in and after the Latin West 19

2 Deleuze and External (or Ontological) Relations 25
  The Circle of the Proposition 30
  The Complex Theme of the Proposition 32

3 Poinsot and Deely on Relations and Signs 39
  Objective Being 42
  The Doctrine of 'Species' 45
  Ideas 46
  Formal Signs 49
  Scotist and Thomist Accounts 51
  Objective Being as *Umwelt* 57

4 *Umwelten* 59
  Jakob von Uexküll and *Umwelten* 59
  The Tick as an Interpreter – the Functional Cycle 62
  Deleuze and Guattari's Appropriation 64
  Contemporary Value and Semiotic Use 66

Species-Specific Objective Worlds   74
Heideggerean *Umwelten*   78
The Transformation of *Umwelt* into *Lebenswelt*   83

5 Autopoiesis and Languaging   85
Background and Context   85
Cognitive Systems   92
Living Systems   95
Languaging   103

Conclusion   133

Notes   145

Bibliography   167

Index   177

Preface

The Primacy of Semiosis is concerned with the ontology of relations and semiosis (the action of signs). The book focuses on the claim that relations are 'external' to their terms and seeks to give an ontological account of this purported externality of relations. The argument is that an understanding of the ontology of relations allows for a compelling account of the action of signs, that is, how things come to stand for something other than themselves.

In this book, I develop the creative proposition, first made by John Poinsot (aka John of St Thomas) in 1632, that ontologically, signs are relations (whose whole being is in 'being-toward' – *esse ad*). Furthermore, relations are univocal in their being as relations. This univocity of being is antecedent to the division between *ens rationis* and *ens reale*. Thus the ontology of relations presented here is neither mind-dependent nor mind-independent insofar as the rationale of the relation is concerned.

Three principal theorists are invoked in this account: Gilles Deleuze, John Poinsot, and John Deely argue that there is a compatibility and mutual enrichment between Deleuze's account of relations and the relatively unknown semiotic of the late-Latin scholastic John Poinsot (as translated and interpreted by the contemporary post-Peircian semiotician, John Deely).

To further illuminate this material and the relevance of an ontology of relations for cognition and theories of language, I give an account of the ethologist Jakob von Uexküll's *Umwelt* sign theory and of the biologist Humberto Maturana's autopoietic theory of 'languaging.'

In engaging with this subject matter, the book presents a semiotic that subverts the opposition between realism and idealism. In other words, it presents a semiotic that is as real as it is ideal, that is, a semiotic in which what have been called 'nature' and 'culture' interpenetrate (à la Bruno Latour) in an expanding collective of humans and non-humans.

In conclusion, in addition to emphasizing the ethico-political implications of this ontology of relations, the book makes suggestions for interdisciplinary research that would complement and further develop this work.

Abbreviations

ATP   Gilles Deleuze and Félix Guattari. *A Thousand Plateaus: Capitalism and Schizophrenia*, trans. Brian Massumi. London: Athlone Press, 1984.
D   Gilles Deleuze and Claire Parnet, *Dialogues*, trans. Hugh Tomlinson and Barbara Habberjam. New York: Columbia University Press, 1987.
DR   Gilles Deleuze. *Difference and Repetition*, trans. Paul Patton. London: Athlone Press, 1994.
FCM   Martin Heidegger. *The Fundamental Concepts of Metaphysics: World, Finitude, Solitude*. Indianapolis: Indiana University Press, 1995.
GL   Keith Ansell Pearson. *Germinal Life: The Difference and Repetition of Deleuze*. London: Routledge, 1999.
LS   Gilles Deleuze. *The Logic of Sense*, trans. Mark Lester with Charles Stivale, ed. Constantin V. Boundas, New York: Columbia University Press, 1990.
NB   John Deely. *New Beginnings: Early Modern Philosophy and Postmodern Thought*. Toronto: University of Toronto Press, 1994.
TDS   John Poinsot. *Tractatus de Signis*, arranged in bilingual format by John Deely in consultation with Ralph A. Powell. Berkeley: University of California Press, 1985.
WIP   Gilles Deleuze and Félix Guattari. *What Is Philosophy?* trans. Graham Burchell and Hugh Tomlinson. London: Verso, 1994.

THE PRIMACY OF SEMIOSIS:
AN ONTOLOGY OF RELATIONS

Introduction: The Drama of Relation and Its Characters

Inter-esse – To be between – To be interesting

Relations are in the middle and exist as such.

Deleuze (1987, 55)

How what one does interests others, how it 'counts' for others, is not opposed to, but rather an element in the way one becomes interested in what one does. Who is interested, how can one interest others, at what price and according to what methods and constraints? These are not secondary questions relating to the 'diffusion' of knowledge. They are ingredients of its identity, of the manner whereby it exists for others and situates them.

Stengers (1996, 48–9; my translation)

This work is about the being and dynamic becoming of relations and that which is relative – in particular, the relations among things, objects of thought, and signs. It is an exploration into the ontological principle of the univocity of being and non-being, that is, a hunt for the single voice that raises the clamour of being (Gille Deleuze's quest in *Difference and Repetition*); for a fundamental onto-logic or, rather, semiotic, that should, as Heidegger notes in his introduction to *Being and Time*, pay heed to Aristotle's problem of the unity of Being as over against the multiplicity of categories applicable to things. We are going to get positively medieval and attempt to achieve the clarity that Heidegger claims the Thomist and Scotist schools never had.

Why write about the being of relation? I will take the risk of claiming that the concept of relation is like a skeleton or abstract key that allows us to move from Duns Scotus to John Poinsot, to Charles Sanders Peirce, to Gilles Deleuze and Félix Guattari, Immanuel Kant, Humberto Maturana, Martin Heidegger, John Deely, Alfred North Whitehead, Bruno Latour, and Isabelle Stengers (to mention a few members of the cast). All these thinkers are in one way or another concerned with relations and their being. Their understanding of the being of relation will determine the structure of their thought and the extent to which it is able to short-circuit the realist/idealist oscillation in Western philosophy; to provide the ontological foundations *in relation* both for a minimal correspondence between thought and things and for its more complex reformulation in terms of a collective of humans and nonhumans involved in a double individuation, a conjoined genesis of subject and object – in other words, what Deleuze and Guattari call the 'truth of the relative' rather than 'the relativity of truth' (1994, 130). The inherent subjectivism of some modern and much postmodern thought (in its assumption that language and thought can have no relation to anything other than their own products) has yet to wake up to this possibility. What will thus be envisioned is what postmodernism might turn out to be (using John Deely's Latin construction in the subjunctive mood – *Quid sit postmodernismus?*)[1] if not a circular, or more complex, dead end.

This focus on the being of relations was not the target of my original research. Initially I was exploring the kind of vitalist ontology that can be found in Deleuze and Guattari's work, together with some of their sources of influence, in particular the work of the philosopher and 'psychobiologist' Raymond Ruyer. However, the more I read and thought about their work and its conceptual geography or 'ecology of ideas,' the more I became persuaded that the question of the ontology of relations was crucial to understanding the dynamics of their thought; more generally, this question also provided an astoundingly fruitful way of approaching the history of philosophy – all the more so when one becomes aware that the possibility of external relations has been largely denied in modern thought from Ockam to Kant, with the notable exceptions of John Poinsot (on whom more later), William James, Bertrand Russell (in his work on external relations), and Deleuze and Guattari, whose philosophy is always concerned with relations (or *interbeing*) in one way or another. Interbeing: the 'hallucination point of thought,' as Deleuze puts it, that is repugnant to thought yet which thought must be forced to think.

So this work is concerned with the being of external relations – and for a particular reason. I will argue (à la Poinsot and Deely) that without an understanding of what external relations *do*, it is impossible to have a coherent account of the action of signs (semiosis); furthermore, without this understanding we cannot know how we communicate, nor can we understand the being of our experience – how we become with the world. This book will constantly emphasize the semiotic realization that 'ideas' or 'concepts' are signs, provenating relations that produce awareness of something other than themselves, rather than being the direct objects of our awareness (as assumed in the inherently subjectivist, classical modern philosophy of, for example, Descartes and Locke).[2]

As I have mentioned, this concern with relations emerged slowly during my research period and in a sense forced itself upon me. I was not looking for it. In retrospect, what happened was that while I sought ways to organize my research materials – that is, to relate them and find a plot – it became more and more apparent that the being of relations and what they do was the main story that had to be told.

What came as a surprise was that this story seemed to be taking me away from the almost standard approach to semiotics (the study of the action of signs) that was being presented in the contemporary academy. It became apparent that the works of Peirce and his major historical predecessor, Poinsot (1589–1644), were relevant to an understanding of what Deleuze and Guattari were doing in their work and that there was little material on Deleuze and Guattari that seriously engaged with relations. This is not to say that there was no material that affirmed the importance of external relations for Deleuze; just that this material never really clarified what external relations were in their proper being.[3] For that matter, neither do Deleuze and Guattari really elaborate on this 'logic of relations.'

A word of warning. I make no claims to absolute mastery of the materials engaged with in the pages that follow. I present here a tentative exploration of a logic and critique that I had been largely unacquainted with and that woke me up from a certain undogmatic confusion. I will indicate where I feel that further research would be valuable – research that time constraints or my personal capacities did not allow. No doubt the reader will find many other questions that should be ignored or, perchance, pursued.

One of the factors that drove me to look more closely at the status of relations and semiosis in Deleuze and Guattari's work is the following: Deleuze's constant emphasis on external relations, which he says he unearthed in the work of Hume and which he regards as Hume's great discovery. This is surely one of the best examples of Deleuze mounting on the back of another philosopher and producing an immaculate conception. The following extract from Deleuze (1995, 5–6) gives some insight into this process and to many of the themes of this book:

> I belong to a generation, one of the last generations, that was more or less bludgeoned to death with the history of philosophy. History of philosophy plays a patently repressive role in philosophy; it's philosophy's own version of the Oedipus complex. 'You can't seriously consider saying what you yourself think until you've read this and that, and that on this, and this on that.' Many members of my generation never broke free of this; others did, by inventing their own particular methods and new rules, a new approach. I myself 'did' history of philosophy for a long time, read books on this or that author. But I compensated in various ways: by concentrating, in the first place, on authors who challenged the rationalist tradition in this history (and I see a secret link between Lucretius, Hume, Spinoza, and Nietzsche, constitued by their critique of negativity, their cultivation of joy, the hatred of interiority, the externality of forces and relations, the denunciation of power ... and so on) [...] But I suppose the main way I coped with it at that time was to see the history of philosophy as a kind of buggery, or (it comes to the same thing), immaculate conception. I saw myself as taking an author from behind and giving him a child that would be his own offspring, yet monstrous.

I have not been bludgeoned to death by the history of philosophy. In fact, one of my main introductions to philosophy was Deleuze and Guattari's *A Thousand Plateaus*. But during my time in the contemporary academy (primarily in Australia), I could not help but notice a certain detour of thought that has occurred through the dissemination of something called 'postmodern theory.' This 'theory' often appears ignorant of Peirce, and would certainly know little or nothing of the semiotic of Poinsot's *Tractatus de Signis* (1632),[4] which, as Deely puts it in his 'Editorial Afterword' to the first bilingual edition, 'is nothing less than a judicious assessment of the philosophical and theological thought of the Latin West, taken in its historical totality as synthesizing influences of ancient Greece, Rome, Byzantium (Constantinople), and Islam.'

For the present I simply note that Deleuze's 'hatred of interiority' and his development or 'buggery'[5] of the Stoic incorporeals into an abstract semiotic machine of language would have found an unexpected ally in

Poinsot – and that Guattari, in his final work, *Chaosmosis* (1995, 30), would have found in Poinsot one of the greatest theorists of the 'incorporeal and virtual part of assemblages of enunciation,' which traditional scholastic realism – and, of course, certainly not nominalism (the 'modern' way of William of Ockham) – could truly grasp.

Other theorists who will emerge during this study include the ethologist Jakob von Uexküll, with particular reference to his concept of *Umwelten* (species-specific worlds), which provides a fine way of appreciating how experiential worlds are constructed that are neither objective nor subjective in terms of the traditional modern dichotomy, but that operate with a trichotomy or triadic relation involving the organism experiencing, the object experienced, and the basis on which the object exists as experienced – namely, the sign relation. The *relation* in which the sign consists is the refrain of this book.

In order to articulate the being proper to this relation, we will start, in chapter 1, with a short history of the concept of relation, using Julius R. Weinberg and Deely as our principal guides. Weinberg's essay 'The Concept of Relation' (1965) is one of the rare works that thematically considers this question.

This will allow us to re-enter the *Umwelt* of Deleuze and Guattari with a greater appreciation of what they are doing in developing an event-centred ontology based on the univocity of being that transcends the distinction between 'mind-dependent being,' or *ens rationis*, and mind-independent being, or *ens reale*, rather than an ontology focused primarily on *ens reale* or mind-independent being (such as Aristotelian substance), or an epistemology based on *ens rationis* (Kant). This will allow us also to see how other theorists, such as Humberto Maturana and Francisco Varela, deal with the question of relation and semiosis and the extent to which they succeed in extricating their analyses from idealism or realism.

Thus a search for a univocal logic of relations indifferent to being 'in voce' or 'in re' and prior to this distinction: 'If Being is the unique event in which all events communicate with one another, univocity refers both to what occurs and to what is said ... Univocal Being inheres in language and happens to things; it measures the internal relation of language with the external relation of Being. Neither active nor passive, univocal Being is neutral. It is *extra-Being*, that is, the minimum of Being common to the real, the possible, and the impossible' (Deleuze 1990, 180).

By concentrating on a largely ignored ontology of relations we will become acquainted with a semiotic that is irreducible to a realism (in which 'reality' is an external 'given' untainted by observation), an idealism (in which 'reality' is a consequence of mental acts), or even a Kantianism (in which what the mind knows is more its own workings than exteriority): 'It is something much richer than either reduction, something more collusive even than the rapport between fly trap and fly in the realm of insects and flowers. It is, in a phrase, semiotic reality, the true reality of human experience, wherein the line between what is dependent upon and what is independent of interpretive activity can never be finally drawn, because that very line itself shifts with each new achievement of understanding whether "speculative" or "practical"' (Deely 1988b, 72).

This is more than interesting, because it inexorably leads us to an image of thought that is not restricted to the representation, correspondence, or adequation of a pregiven known to a pregiven knower, but that consists rather in the reciprocal production and specification, or 'double individuation' of the knower and the known. Ultimately, this involves an ontological or semiotic relation in place of a purely epistemological one.

But what were the steps to this new image of thought, which in hindsight appears so *obvious*? There is no problem of knowledge if we are not 'inside,' isolated behind a screen of representations, and the world is not 'outside' and intrinsically unknowable *as a matter of principle*.[6]

As already mentioned, the question of relations forced itself upon me as a problem that mutated into the focus of my research; it was not simply a question of how to organize and relate together a variety of materials. Deleuze's constant insistence on the 'exteriority' of relations to their terms as essential for any pluralistic philosophy that affirms the possibility of constructing novel relations not derived from the 'essence' of things, seemed worthy of thought. For Deleuze, James, and Russell (among others), Hegel's thought assumes that there *must* be an absolute, self-enclosed system with no loose ends, wherein everything is internally related in a single, all-inclusive whole – that is, like a pool of treacle, as opposed to an irregular mosaic without a bedding but with relations that are distinct from the relative pieces. Neither a One nor a Many, but rather a 'fusional' Multiplicity for which a logic of relations irreducible to their terms (although existentially inseparable from them) is required. The trick is to realize that 'things' cannot be understood apart from their relations, or assemblages, but that this does not require one great big only-internally-related blob. We do not have to choose between complete disunion and complete union.

My hope is that some novel relations will be constructed throughout this reflection and engagement with relations. Michel Serres, who saw his work as a 'general theory of relations,' notes that 'relations are, in fact, ways of moving from place to place, or of wandering' (Serres and Latour 1995, 103). I am glad to have wandered with relations. They always took me somewhere unexpected in an open multiplicity that could not be totalized by any addition, and in which subtraction always left a remainder.

This particular trip or stroll went the following way, although it always overtook and surprised the non-punctiform 'me' and made the multiplicity that I am become something else again, in the laying down of a path through walking it:

Following Deleuze's hatred of interiority and his suggestion that relations be made 'the hallucination point of thought,' it seemed necessary to look more closely at the ontological status of relations. It 'occurred' to me (or *it* happened to me) that Deely's detour by way of John Poinsot's *Tractatus de Signis*, and the ontology of relations contained therein, provided a fascinating complement to Deleuze's *univocal* ontology, which had been inspired, in part, by Duns Scotus and Avicenna.

Poinsot's genius lay in moving *from* a theory of relations (in which all of reality is composed of two kinds of relative beings: [1] individuals, who are relative – i.e., who cannot be understood apart from their relations, and [2] their actual external or ontological relations – e.g., the eye, which cannot be understood apart from its relation to light) *towards* a semiotic in which concepts (as signs) are relations that bring into awareness something other than themselves. Furthermore – and this is perhaps the crucial insight – ontological relations are *univocal* in their being. They are indifferent, or superordinate, to the division of being into *ens reale* and *ens rationis*. A relation is a relation whether it is assumed to exist extramentally or intramentally. Its foundations or conditions are external to the relation itself, and it is this uniqueness of the ontological status of relations that allows them to 'pass' freely between 'mind' and 'matter.' Relations do not respect any ontological Iron Curtain. This is what allows for a 'realistic realism' (à la Latour), or for a compenetration in experience between mind and nature that knows no final boundary (à la Deely); it also allows for a semiotic reality or collective in a process of *becoming* that is generative of relations. In fact, as Deely emphasizes, Poinsot's ontological analysis of signs as relations only develops its full power when there is included within it a post-Peircian analysis of how signs *become*, or grow, and how they can do this without the need for physically existent terms.

The difficulty of engaging with Poinsot is that he walks a tightrope between Scotism and Thomism (something that, perhaps for economy of presentation or didactic clarity, Deely tends to gloss over). Poinsot allows for representation (*esse repraesentatum*), but cognition does not terminate in a representation or first become aware of the representation as an instrumental sign. The representation is treated as a formal sign (ontological relation) that disappears before its object, and an object is anything to the extent that it is a terminus of a relation of feeling or cognition. Things are first of all objects, but this does not stop the objects of awareness from also being things that exist independently of the awareness in which they are partially objects as well. Representations found a relation to something other than themselves, and when that object is physically existent the relation is also a physical relation allowing for knowledge of something not simply contained within an intramental sphere. A knowledge of an extra- (or pre-) mental world is possible, because the ontological relation is indifferent to what is and what is not independent of thought.[7] None of this precludes an awareness of objects that have no physical existence.

Without daring to give a 'scholastic' account,[8] and restricting ourselves to the notion of objective being, we can say that Duns Scotus certainly diverges from classical Thomism in developing the notion of objective being (*esse objectivum*) as entitatively immanent to the knower. *Scotus identifies the notion of concept (i.e., that which is known) with objective being*, which is constituted in and by the intellect. It is an 'intelligible' representative imitation, or a resemblance that corresponds in me to something outside of me.

Poinsot attempts in an original way to avoid the concept of entitative immanence by developing an account of the concept (expressed *species* or 'specifying form') as a formal sign. All of these perhaps unfamiliar terms will be explained later in the text. Although Poinsot retains objective being, it is not entitatively immanent but suprasubjective (like the *Umwelt*). It is not the concept, as formal sign, that is known, but rather objective being as a pattern of univocal relations, some of which may also at the same time be physical relations. In this sense, objective being is not representative. It is not a middle term that is known first and then on the basis of which something else might be known. It is a pure 'nonmediating' relation – it does not get in the way. Thus, Poinsot seeks to retain a certain Thomistic realism, while at the same time, and perhaps in spite of himself, he opens the way for a semiotic in which concepts are formal signs that bring into awareness something other than themselves – but these 'objects' need not have extramental, physical existence, or they may mix up physical and ideal being.

As Deely notes (1998, 233), a knowledge of 'essences' is not 'a special intuition, or immediate insight *into* what things are "beyond their sensible appearances." On the contrary, a "grasp of an essence" normally consists in those very sensible appearances themselves subsumed under the pattern of a set of relations abstractly taken apart from the instances, and supposed to consider the unique character of some object, whether real or fictional.' Or as Deleuze and Guattari would say: 'The concept speaks the event, not the essence or the thing' (WIP, 21). Thus, the bird as an event or pattern of relations – colours, postures, songs.

Through a study of the concept of *Umwelten* as species-specific *objective* worlds, all these ontological and semiotic issues become more concrete. The *Umwelt* is rescued from Jacob von Uexküll's overly subjectivist (Kantian) interpretation and becomes no longer a subjective bubble, but rather a limitless interface through which ontological or 'pure' relations and 'becomings' easily 'pass.' This does not mean that relations now move from a closed, monadic subjectivity to an extramental world. Subjectivity is constitutively open, or has a being-toward, as do all relative beings. *Umwelten* are suprasubjective. All of this amounts to a semiotic wherein (as Guattari emphasized in his final work, *Chaosmosis* [1995, 22]) the interpretant of the Peircian triad is foregrounded as the active mediator between the physical universe of things and the objective universe that includes things but is not reducible to them. This is an expanded conception of subjectivity that includes not only words and images but all the 'machinations' that go to make up those words and images. We are semiotic, existential terrritories rather than brains in vats, and these territories or ecologies are not contained within our physical anatomy, nor are they known only as immanent representations. The question becomes this: Where does your cognition or subjectivity terminate if it is a suprasubjective process and not a stable substance? The 'self' becomes a sign *relation* or interpretant rather than an unrelated, ontological entity.

What is being constantly emphasized is a kind of semiotic ontology in which relations become crucial at every level of analysis and allow for the interweaving of corporeal and incorporeal factors. Relations are an intrinsic dimension of being, and every being becomes the active centre of a web of relations with other beings. The relations are, however, in what they are as relations, suprasubjective. They are not reducible to the relative being that enters into or generates these relations. A dilemma of much thought is the difficulty of thinking beyond the One or the Many and entertaining the concept of a multiplicity of different things or beings that are nevertheless in mobile relationships – the concept of a place where, *sometimes with the greatest difficulty,* new relationships can be constructed. As Guattari so often emphasized, this amounts to an 'ethico-aesthetic paradigm' in which one takes responsibility for the relations and existential territories, or worlds, that one seeks to construct with others (whether human or non-human).

Autopoietic theory provides an interesting contemporary version of *Umwelt* theory; and if one ignores many of Maturana's idealistic statements, which make cognition a closed bubble (à la von Uexküll), it can offer valuable distinctions – in particular, the distinction between an organism and its relational domain, or domain of interactions. Thus, 'behaviour' is a relation between a living system and its medium, and therefore behaviour does not take place in the anatomo-physiological domain of the organism. The analysis of language as a relational activity, and the claim that objects and consciousness arise in languaging, are also compatible with many aspects of the semiotic approach with which we have engaged.

The problem is always the 'radical' constructivism that Maturana espouses, in which there can never be an aspectual coincidence or compenetration between objects of awareness and things of a prejacent environment. Maturana thinks that we live in a bubble of cognition and that we can say nothing about the 'substratum that we need for epistemological reasons.' Varela has certainly distanced himself from this approach, and seeks to develop a 'naturalized phenomenology' or enactive approach that has definite affinities with Guattari's work. In fact, Guattari refers to the work of Maturana and Varela in *Chaosmosis*, arguing that the concept of autopoiesis deserves to be rethought. Isabelle Stengers makes similar claims in *Cosmopolitiques* (1996), arguing that we should be wary of Maturana's general epistemology. To be fair to Maturana, he will argue that they have misunderstood him and not appreciated the distinction he makes between the autopoietic system and its domain of relations. To be fair to Maturana's critics, these distinctions are often made in seminars or articles that are not easily available. In any case, it is significant that Guattari sought to make use of an enlarged concept of autopoiesis and certainly entered into dialogue with Varela. One of the main points of intersection in their work is the notion of 'enaction,' or reciprocal specification between knower and known, rather than adequate representation of a pregiven world wherein knowledge becomes ontological and truth becomes production – and all the more real for that. Here, perhaps, there is a tension with Deely's early attachment to the language of truth as adequation – a term he uses to assert the interpenetration of the physical and ideal, or *physis* and *nous*. However, Deely's work, taken as a whole in its processual dimension, seems to be compatible with the semiotic and ontologic of Deleuze and Guattari, and vice versa. This is not to suggest that they say the same things (which would not be very interesting), but rather that there is a compatibility between them – particularly at an ethico-political level where we take responsibility for the collective worlds or *Umwelts/Lebenswelten*, be they corporeal or incorporeal, that we co-construct with *others* (be they human or otherwise) in the micro- and macro-politics of everyday existence. What world do we want to invent and make exist collectively? Guattari (1995, 83) tells us: 'I is an other, a multiplicity of others, embodied at the intersection of partial components of enunciation, breaching on all sides individuated identity and the organized body. The cursor of chaosmosis never stops oscillating between these diverse enunciative nuclei – not in order to totalize them, synthesize them in a transcendent self, but in spite of everthing, to make a world of them.'

I will take the risk of claiming that the following pages constitute faltering steps towards a novel relational corpus of knowledges and practices that need to be developed collectively by a community of inquirers. Philosophy requires invention in order to stay alive, and if these kinds of less familiar materials are not engaged with, philosophy risks becoming solely 'history of philosophy,' taught by apparently subtle connoisseurs of particular doctrines, when in fact philosophy can be (and sometimes is) a creative and experimental metaphysical activity enriching the life of a collective of humans and non-humans.

1 An Even Briefer History of Relations

> It will be readily admitted that the concept of relation ... is fundamental to modern science, logic, and philosophy. There is no doubt, also, that the need for this concept has been felt throughout the history of civilization since the time of the Greeks. It is not, however, so readily admitted or much realized that many aspects of ancient, medieval, and early modern philosophy prevented a clear understanding of this concept.
>
> Weinberg (1965, 61)

> Relations are in the middle and exist as such. This exteriority of relations is not a principle, it is a vital protest against principles. Indeed if one sees in it something which runs through life, but which is repugnant to thought, then thought must be forced to think it, one must make relations the hallucination point of thought.
>
> Deleuze and Parnet (1987, 55)

This chapter is not intended (assuming this were possible) to give anything like a complete philosophical history of relations. Its purpose is to provide a brief account of the 'classical' theory of relations insofar as it is relevant to this book.[1]

As Weinberg (1965, 68) notes, Aristotle's views on the subject of relations have affected 'almost everything that has been said on the subject for the past two thousand years.' So we will start with Aristotle, particularly as this affords us a manner of entry into the central concerns of Poinsot's *Tractatus de Signis*.

Aristotle is interested in the really real – that is, the way things are independently of the mind – *extra-animam*. He uses the term 'substance' for the purported individual things or fundamental natural units that are assumed to have independent existence – for example, 'Socrates and this ox here.' The problem with this way of approaching things is that relations between individual substances become metaphysical nuisances. (Whitehead develops his philosophy of organism through a sustained critique of this concept of substance, which he replaces with 'events' in relation as the ultimate units of natural occurrence. Deleuze and Guattari also propose an event-centred ontology, with due reference to Whitehead.) What we need is a philosophy of the event that ousts the verb 'to be' and its attributes.

Aristotle thought that these ultimate substances had a basic enduring self-identity that could be affected by a number of 'accidents' or manners of being – for example, quantity, quality, position, when, where, relation – that were dependent on substance. Thus the affections were accidental in character. This is the Aristotilean categorial schema. A substance as such must be changeless and any changes can only be *in other features (accidents) which are not essential to the underlying 'changelessness' of the entity or substance.* Whitehead and Deleuze and Guattari's ontology (or schizoscholasticism) is largely based on abandoning the notion of an unchanging subject of change (a subject and its attributes or predicates) for situations in which entities become individuated and exist through intrinsic processes of change or becoming wherein each entity or existential territory cannot be understood apart from its relations with others.

What we need to be clear about for our present purposes is what may turn out to be the peculiar notion of relation in the Aristotelian categories ... and the fact that, as Weinberg (1965, 63) notes, very few philosophers seem to have realized why 'relations cannot really be fitted into a substance-accident ontology.' Remember that for Kant, categories were things of the mind, or mental entities – the subjective forms of understanding – whereas for Aristotle the mind did not impose its own relations on the sensory manifold. Aristotle, in 'realist' mode, claimed to have discovered pre-existing relations existing independently of human thought. Kant, as the quintessential classical modern philosopher, claimed that relations are the product of the mind's own constructions, since the mind can know nothing of an order of being *that would not be changed by being known.* Kant's categories only apply to appearances, or *phenomena*, never to a mind-independent order of being. As might become mind-blowingly evident, neither of these alternatives is adequate in accounting for our experience or for describing how semiosis (the action of signs) actually works.

As we have noted, in the Aristotelian schema all the categories of being, other than primary substance, are dependent and accidental. What is significant is that Aristotle included a category of 'the relative' as one of the 'accidents' of being, but he became concerned by some strange properties that relations seem to possess. In the *Categories*, Aristotle makes two attempts to categorize the relative. The first of these is as follows: 'Those things are called relative which, being either said to be *of* something else or *related to* something else, are explained by reference to that other thing.'[2] Now Aristotle recognizes that this definition contains some ambiguity as to whether relation constitutes a distinct category of being within the substance-accident scheme, and decides that he has to modify it:

> Indeed, if our definition of that which is relative was complete, it is very difficult, if not impossible, to prove that no substance is relative. If, however, our definition was not complete, if those things are only properly called relative in the case of which relation to an external object is a necessary condition of existence, perhaps some explanation of the dilemma may be found.
>
> The former definition does indeed apply to all relatives, but the fact that a thing is *explained* with reference to something else does not make it *essentially* relative.[3]

As Deely (1974, 867) notes astutely: 'This distinction between what must be *explained* by reference to something without having itself to be a relation, and what is *essentially* a reference to something other than that on which it is founded or based, is the first recorded glimpse of what was to become the Latin distinction within the order of relation between what is relative *secundum dici* [according to the way it must be expressed in discourse] and what is relative *secundum esse* [according to the way it has being].' Articulating this distinction and showing how it is relevant to semiosis and to an order of being – the ontological status of the being of relation – that is neither substantial nor accidental, neither subjective nor objective, but rather preceding any categorial schema, is what this story is about. That is, the being *of* the middle, distinct from the terms of the relation; the exteriority of relations to their terms; or an event of interbeing.

We have now reached a threshold. This distinction between *relatio secundum dici* and *relatio secundum esse* was discussed throughout the medieval period by the Christian commentators (at least from the time of Boethius' commentary on the Aristotelian *Categories* in the sixth century), but, as Deely (1974, 869) notes: 'To disengage as such the full notion of ontological relation (*"relatio secundum esse"*) in its properly philosophical import, it seems, was the unique privilege of Poinsot among all the Latin scholastics who, for more than 1100 years, debated the question of the relative raised by Aristotelian texts.'

The difficulty in grasping this distinction between relative terms and the relations themselves is twofold. First, apart from Poinsot's TDS (first published in 1632), its proper thematic articulation has almost totally disappeared from our conceptual landscape since the time of William of Ockham and the rise of nominalism around 1350, which denied an ontological status to relations independent of their terms. Second, Aristotle used the expression *to pros ti* to refer not only to relations themselves, but also to the things that *have* relations.

This contributed to the only slowly dawning (and soon to fade) awareness that every 'thing,' or term, is 'relative' in two different ways: first, it can only be understood *with reference to* other things (*relatio secundum dici*); and second, there are the ontological *relations* that the 'thing' is actually involved in (*relatio secundum esse*). Subtle perhaps, but the growing awareness of this distinction provides us (as Deely repeatedly emphasizes) with a powerful tool for rereading the history of philosophy and, ultimately, for inventing what a 'postmodern' philosophy could be once divested of its latent semiological idealism: a metaphysical materialism of the event that combines the physical and mental, the mind-dependent and mind-independent.

But first we need to develop a terminological consistency.

Terminology

1. *Relatio secundum dici* (relation according to the way it must be expressed in discourse) Following Deely's translation of this term in Poinsot's TDS, *relatio secundum dici* will be rendered as 'transcendental relation.' Poinsot equates transcendental relation with the older terminology of *relatio secundum dici*, and this provides us with an English term (which, of course, still needs to be conceptually developed).

The medieval notion of *transcendental* came to be used (after the thirteenth century) to refer to those properties of being which appear to transcend the Aristotelian categories of being.[4] They surpass or run through all of them. This, of course, was Aristotle's worry in his categorization of the relative. Nothing can be understood or explained without at least implicit reference to something other than itself, and thus all of his categories seemed to be 'relative.' But to be relative is not actually to be a relation.

2. *Relatio secundum esse* (relation according to the way it has being) Again following Deely's translation of TDS, *relatio secundum esse* will be rendered as 'ontological relation.' As Deely explains in his editorial afterword to Poinsot's TDS (page 463), this provides, 'faute de mieux,' a less cumbersome term. More important – in fact, crucially important for this story – ontological relation does all the work that the more recent term 'external relation' achieves.

Discussion in and after the Latin West

The crux in discussions of the relative in the Latin West prior to Poinsot was whether there was a mind-independent category of ontological relation – that is, a relation whose whole manner of being was essentially toward another. Or was relation all in the mind, there being no real 'interbeing,' or communion, or intersubjectivity, among individual existents or subjects? *To be able to really be a relation*, although existentially dependent on some relative foundation, *or to only be something that is relative to other things*, but without there actually being a relation 'external' to its terms: that was the question.

By the thirteenth century the general consensus among those who had the time and the interest to consider this question was that there are indeed relations existentially inseparable but analytically distinct from their foundations, in relative things (e.g., fatherhood, or the equality of atomic weight between two atoms that cannot be identified with the weight of each of them); but with William of Ockham this consensus gives way to a *nominalism*,[5] in which there are no mind-independent relations distinct from their terms. Ockham accepts order and unity in the universe, objective similarity, causal connection; but he insists that this unity, causality, and so on consists only in the terms themselves, and is conceived by relational concepts in the mind. This is the view that Kant would radicalize: it is through a property of our mind, the form of outer sense, that we represent the shape, magnitude, and relation of things to one another.

Weinberg (1965, 117) notes that the rise of nominalism can be partly explained by the influence of a substance-accident ontology of relations. Apart from Poinsot's neglected work, it is not until Charles Sanders Peirce, William James, and (particularly) Bertrand Russell that we start to achieve a clearer grasp of the nature and importance of relations.

Gilles Deleuze (1991, 99) makes this claim in his first book, *Empiricism and Subjectivity*: 'Relations are external to their terms. When James calls himself a pluralist, he does not say, in principle, anything else. This is also the case when Russell calls himself a realist.'

Weinberg (1965, 117) claims that a 'radical innovation in metaphysics is involved in his [Russell's] view that dyadic relations are not reducible to monadic attributes of their terms,' and that 'We owe to Russell, more than any other single philosopher, a clear understanding of the nature and importance of relations.'

Deely would also agree that Russell, like Thomism, recognized the importance of the independent reality of relations for a pluralistic realism, and that Russell, again like Thomistic philosophy before him, allowed for the reality of relations as something external to the related subjects and not merely an attribute of a subject conceived in a certain way by the mind. A unique *esse ad* (being-toward) that is not 'in' something – although neither are relations floating around on their own. No 'thing' – no relations; no relations – no thing:

> It was the genius of Russell, in effect, to seek in the reality of relation a way through the mind-dependent structures of discourse to the mind-independent reality of things. It was the genius of St. Thomas, after all those years, to have given rise to a tradition that has within its resources the wherewithal to uncover the very path whose existence Russell suspected but failed to uncover. This discovery is not something to crow over. Only one man – John Poinsot – in the long tradition of Thomistic thought, seems ever to have suspected, as Russell did, that the path was there (Deely 1975, 306)

Deely also claims (1982, 199) that James 'among the moderns came perhaps closest to a semiotic understanding of this matter [of relations].' James is critical of atomistic empiricism and its assumption that there are no real connections between perceptions or sensations; but he is also critical of Kant's 'solution' to how to join together the putatively isolated bits of sensation. James develops a 'radical empiricism' in which he argues that conjunctive relations are just as immediately given as disjunctive relations.[6] Deely likewise argues (ibid., 115) that the 'initial synthesis of sensations made by the mind is not arbitrary or habit controlled, as the early moderns, notably Hume, opined, but *naturally determined* by semiotic means.'[7] 'Sense data' are neither intrinsic properties of physical things, nor merely subjective constructs, but rather realistically relational and 'two-faced' or Janus-like.[8]

For James, as for Deleuze, the importance of emphasizing pluralism and the externality of relations lies in its critique of absolutisms or monisms,[9] which claim that relations are all internal to their terms and that relations cannot be changed without changing the 'essence' of the thing. Moreover, in monistic accounts, 'relations' aren't really relations because they are not distinguished from their terms. All that James and Deleuze require is that a 'thing' be able to pick up and drop and create new relations which are not simply deterministically derivative of some unchanging essence.[10] In *Dialogues* (Deleuze and Parnet 1987), Deleuze gives the simple example of the glass of water that can be taken off the table without changing its putative essence. In *A Pluralistic Universe*, James (1977, 146), refers to the log that can take up new carriers and drop old ones: 'The difference I try to describe amounts, you see, to nothing more than the difference between what I formerly called the each-form and the all-form of reality. Pluralism lets things really exist in the each-form or distributively. Monism thinks that the all-form or collective unit is the only form that is rational. The all-form allows of no taking up and dropping of connexions, for in the all the parts are essentially and eternally co-implicated.' The main point here is not to deny interrelations but rather not to subsume them into a bloc-holism that is ultimately non-relational!

What will be emphasized in this book is not a simplistic realism, adequation, or correspondence theory of truth (e.g., in which colour is considered to *be* in the grass), but rather a more 'realistic realism' (to use Latour's expression; 1999a, 15), or a semiotic 'truth of relations,' in which a text can truly speak of the world by keeping something constant (a pattern of relations) through a series of transformations; a *relationism* in which discourse and things interact and where's there's more to life than things and words and brains in vats – to wit, a relational collective of coemergent properties (such as colour) that is all the more real for its relations, a richly articulated or vascularized collective in which relations are like blood ... circulating. Says Deely (1982, 115): 'The world appears thus (e.g., coloured) only to a subject, but it really *is* that way *given that totality of conditions*.' A semiotic reality thus appears in which 'we speak truthfully because the world itself is articulated' (Latour 1999a, 296). Or, in other words, we arrive at a non-modernist truth in which facts are neither real nor fabricated and all the more *realistic* through sidestepping this polemics – a world in which construction and autonomy have become *synonyms*. The more affects and relations a 'thing' has, the more autonomous it becomes in a manner strikingly similar to Hans Jonas's portrayal of Spinoza's theory of organism, although not restricted to the 'living.' Autonomy comes together with openness: 'The more individuality is focused in a self, the wider is its periphery of communication with other things; The more isolated the more related it is' (Jonas 1965, 57).

To avoid any suggestion that Kant is being portrayed in this book as a radical idealist *denying* any external reality ('what you eat is not dust'), let us make a brief detour by way of the 'Konigsberg broadcast.'[11]

Deely reads Kant's epistemology as a failed attempt to steer a course between realism and idealism. As we shall see, in Deely's analysis Kant is barred from knowledge of how the world really (realistically) works because of his emphasis on the way the human species – and therefore every human subject – processes experience. From the perspective of the primacy of relations, we shall treat Kant's transcendental idealism in a similar manner.

Having said this, nonetheless, there are a number of statements in Kant's writings that do partially qualify this picture.

First, Kant does have something to say about how the domain of the noumenal ground relates to the way humans experience the world around them. However, this relation is itself not observable but only *stipulated of necessity* – it is specified as an epistomologically necessary, minimal constraint. In *Critique of Pure Reason*, Kant (1978a, A287/B344) notes that it is possible that our human way of knowing the world is only one specific manner of doing so. He wonders 'whether there may not be objects' for a 'quite different intuition and a quite different understanding from ours.' If so, we need to assume a ground permitting a variety of realizations of noumenal 'stuff' – that is, alternative appearances and phenomena. Beyond that abstract notion of relation as necessary condition, Kant also regards things-in-themselves (to which the world has been reduced) as the 'true correlate of sensibility.' Ontologically speaking, what we experience is not a world separate from the noumenal, but rather its specific human reflection.

Second, a radically idealist reading of Kant finds it difficult to account for his statements concerning the function of the human senses. The senses play an important role in Kantian cognition; furthermore, all sensible representation is 'a modification by the object in question' (Kant 1992a, para 4). Here we have a relation in principle between what really is out there and how humans are able to experience it. For Kant (ibid., para. 3), sensibility is 'the receptivity of a subject in virtue of which it is possible for the subject's own representative state to be affected in a definite way by the presence of some object.' However, we should add, we are not in a position to know the putative unconditioned ground of our experience in the same definitive way in which we can know what appears to us. Kant (1978a, A15/B19) carefully distinguishes between these 'two stems of human knowledge': objects that are 'given to us' through our senses and the 'thought' that we add via our understanding. Furthermore, Kant (1978b, para. 15, 17–20) distinguishes 'sense' as our faculty of intuition in the presence of an object from our 'outer sense' as the affection of the body by physical things.

Third, idealist readings tend to use 'idea' to cover a variety of distinct terms in Kant, such as *Anschauungen* (lookings-at/intuitions), *Vorstellung* (mental projection), and *Idee*. Kant strictly forbids us to use 'idea' in conjunction with appearances and phenomena of the world before us. As he says, 'the idea is a concept of reason whose object can be met with nowhere in experience' (1992b, 590). In other words, mere ideas are clearly separated from our realizations of the actual world. In contrast, appearances and subsequent phenomena are conditioned by a ground outside the human faculties – that is, the *Ding-an-sich*. Earlier, in the *Prolegomena* (1985, 374), he wrote: 'All cognition of things merely from pure understanding or pure reason is nothing but sheer illusion, and only in experience is there truth.' It is not surprising, then, that Kant (1967, 253) reprimands Fichte's idealism for having merely conjured up a 'real object out of logic.'

Kant intended to provide a new explanation of cognition by retaining certain aspects of the rationalism of idealism, on the one hand, and the receptivity of empiricism, on the other (1978a, A13/B61ff.) In this he had only limited success. The weight of his descriptions is heavily on the side of how we process sensible information, rather than on the constraints that nature imposes on us. An inquiry into the primacy of relations demands a more positive approach to such 'constraints,' or encounters, rather than the minimalist acknowledgment that Kant accords them.

One place to look for such a positive approach is in the work of Bruno Latour and Isabelle Stengers, for whom the main partner to be questioned in our arguments about the world is, strangely, the world, yet a world that is not a self-identical, formless matter which cannot be known in any positive way, but rather a richly articulated collective of humans and non-humans where no one is in command.

2 Deleuze and External (or Ontological) Relations

Deleuze emphasizes external relations from his first book, *Empiricism and Subjectivity*, onwards. How does he understand external relations, and why does he seek to affirm them?

First, let us look at what Deleuze does in his later article on David Hume (1972), which provides us with one of the most compact statements Deleuze ever made on these questions.

What Deleuze does is creep up behind Hume and argue that he allows for an autonomous logic of relations whose development will continue with Bertrand Russell and William James. This is not the way that Hume and empiricism have normally been digested by the history of philosophy, which presents empiricism as the theory that everything in the understanding comes from the senses – 'the intelligible from the sensible;' in other words, empiricism has long been seen primarily as the opposite of rationalism.

For Deleuze, one of Hume's originalities lies in the realization that relations are external to their terms and that this can only be understood in opposition to 'rationalist' philosophies that deny the 'paradox' of relations. In fact, Deleuze claimed that he wrote on Hume precisely to escape the rationalist history of philosophy and its denial of external relations.

What Deleuze is targeting are those metaphysically essentialist philosophies which seek to make relations *reducible* or internal to their terms or essence, or to include them within a more encompassing unity. The logic of Western philosophy (with the notable exceptional elaborations of Thomist and Scotist thought by Poinsot and Peirce) had largely been based on an interpretation of the Aristotelian form of logical judgments whereby relations were treated as attributes of a subject and those relations that could not be treated in this way (i.e., ontological/external relations) were largely ignored or illegitimately reduced to attributes of a subject or substance.

Deleuze argues that if, for Hume, ideas contain nothing other than sensible impressions, then the relations between ideas are external to ideas and may vary without the ideas varying – there being no absolute unity or transcendent totalizing whole to be maintained.[1] The possibility for change, as Deleuze will affirm, is clearly the guiding force in this novel reading of Hume's empiricism. Rather than tying relation to the 'essence' of its term, Deleuze/Hume's empiricism allows for new relations to be created between 'things/terms'; these would modify the open and changeable multiplicity in which these terms participate. Deleuze seems to have honed in on Hume's statement that relations are not properties of things, but rather arise 'from the comparison which the mind makes betwixt them.'[2] So Deleuze is emphasizing the hesitation in Hume between a psychological atomism and a theory of association or continuity based on habit and 'the principles of human nature.'[3]

As Deleuze argues in his Hume essay, the irreducibility of relations to their terms allows for a 'world of exteriority' whereby thought can have a relation with the 'Outside' of thought, a world where one communicates by way of external relations. He credits Hume with undoing the constraining form of the judgment of attribution and allowing for an autonomous logic of relations.

At this juncture, and simply for the historical record, let us note that Poinsot had achieved a full thematic statement of this logic of relations some hundred years prior to Hume (in 1632, and with much greater force and subtelty), and that the Thomist and Scotist schools had clearly grasped the basic notion of ontological or external relation as early as the fourteenth century. Of course, this concept was to wither away from about 1350 with the rise of nominalism. Given that Poinsot's work 'fell deadborn from the press' with the rise of classical, modern, nominalistic philosophy in the seventeenth century, it is to the young Deleuze's credit that he was inventive enough to discover external relations in Hume, where few had sought to find them. Nevertheless, Hume's external relation still falls short of Poinsot's ontological relation, for whereas this includes both *relatio realis* and *relatio rationis*, Hume's 'comparison' is only *relatio rationis* – thus it is external but not ontological.

Deleuze and Guattari make external relations do a lot of work, and in *Dialogues*[4] Deleuze adds a few more details to the Hume story, explaining why he wrote about empiricism (D, 54–9). I will quote and annotate extensively from these pages, as they provide one of the finest statements Deleuze ever made on relations:

> Things do not begin to live except in the middle. In this respect what is it that the empiricists found, not in their heads, but in the world, which is like a vital discovery, a certainty of life which, if one really adheres to it, changes one's way of life? It is not the question "Does the intelligible come from the sensible?" but a quite different question, that of relations. *Relations are external to their terms.* "Peter is smaller than Paul," "The glass is on the table": relation is neither internal to one of the terms which would consequently be subject, nor to two together. Moreover, a relation may change without the terms changing. One may object that the glass is perhaps altered when it is moved off the table, but this is not true. The ideas of the glass and the table are not altered. Relations are in the middle, and exist as such. (D, 55)

The critical issue for Deleuze is that this logic of relations is particularly crucial with respect to philosophy's problem of being, IS, and the judgment of attribution (Aristotelian substance/accident categorial schema). He argues that it is primarily the English and the Americans (Russell, James, Whitehead, Peirce) who have developed this reflection on relations and that in order to free relations from the verb to be, AND must be substituted for IS. This contaminates the whole of the categorial schema (as we have already seen with our meditation on transcendental and ontological relations in chapter 1).

Furthermore, this AND is not a specific relation; rather, 'it is that which subtends all relations, which makes relations shoot outside their terms, and outside of everything that could be demined as Being, One, or Whole. The AND as extra-being, inter-being' (D, 57).

'Thinking *with* AND, instead of thinking IS, instead of thinking *for* IS: empiricism has never had another secret. Try it, it is an extraordinary thought, and yet it is life' (D, 57).

Deleuze notes that it was Jean Wahl who introduced him to the British empiricists, particularly by way of Wahl's *Vers le concret* (1932), which has extended chapters on Whitehead and James. The section of *Dialogues* I am quoting from and discussing is titled *On the Superiority of Anglo-American Literature.*

The conclusion to William James's *A Pluralistic Universe* (1977, 145) is 'remarkably' resonant here: 'Pragmatically interpreted, pluralism or the doctrine that it is many means only that the sundry parts of reality *may be externally related.* Everything you can think of, however vast or inclusive, has on the pluralistic view a genuinely 'external' environment of some sort or another. Things are with one another in many ways, but nothing includes everything, or dominates over everthing. The word "and" trails along after every sentence. Something always escapes.'

Deleuze will give another twist to this story of external relations, which is one of the most important aspects of his and Guattari's later work – MULTIPLICITY (for Deleuze, philosophy is the theory of multiplicities). The critical point here is that the word AND is not conceived as numerically additive (as in 'one more' glass of wine). Multiplicity has become a noun, as opposed to the multiple, which as an adjective is 'still subordinate to the One which divides or the Being which encompasses it.' (D, 57). In the preface to the English-language edition of *Dialogues*, Deleuze strongly emphasizes the concept of multiplicity as a characteristic of empiricism, in contrast to rationalist philosophies, which start with the One, the Whole, the Subject, and then speculate on how such abstractions are embodied 'in a world that has been made to conform to their requirements (this can be knowledge, virtue, history ...)' (D, vii).

Deleuze's empiricism starts instead with multiplicities that are *states of things* rather than unities or totalities. The essential point for Deleuze is that every 'thing' is in fact a multiplicity of irreducible dimensions, an open continuum/becoming of inseparable relations that cannot be reduced to their terms (ENTITY = EVENT). These relations are not like fixed ropes or lines between self-identical metaphysical subjects, but mobile, fieldlike relationalities that can be modified without having to change the purported static 'essence' of the terms. These terms are *essentially relative but distinguished from the relations*, and a change in the mobile field of actual relations that the terms are involved in will qualitatively alter the processual multiplicity or continuum that the terms 'are.' As we have seen with the distinction between transcendental and ontological relations in experience, every 'thing,' or term, is relative in one of two ways:[5] (1) the very being of a thing or individual requires that it be understood in relation to and as dependent on factors outside itself – every thing is transcendentally 'relative'; or (2) the relations that the thing/term/being/subject are in fact involved in are the external/ontological relations. The interbeing or intersubjective field that is 'between things.' Relations are external to their terms.

For example, I could take an empty plastic milk crate and place it in a garden pond as a support for a fountain and haven for small fish. I have not changed the purported essence of the 'milk crate,' but the relations or interactions that the 'milk crate' is involved in have changed, and the 'milk crate' can now only be understood in relation to the new assemblage of relations that it has actually entered into. (It is slightly more complex than this, requiring a semiotic analysis of how the *objects* of human experience are constituted, and come to be distinguished as *things* in a prejacent physical environment, but we'll get to that eventually. The trick is that every thing is first of all an object of experience *and many objects are not things – and many things may never become objects.*)

Deleuze simply gives the example of a glass on a table (D, 55). When the glass is moved off the table, the relation between the two has changed but not the idea of the glass and the table. He argues, furthermore, that the very book *Dialogues*, ostensibly written by Gilles Deleuze and Claire Parnet, is 'between' in several senses: not only between Deleuze and Parnet, and between other books with Félix Guattari, but also in the sense that it is a multiplicity of external bifurcating lines/relations that cannot be attributed or reduced to individuals – *particularly as the 'individuals' were also qualitatively changing as the book developed.* It becomes a book without a subject (or an object). To think this can be difficult, because, in the process thought itself becomes 'subjectless.'

So, as we have seen, Deleuze extracts external relations from Hume and subsequently continues to use this tool as a vital part of his philosophical work, which reaches (perhaps) its most extraordinary development with Félix Guattari in *A Thousand Plateaus* (ATP). However, before moving into the land of plateaus I would like to engage with Deleuze's *The Logic of Sense* (LS), which undertakes an important development of the use of external relations that will enable us to feel the resonance between Deleuze and Poinsot/Deely's understanding of the *relation* between words and things, or propositions and states of affairs.

The Logic of Sense (together with *Difference and Repetition* [DR]) is recognized as a turning point in Deleuze's oeuvre, wherein he, by his own admission, starts to 'do philosophy' instead of merely producing 'readings' (remarkable though they may be) of other thinkers (e.g., Nietzsche, Spinoza, Hume, Bergson, Kant). What is Deleuze doing in LS?[6] In the preface, he tells us that he is presenting a series of paradoxes that will form a theory of sense, one that develops out of an engagement with Lewis Carroll's work and Stoic philosophy. The work is paradoxical because 'sense is a nonexisting entity.' For our purposes we will connect primarily with the Stoic series.

As Jean-Jacques Lecercle astutely observes in his fine introduction to LS,[7] although various theories of meaning have been developed in analytical philosophy (e.g., those of Frege, Russell, Wittgenstein, and Strawson), Deleuze, for reasons that I hope will become apparent, largely ignores this tradition and returns to Stoic semiotics (one of the first theories of the sign, or philosophies of language).[8] Note that Deely also returns to an earlier tradition (that of Poinsot's semiotics) for a logic of sense that we will use here to intersect with Deleuze's logic.

For Deely (1990, 18), the main problem of so-called linguistic philosophy is that it fails to give an account of how we can talk about non-existent things, this being one of the most notable features of human language. Linguistic philosophy attempts to treat language as primarily involved in mirroring or developing a point-by-point correspondence with an external, non-linguistic reality. In the analytical approach, meaning and truth only occur when there is a direct referential correspondence between words and things. For similar reasons, Deleuze and Deely both consider this approach completely inadequate.

The Circle of the Proposition

Deleuze demonstrates that the commonly recognized functions of denotation, manifestation, and signification are incapable of accounting for their own genesis, as they are involved in a relation of circular, reciprocal presupposition; and that the proposition in fact presupposes an element or 'stratum' that is unconditioned and thus capable of generating denotation and the other propositional functions. This 'fourth dimension' of the proposition is sense, or *that which, in the proposition, is expressed*. It is an incorporeal event, one that is related to the proposition and the denoted states of affairs but irreducible to neither and not derived *from* their correspondence. Sense becomes an external or ontological relation, an interface, 'the boundary between propositions and things' (LS, 22).

The tradition that Deleuze presents (which has often been recapitulated in the secondary Deleuzian literature) goes briefly like this: The Stoics discovered another dimension to the proposition – *sense*, or the *lekton*, which Deleuze claims was subsequently rediscovered by Gregory of Rimini in the fourteenth century (on whom more later), and again by Meinong at the end of the nineteenth century (as well as by Husserl, although with some qualifications). Here is how Deleuze sets up the problem:

> The question is as follows: is there something, *aliquid*, which merges neither with the proposition or with the terms of the proposition, nor with the

object or with the state of affairs which the proposition denotes, neither with the 'lived,' or representation or the mental activity or the person who expresses herself in the proposition, nor with the concepts or signified essences? The Stoics said it all: neither word nor body, neither sensible representation nor *rational representation*. Better yet, perhaps sense would be 'neutral,' altogether indifferent to both particular and general, singular and universal, personal and impersonal. (LS, 19)

The answer for Deleuze is that we can infer sense as that which has neither physical nor mental existence – or rather, it has that *minimum of being* which allows it to be irreducible to either of these two distinctions and which enables their very distinction. This notion of minimal being (the *ens minimum* of the latin West)[9] is a crucial piece of this puzzle, and we will return to it. For the moment, suffice it to write that *sense and ontological or external relation* have the same minimum of being that allows them to be indifferent to the mind-dependent, mind-independent distinction, and that it is Poinsot (rediscovered and translated by Deely) who appears to first fully realize the implications of this unique ontological feature of relation for a science of signs or semiotic – a science that would be displaced (historically) by the rise of the essentially unsemiotic, nominalist, national-language modern philosophies.

In *Dialogues* (62–76), Deleuze explains why he chose to write about the Stoics. He claims that their great strength and originality lay in no longer separating the sensible from the intelligible, but in distinguishing between things and events that could not be reduced to their spatio-temporal manifestation. The event (or sense) is an 'incorporeal vapour,' an infinitive that is the expressed of the proposition and an attribute of things ('to redden,' 'to turn green,' 'to cut,' 'to die,' 'to love'). Deleuze sees this as another way of avoiding the IS: 'The attribute is no longer a quality related to the subject by the indicative "is," it is any verb whatever in the infinitive which emerges from a state of things and skims over it' (D, 63). Deleuze gives the example of the event of cutting[10] (another is that of the battle), which belongs to a different order of being from the knife, or the flesh, or their conjunction. It is not a physical property of things: it *insists* in them and *subsists* in language – that is, the event is not a thing but an infinitive (or, as Poinsot would say, *a relation*). Events are 'where' language and things are linked: the proposition designates things and expresses events, and events are attributed to things and expressed in propositions. That which is expressed is neither the thing nor the proposition but a 'non-existent entity,' or an ontological relation that allows there to be this interface. The 'sense' of the proposition has a kind of ontological parity with the events that are happening to things; it is the univocity of ontological relation, which is the imperceptible event of sense: 'We will not ask therefore what is the sense of the event: the event is sense itself' (LS, 22).

This is a complex and inspired attempt by Deleuze to construct an ontology based on relational becomings, inspired by empiricism and external relations, which act as signs relating 'the interiority of language to the exteriority of being' (LS, 185). He is constructing an ontology/logic of sense that is effectively a *semiotics based on ontological or external relations* – but doing so with unfamiliar and complicated tools that he must constantly reinvent and adapt for his own ends. In his later work with Guattari, a semiotics inspired significantly by Charles Sanders Peirce and Jakob von Uexküll will complexify this logic of sense and give it its full amplitude as a social pragmatics concerned with the creation and articulation of relations in mobile assemblages, rather than with the representation of things (the traditional 'realist' image of thought as the more or less successful representation or resemblance by an individualized subject of the way things are). An 'ethico-aesthetic' paradigm, as Guattari will characterize his final work, *Chaosmosis*; a semiotics rather than a traditional ontology, epistemology, or semiology.

But what happened to Gregory of Rimini?

As we have noted, Deleuze traces a line from the Stoics through Gregory of Rimini to modern analytic logic (e.g., Meinong's 'extra-being'); and it might help us to follow this buried line a little farther.

The Complex Theme of the Proposition

Who was Gregory of Rimini, and why would Deleuze refer to this almost totally ignored thinker?

In his fine article, 'The Coalescence of Semiotic Consciousness' (1986a, 6), Deely contends that the most important period in the development of a 'semiotic consciousness' that would surpass the traditional ontological-epistemological analysis of knowledge was 1350 to 1650; and he observes that this is one of the most poorly researched periods in the history of philosophy – a kind of 'black hole' between Ockham and Descartes during which there emerged a complex reflection on language, the nature of concepts, and the action of signs.

Gregory of Rimini (1300–58),[11] of the Eremite Order of Saint Augustine (who died on the edge of the black hole of philosophy), is often placed in the Ockhamist or nominalist school. Yet his novel ideas on what a proposition actually signifies (i.e., the 'object' of the proposition) distance him from Ockham, who is specifically criticized by Gregory of Rimini; Gregory is in many ways much closer to Scotus.[12]

Deleuze does not actually say a great deal about Gregory, and refers with praise to H. Elie's *Le Complexe significabile* (1936) as providing the filiation between Gregory and phenomenology (Husserl, Meinong). What is remarkable is that in 1968-9 Deleuze makes a connection between the Stoic origins of the problem of the lekton as the incorporeal 'expressed of the proposition' and Gregory's theory of the '*complexe significabile*.'[13] Deleuze clearly enjoys discovering/inventing this tradition, which he will adapt to his own uses and seek to rescue from its modern phenomenological and analytical interment in the 'tomb of individual consciousness.'[14] For someone who has 'a hatred of interiority,' this is important. It is also important for our story, as it is Poinsot who at the end of the black hole of philosophy, with his *Tractatus de Signis* (1632), provided a synthesis that condensed the previous three hundred years of scholastic thought on sign relations, as well as an alternative path to the one taken by the mainstream modern philosophy of representation in its denial of external or ontological relations (e.g., by treating 'ideas' as the direct objects of awareness, or in other words as *representations*, rather than as imperceptible sign relations of *which we are not directly aware*). Poinsot was virtually ignored for the following three hundred years; it was Peirce who began to reinvent in his own terms a semiotic that could escape the prison house of interiority and its screen of concepts.[15]

To get a better understanding of Gregory of Rimini, we must try to step back to the 'subtle doctor,' Duns Scotus (1266–1308), who just preceded Gregory and whose 'subtle' doctrines had a determining influence on the debates around cognition and metaphysics over the following three hundred years, up to Poinsot's synthesis – and who influenced much of the structure of modern philosophy. The goal here is not so much to give an exegetical account of Gregory's understanding of the object of the proposition, but rather to outline the constellation of issues that were emerging during this period. This will allow us to better appreciate the importance of Poinsot's work and its relevance to Deleuze and Guattari's philosophy of multiplicity.

As we noted in chapter 1, during the thirteenth century the medieval notion of transcendentality or the transcendentals, as that which surpassed the Aristotelian categories by being common to all of them (*ens vagans*/vagrant being), gave rise to a metaphysical reflection on being-as-being (*ens inquantum est ens*). Metaphysics became ontology in the thirteenth century, and with this emerged the possibility of an awareness of a domain of being irreducible to things (*ens reale*) or thought (*ens rationis*).

To the extent that Scotus is remembered today, it is for the concepts of the univocity of being, the formal distinction, and objective being (*esse objectivum*). How are these interrelated, and why were they relevant to Gregory of Rimini and John Poinsot, as well as (today) to the very structure of modern philosophy?

Let us start with univocity as the least difficult entry point, although univocity is really a corollary of the formal distinction.

Duns Scotus wants to specify the proper object of metaphysics as an abstract science of being, distinct from theology and physics. Theology is concerned with God through the concept of 'infinite being'; physics is concerned with the being of individual things. Thus if metaphysics is to be something other than a physics, it must have a univocal concept of being that is not restricted to the being of material things but grasps being in a universal way, or being-as-being. The object of metaphysics, as something real and common, cannot be formulated in either logical or numerical terms. It is not simply a being of reason, nor is it a being of individual existents that are numerically and irreducibly distinct from one another. For metaphysics to have an object, it must consider the concept of being at the highest level of abstraction so that it can be said in one and the same way of everything. This is the 'univocity' of being. Being is said in the same sense of everything (including God and creatures).[16] As Deleuze remarks (DR, 35): 'In the greatest book of pure ontology, the *Opus Oxoniense*, being is understood as univocal, but univocal being is understood as neutral, *neuter*, indiffent to the distinction between the finite and the infinite, the singular and the universal, the created and the uncreated.'[17] So here emerges a concept of being distinguished by Duns Scotus from the being of individual things, from logic (beings of reason/*ens rationis*), and from theology (infinite being).

For Duns Scotus this is a 'formal distinction,' a 'formality,' one that goes beyond the Aristotelian division of distinction into only two types, 'of reason' or 'of nature' – a subtle, Scotist third distinction *between* things and thought. Nevertheless, for him this distinction is on the side of the nature of the thing (*ex natura rei*). It is not an abstraction of the intellect but has a foundation in things between essence and existence, between the universal and the particular.[18]

Thus, univocity of being arises from awareness of the fact that the real is neither pure universality nor pure individuality. This distinct univocity relates to a real distinction in the thing, or rather 'on the side of the thing.' The concept of univocity of being corresponds to a real third distinction '*ex natura rei*,' and this is of key importance for Scotus. The being 'as known' (i.e., in the scholastic use of the term, its '*objective*' reality) is identical to its 'formal reality' or real being.

Which brings us to the Scotist doctrine of *esse objectivum* or 'objective being,' a doctrine that right from the start must be emphasized as concerning *that which exists in awareness* – whatever is, is, for us, first of all an 'object' of an act of awareness. For Scotus, reality has a formal being in its mind-independent reality *and* an objective being in thought. Yet the modern philosophy of representation and its epistemology has in effect abandoned any real knowledge of a mind-independent reality, or (with Heidegger) had developed a 'novel' approach in which human discourse reveals 'Being' itself.

If, for Scotus, metaphysical being is a concept prior to the distinction between mind-dependent and mind-independent – 'being' as the first natural *object* of our understanding (*ens ut primum cognitum ab intellectu nostro*) – it is nevertheless an object of awareness, and to this extent it is, for him, a representation – it has an *esse repraesentatum* in the intellect that apprehends it. An object is an object to the extent that it is an object of cognition. This, then, is the beginning of the modern notion of the object as a representation in thought (an *esse objectivum*). And from here much confusion will develop, because Scotus conceives of the objective being as an 'instrumental sign,' that is, as something of which one is directly aware, something that then, subsequently, leads to an awareness of something else. Concepts become signs that we are directly aware of – they subsequently make one aware of something else – but for Scotus and the modern philosophy of representation, ideas are first of all directly perceived and *then* related to something else. This, we will come to realize, is the heart of the problem of cognition, and it is Poinsot who manages to overcome the inevitable problems that Scotus' *esse objectivum* would lead to. For if the objective being of a thing is its representation to a *cogito*, what is the relation between the representation and the thing that is represented?

But what happened to Gregory of Rimini and the *complexe significabile*? As the reader will have undoubtedly realized, Scotus' formal distinction and *esse objectivum* of the concept might be related to the 'sense' of the proposition that Deleuze traces from the Stoics through Gregory to

Meinong, Frege, and Husserl. Just as metaphysics has a univocal concept of being, there is something special about the 'object' or 'sense' of the proposition.[19] In fact Gregory appears to define the principal themes of the philosophy of sense as they will reappear in analytical philosophy

In the fourteenth century, as today, there were three possible conceptions of the object of a proposition: that of Ockham, for whom the object of the proposition was the reflexive act of thinking it; that of Walter Chatton, for whom the object concerned the extramental thing; and that of Gregory of Rimini, for whom the object of the proposition (and especially of scientific propositions) was the 'total and adequate signified.'

The object of the proposition is its *esse objectivum*, to be distinguished from the reflexive act of thinking of the object of the proposition. Neither is the expressed of the proposition the thing in its concrete reality. This distinction is similar to Meinong's *objective*. For example, the 'being-blue-of-the-sky' (the objective) is a distinct 'something' separate from the sky, yet irreducible to a mental entity or to the linguistic expression.

To recapitulate: for Gregory the object (or 'conclusion') of a proposition is not self-reflexive. One's attention is not on the act of concluding, but goes directly to the meaning of the conclusion. What is designated is what is signified, and this is neither the extra-mental thing nor the act of thinking the conclusion. Ockham, however, reduces the direct intellection of the propositional act to a reflexive form of intellection. Gregory understands 'objectively' what Ockham understands subjectively. For Ockham, it is the proposition itself that is known – it does not lead directly to something other than itself ('only propositions are known').[20] For Gregory, the object of a proposition is what the proposition signifies – that is, its 'total complex signified' – and the intellect gives its attention to this directly, not self-reflexively.

In *Difference and Repetition* (DR, 156), Deleuze gives a brief account of Gregory's complex theme as 'sense': 'It is distinguished from the proposition itself because it relates to the object as though it were its logical attribute, its "statable" or "expressible." It is the *complex theme* of the proposition, and, as such, the first term of knowledge.' Sense is extra-propositional.

Both Deleuze and Muralt note that Gregory of Rimini's analysis finds a precursor in Stoic logic, where the object of the proposition is that which the proposition expresses, – that is, the lekton (for the Stoics this is the only incorporeal entity in the material universe). What is even more remarkable is the manner in which contemporary reflection continues the Gregorian approach to the logic of sense. For example, Muralt (1991, 138) claims that Husserl effectively repeats Gregory when he analyses the sense of the 'expressions' of human language and the subjective acts of consciousness that correspond to them. Thus Husserl also distinguishes between the objectivity expressed by the linguistic expression and the objectivity signified by it. Husserl sees this distinction arising in the comparison of expressions which, while naming the same thing, have a different sense (e.g., equilateral triangle and isogonal triangle, morning and evening star). Frege also uses this distinction between the *Sinn* (sense) of a proposition and its *Bedeutung* (objective signification).

One of the challenges of this book will be to show how Poinsot succeeds in incorporating both elements of Scotus' 'objective being' (*esse objectivum*) and Gregory's object of the proposition without falling into the representationalist theory wherein the representation becomes the absolute term of cognition.

Now what is the being of the *complexe significabile*, or the signified of the proposition? It is not a physical thing, but it is nonetheless *aliquid* (something) that is more than a psychological act. It has the being of an 'object,' *esse objectivum*, which constitutes, for Duns Scotus, the being of the known in the knower; and it will be Poinsot who shows how this *esse objectivum* can be understood in a relational rather than an entitative sense – as an interface or pure relation, rather than as an obstacle or impenetrable screen between mind and matter. It is what Deleuze and Guattari will call the 'outside' of thought, which is not the external world but rather that from which the opposition external/internal can even arise.

Poinsot will clarify how there can be a relation between the object (or 'propos' or expressed) of the proposition and physical things or states of affairs (although experience, cognition, and semiosis will not be reducible to this paradigm case). It is that which in a proposition is indifferent or neutral to the mind-dependent or mind-independent distinction. It can relate being and 'non-being' because it remains a relation in either case. It is, as we will come to understand, the univocity of the sign relation, the univocity of sense (the 'extra-being,' to use Meinong's terminology). What Deleuze and Poinsot do is make this objective being an event or relation – a metaphysical field of objective, external, ontological sign relations. Deleuze and Guattari will become more interested in the onto-ethology or ecology of relations from

Spinoza to von Uexküll and Bateson – the power to affect and be affected – and in a philosophy of expression and invention, rather than in recognition. Poinsot will use an understanding of ontological relation to show how semiosis (the action of signs) works through the univocity of being and non-being in the sign relation to bring about a semiotic 'objectivity' or 'reality' that provides a mobile mixture of objects that are *only* objects of awareness, together with objects of awareness that are *also* things; a philosophy of experience that provides for a permeable osmosis between things and thought, nature and culture, the mind-dependent and mind-independent, involving a semiotic 'outside' of thought that is 'an outside more distant than any external world because it is an inside deeper than any internal world' (WIP, 59).

What must be emphasized is that we are concerned here not with a traditional image of thought as an adequation with an external, self-identical, 'objective' world (in the modern philosophical sense), but with an encounter with an exteriority beyond any external (or internal) world. Creation, or an 'ethico-aesthetic' paradigm, takes precedence over recognition and resemblance.

As François Zourabichvili (1996, 34) has elegantly expressed the matter, it is not a question of whether rocks, animals, and other human beings exist; this is not the issue: 'The question is to know under what conditions the thinking subject enters into a relation with an unknown element, and if for that it's sufficient to go to the zoo, walk around an ashtray on the table, chat with one's friends, or travel around the world. The question is to know what determines a mutation in thought and if it's really in this way that thought has an encounter.'[21]

What is at issue is the possibility of an encounter with an Outside irreducible to an external or internal world, a univocal Outside of thought composed of relations external to their terms.

3 Poinsot and Deely on Relations and Signs

> It is not simply a question of stating the exteriority of relations, but of producing the concept. What is the status of this unrecognized and yet encountered object? It is the sign that escapes representation.
>
> Zourabichvili (1996, 36–7)

Duns Scotus is a crucial figure in that his concept of *esse objectivum* set the stage for a set of controversies regarding the nature of signification and the status of concepts as signs. Gregory of Rimini's *complexe significabile* is one example of a decidedly Scotist treatment of the nature of the object of a proposition, and as we have noted, this issue is also engaged with by modern analytical philosophy and phenomenology (e.g., Husserl and Meinong). What is less often appreciated is just how much these questions were debated throughout the late scholastic period leading up to Poinsot's semiotic synthesis in 1632.[1]

The point of departure was Scotus' development of Avicenna's proposal that being-as-being should be held to be the first natural object of our understanding. This was not the Aristotelian being of the things of a mind-independent world, nor was it the being of thoughts or reason; rather, it was being-as-being as an object of cognition. And here everything started to become complicated. For Scotus and Poinsot, something was an 'objective being' *to the extent that it existed in awareness.* The sun and the sea were 'objective beings,' but so were unicorns – they also existed 'in' our awareness. So, within experience, all beings were by definition objective beings. However, not all of them were physical things or events. (We will keep returning to this question of 'objective being,' as it will provide us with a conceptual tool for dealing with all the material that will be presented in this book.) This notion of 'objective being' (the status of the immanence of the known in the knower) was the principal point of contention in the debates between the medieval schools – principally Thomist and Scotist – over the last of the Latin centuries.

Linked to this problematic was the growing realization that concepts or ideas act as signs – they bring something into awareness other than themselves. The centre of gravity of the debates concerned the definition and action of signs. Throughout the period between Duns Scotus and John Poinsot a complex terminology started to appear and to be refined. Descartes, 'the father of modern philosophy,' would unfortunately ignore this accumulated capital of reflection on the structure of experience and assume that ideas are not signs, but rather the direct objects of experience (such as sensible things) that represent themselves. Scotus' objective being mutated into an *object for a 'cogito,'* or subject (it became immanent to a cogito), and an insurmountable wall (overcome only by God) was thus created between objective being (as known) and the 'formal reality' of things.

As Deely (1978, 5) clearly informs us, the definition of signs that laid the foundation for the Western interrogation on signs was the one laid down by Augustine in the fifth century: 'Augustine defined a sign as "something that, besides the impressions it conveys to sense, makes something else come into cognition."[2] Translating more freely, we can say that Augustine defines the sign as anything that, on being perceived brings something besides itself into awareness.'

By the time we reach the period we are dealing with (1350–1650) there was growing debate in the medieval schools over the nature of signification, the question of universals, the structure of propositions, the understanding of concepts as signs, and so on. Deely (1986a, 10–11) gives us a critically important example of this development of semiotic terminology, which I will attempt to present with little modification. He contends – and extensive historical research supports him – that the most important and relatively neglected centres of semiotic inquiry during the period in question were in the university traditions of Spain and Portugal (principally Coimbra in Portugal and Salamanca and Alcalá in Spain).

The example Deely gives us when emphasizing how much questions of semiotic were a principal theme of reflection is taken from the work of Petrus Fonsecus (1528–99) the leading professor at Coimbra, whose students and collaborators, the so-called 'Conimbricenses,' wrote a treatise *De Signis* in 1607.[3] Fonseca himself had already by 1564 given a detailed account of a way of characterizing the action of signs – a way that had its origins at least as far back as the fourteenth century (perhaps with Aegidius). The main issue of reflection was whether Augustine's definition of the sign was in fact *too restrictive* in requiring a sensible aspect, in requiring a sign to be something *that on being perceived* would bring something other than itself into awareness.

In this nascent semiotic doctrine, signs are divided into 'formal' and 'instrumental,' 'the former being the "forms" (*species expressae*) or ideas within the mind whereby experience is structured, the latter being words and, more generally, any sense perceptible item or object of experience which functions as a sign, i.e., to bring something other than itself into awareness' (Deely 1986a, 10). Or, as Pedro de Fonseca puts it in 1564:

> Formal signs are similitudes or a certain type of forms of things signified [*species*, as Albertus Magnus had already intimated c.1250–2] inscribed within the cognitive powers, by means of which the things signified are perceived. Of this sort is the similitude which the spectacle of a mountain impresses upon the eyes, or the image which an absent friend leaves in another's memory, or again the picture one forms of something which he has never seen. These signs are called 'formal,' because they form and as it were structure the knowing power.
>
> Instrumental signs are those which, having become objects for knowing powers, lead to cognition of something else. Of this sort is the track of an animal left in the ground, smoke, or a statue, and the like. For a track is a sign of the animal which made it: smoke the sign of an unseen fire: a statue finally is a sign of Caesar or someone else. These signs are called 'instrumental,' either because through them as instruments we signify to others our ideas; or because just as an artist must move his instrument in order to shape his material with it, so must powers able to know first perceive these signs in order to know anything through them.
>
> Hence may be gathered the most striking difference between instrumental and formal signs: since indeed formal signs do not have to be perceived by us in order for us to come to an awareness of the thing signified by the perception they structure; but unless instrumental signs are perceived, they lead no one to an awareness of anything.[4]

So here we see a distinction being made between instrumental signs, which are sense perceptible, and formal signs, which are not. Fonseca, nevertheless, downplays this criticism of Augustine's definition. He accepts a distinction between perceptible and imperceptible signs, but as a nominalist he does not understand a common mode of being (ontological relation) operating in both types of sign. As we shall come to see, this terminology 'instrumental/formal' remains insufficient until it is understood how *both* kinds of sign serve as the foundation for an ontological relation that is other than or external to its foundation or 'vehicle.' Fonseca does not realize this and makes the formal sign a purely subjective determination (it is not distinguished from its foundation). For Poinsot the sign-vehicle founds a relation to something other than itself. This 'ontological' or 'external' relation is what is proper to both instrumental and formal signs; as a pure relation, it cannot be perceived but can be *understood*. Poinsot realizes this (and Peirce and Deleuze[5] will start from this realization of thirdness as external to its terms, operating in nature and culture alike).

Now it happens that Poinsot spent some time (1604–6) at the University of Coimbra studying with the group of professors, the Conimbricenses, organized by Pedro de Fonseca (who died in 1599). We now turn to Poinsot, an important figure, in order to appreciate how he developed these semiotic reflections and brilliantly and uniquely grasped *the importance of a theory of relations for the nascent doctrine of signs.*[6] This was Poinsot's singular achievement, and it is John Deely's achievement to have unearthed this 'neglected figure,' who was the first to demonstrate clearly that experience is a *univocal*[7] web of sign relations or semiotic web: 'So an animal, a thing, is never separable from its relations with the world' (Deleuze 1988a, 125).

Objective Being

To understand this move from a theory of relations to a doctrine of signs, we must return to the question of objective being, as it is a crucial and unavoidable element in the development of semiotics.

It seems that no thematic treatment of the history of objective being has yet been written (although André de Muralt intended to write one). My goal here is not to attempt what would be for me impossible – namely, to provide some panoramic view of medieval thought; rather, it is simply to attempt to indicate the relation between Duns Scotus' understanding and Poinsot's, and their distinction from a *traditional* account of the Thomist understanding of cognition and intentionality. Histories of medieval thought never seem to grasp the importance of Poinsot's semiotic, when they mention it at all. The matter is *inherently complex*, and all the more so because it is possible to question the overly realist accounts of Thomism and their critiques of Scotism and thereby to show a compatibility between Scotism and Poinsot's semiotic Thomism.

In a traditional Thomist account of cognition (as also for Scotism), the central issue is the relation between the knower and the known (nearly always thought of as a physical thing). For traditional Thomism there is an immaterial or *intentional direct union* between the knower and the known. How does this occur? A tree or a stone does not exist in the mind according to its material or natural being but as an *intentional being*,[8] or immaterial and spiritual being. The nature of this being is that of a relation or interface; it is not that of an obstacle between the knower and the known that would first be known reflexively before the thing was known. A unity is posited between the knower and the known. Thought has an immaterial, non-entitative nature and does not need to get outside itself to know the intelligible 'essence' of a thing. This intentionality is a descriptive concept that expresses the openness of the mind to what is other than itself. It is a 'being-toward' of thought open to that which is other than itself (normally understood as the intelligible physical environment). This being-toward, or intentionality of thought, will reappear with Brentano and subsequently with Husserlian phenomenology in a more idealistic form (the intentionality never escapes the transcendental subject). Whitehead's notion of 'prehension' is also a version of intentionality. This notion of intentionality remained somewhat 'opaque' in early Thomism; it would be Poinsot who showed how the concept of intentionality could be accounted for more adequately with the concept of relation as indifferent to the opposition between the mind-dependent (*ens rationis*) and the physical or mind-independent (*ens reale*).

For traditional Thomist cognitivism, the emphasis is on a realism whereby what we know directly are the things themselves in their intelligibility, not *copies* of things in the mind (as with Descartes and representational theories). As mentioned earlier, the concept of intentionality is descriptive of the *relation* between the mind and things: 'The "intentional inexistence" (Brentano's later term) of the thing would designate this junction between the knower and the known, and not an intermediary that would introduce itself between them'[9] (Solère 1989, 36).

Following the expositions of Jean-Luc Solère (1989), Jacques Maritain (1959), Mauricio Beuchot (1994), and John Deely (1994a), let us explore further this Thomist theory of cognition and intentionality. The critical point is that the 'intentional objects' of Thomism do not have the same status as the 'representations' of classical modern philosophy (or Husserlian phenomenology). The error, which Cajetan (1468–1534) rather prejudicially attributed to Duns Scotus, is to reduce the representative processes to a material relation whereby the mind, conceived of as a container or entity, would receive into its interiority through a process of absorption or digestion ('abstraction'), copies or phantoms of things. In the Thomist theory, the knower and the known become one in the same *act*, a 'union without confusion.' The intelligence transforms itself into the intelligibility of that which is to be known without thereby losing its own identity. This is the 'mystery' of consciousness (Solère 1989, 18).[10] The intellect actualizes the prospective intelligibility of the known. The active union is between the intellect in act and the intelligible in act. For the scholastics there was a dynamic quality in the concept of intentionality, a capacity of tension or stretching towards another. This *intentio* is the Latin rendition of the Arabic terms *'ma' qul,'* Al-Farabi's translation of the Greek *noema,* and *'ma' na,'* Avicenna's (980–1037)[11] term for what is before the mind in thought. In fact, the term *intentio* became current in scholastic philosophy after the translation into Latin of Avicenna's works and commentaries on Aristotle. The starting point for Aquinas was Aristotle's theory of thought and perception in which cognition was explained in terms of the reception of forms into the soul. The form in the soul (*ma' na*) was simply a meaning, or a cognition, or *an intention* of the same form in reality. For Aristotle, the soul (or mind) takes on the form of the thing perceived without receiving its matter. When I think about or perceive a horse, my mind receives the form of the horse. Aquinas develops Aristotle's account, arguing that the horse has a different existence in nature (*esse naturale*) and in thought (*esse intentionale*).

That which is known acts on the intellect in an 'intentional' way without modifying it entitatively (the scholastic adage: 'When I look at a stone I do not become a stone'). The received form remains distinct and *objective*. It exists for the knower not subjectively but *intentionally*. This intentional or objective existence is neither in the thing as a physically existent subject, nor in the knowing subject; it is strictly suprasubjective (and with language, as we shall see, potentially intersubjective).

How does this action of the known on the knower occur? Again we start with the 'canonical' Thomist account and move towards Poinsot's semiotic transposition. This requires some understanding of the scholastic term *species* (pronounced *spay-chee-ehs*).[12] Deely (1994a, 8) argues compellingly that this is 'one of the least understood and yet philosophically richest aspects of Latin philosophy, namely the doctrine of "*species*" or forms as specificative within cognition.'

Modern western philosophy (particularly from Descartes onwards) chooses to dispense with the doctrine and embrace the aporias of a 'classical' metaphysics of representation in which what the mind knows directly is its own products, positing a beneficent God to make our 'objective' ideas conform to the world.[13]

The Doctrine of 'Species'

Species come in two kinds: *impressae* and *expressae*. What do they do? They are posited as the medium of intentionality whereby the knower knows the known – 'a synergy of intellect and sensible reality' (Spruit 1994, 159). How do the species do this important job of producing/causing cognitive experience of objects?

As Deely (1994a, 127) claims, 'the main sense of the epistemological Latin term *species*, namely, the sense of *giving specification* or *specifying form*, is one that has never been really brought out in modern English discussions or translations of relevant Latin texts prior to the 1985 edition of Poinsot's *Treatise on Signs*.' The basic argument is that both experience and analysis of sensation and perception indicate that cognitive organisms (e.g., human beings) are in some way determined or specified to apprehend something in particular rather than something else, or nothing at all. To perceive a material object is to be in a certain kind of perceptual state as a causal result of the action of that object; thus there is a distinction between 'phenomenal' object (in scholasticism, 'objected object or objective being') and physical object. The distinctions among all the schools of interpretation depend on the ontological status of the being of the object-as-known: 'Species are, as it were, the abutments upon which an analysis of the given leans for support, the reality of which the mind, by that very analysis, is compelled to recognize – with certainty, if the analysis itself has proceeded correctly and under the constant pressure of intelligible necessities. Some determination must, of necessity, actually supervene upon the knower ... The species is nothing but that internal determination (Maritain 1959, 115–16).

The *species impressae* are the means whereby a given physical entity affects its surroundings by way of some specific energy (light, heat, sound, movement, shape) such that a cognitive organism becomes aware of something. Thus there is some 'impression' or specification on the sensory powers, such that there is an actual sensation or cognitive stimulus. There is an interaction or collusion between a cognitive power (such as sight or hearing) and a stimulus generated by some environmental factor. Deely gives the example of the pits of a CD, which specify what kind of output will occur (music, images, text): 'The physical being of the grooves is one thing, that which is specified by them quite another: intentionality lies in the specifying – not as such ... but in what it enables' (Deely 1994b, 271).

Beuchot (1994) gives the following account: In experience we notice that the external senses 'sense' in the actual presence of their objects. For example, the relative distance of an object determines whether it is clearly or poorly perceived. This suggests that the senses are stimulated with greater or lesser intensity by something emitted by the object (the 'species'). The experience of a mirror's reflection of an object that is behind us also suggests that, besides the object, there is something (the species) that causes the reflection in the mirror and allows us to see something that is behind us. Rational analysis suggests that the senses must be specified in some way so as to be aware of a *particular* object, and this occurs through the object giving something of itself, *a form of specification*. The *species impressae* unite the object with the external senses.[14]

Let us now return to Deely's exposition of the 'Semiotic and Scholastic Doctrine of Species' (1994a, 123–143). Deely's account is the most succinct that I am aware of in the literature and has the added merit of clarifying how Poinsot accommodated the doctrine of species to a doctrine of signs. What follows is a paraphrase or 'free rendering' of Deely's account.[15]

Ideas

Deely begins by referring us to the introduction (§8) to Locke's *An Essay Concerning Human Understanding* (1690), where Locke seeks to clarify what he means by the word 'Idea': 'I must here in the Entrance beg pardon of my Reader, for the frequent use of the Word *Idea*, which he will find in the following Treatise. It being that Term, which, I think, serves best to stand for whatsoever is the Object of the Understanding when a Man thinks, I have used it to express whatever is meant by *Phantasm, Notion, Species,* or whatever it is which the mind can be employ'd about in thinking.'

The problem here is that Locke is providing a single term in place of many other Latin terms that contain important distinctions – in particular, the distinction between *repraesentatio* (representation) and *species*. Deely (1994a, 126) argues that Locke is using the term 'Idea' as a representation whose cognitive function is to make 'present within awareness objects regardless of their proximity within the environment. This is the main function of the idea that Locke had in mind, as also Descartes, and it is perhaps not too much to say that this is the principal notion of idea throughout the period of modern philosophy.' However, unless we have an understanding of the distinction between representation and species (or representation and signification), we cannot understand the difference between a metaphysics of representation ('the way of ideas') and a semiotic ('the way of signs').

Deely continues his exposition by giving an account of the doctrine of *species impressae* and *species expressae*. He emphasizes, as we have already noted, that the primary sense of the term *species* lies in *giving specification* or *specifying form*. In Poinsot's late Thomist synthesis, *sensory impressions* are 'bi-relative' qualities that require a collusion or interaction between the stimulus of a physical object *and* a particular sensory power. This analysis distinguishes itself both from a naive realism, such as that found in Ockham's school wherein sense qualities inhere in the object (the knower contributes nothing), and from the position of Suárez, wherein the sense qualities are *images* formed by the mind and it is these images which are directly known (Suárez would be the main scholastic influence on Descartes and Kant). Or, in other words, for Suárez, we have only our 'representations,' which already exist at the level of sensation.

Deely argues that Poinsot's analysis enables us fully to understand the doctrine of the *species* as *specifying* and whether or not this specification of the cognitive powers constitutes an 'idea' in Locke's sense (i.e., a representative image). This is the distinction between *species impressae* and *species expressae* (or, as Deely also renders these terms, between 'cognitive stimulus as such, and cognitive response').

Deely continues by noting that in Poinsot's tradition the most important reason for positing the existence of ideas (beyond their function of bringing objects into awareness that are not physically present) is to allow for the proportion between the 'bare impressions of sense,' which are given directly in experience, and 'objects' as we experience them. We do not just have sense impressions, we perceive objects: a policeman's uniform, a car crashing. This proportioning of sense into experienced objects of awareness is the function of 'ideas.'

The distinction between *species impressae* and *species expressae* (impressed and expressed, stimulus and response) lies in this distinction between bare sensation on one side, and perception or conception on the other. At the level of sensation (analytically distinguished within experience from perception and conception) there are no 'ideas.' Sensation consists in the interactions among things that actually exist in the physical environment and are actually affecting the external senses 'here and now.' At this level of bare sensation there is a proportion between sensory powers and environmental influence – the power of hearing or sight is proportioned to a specific range of stimulus beyond which nothing is experienced (this proportionality varies among cognitive organisms). An actual sensation, as we noted earlier, occurs when a specific sensory power is specified by some stimulus, the sensation being a *relative* being arising in the interaction between sensory stimulus and sensory power. Thus, to respond to the well known question 'Does a falling tree that no one hears make a noise? According to Poinsot, the answer is no.

The *species impressae* is not an idea in the sense of a representation. It is a *theoretical* term of analysis for *the act of causal specification* whereby an actual sensation occurs. The species does not appear, but is rather that by which some physical environmental influence *could be known*. When something does appear in perception, it will be the environmental object, not the theoretically posited act of specification. I do not see (to use vision as one example!) the interaction and specification arising between the thing and the sensory power; rather, I see the thing as an object of awareness. As Deely notes, this epistemological theory is based on a sexual analogy: 'The *species* is a seminal form, the sensory power a maternal womb. The power inseminated gives birth to the object apprehended.' What distinguishes Poinsot's position is that the object apprehended *only* arises in the interaction between the physical thing and the senses. This distinguishes Poinsot's position from that of Ockham and Suaréz. The *species impressae* is an explanatory causal principle or mechanism to account for the way in which the external senses are specified to sense something. The *species impressae* is not an image or idea, in that it does not make physically absent or inexistent things present in awareness; it itself arises within an analysis of cognition that seeks to explain how aspects *of the environment* come to be known. This analysis is based on a distinction made in experience between sensation on one side and perception and understanding on the other.

Species expressae (still not quite the Lockian 'ideas') arise as an element of the analysis of cognition that seeks to explain how a given sensation becomes a sensation *of* something – a sensation *of* an object of perception. As Deely argues, the *species expressae* (or ideas) arise at the interface between sensation and *response*: 'The idea is the cognitive response of the organism to the cognitive experience of a stimulus.' The *species* is now 'expressed' rather than 'impressed.' That noise that is now expressed in my awareness is *of* my baby crying. It is no longer a specifying factor of the external environment acting on my senses that would enable me to become aware of something – I am now actually aware of something that has a manner of being over and above that of a bare sensation. The sensation has become incorporated into an 'object' of awareness, it has been 'objected' such that it is no longer merely a sensation at the level of physical interaction (e.g., sound waves interacting with the ear) but an object of perception and, perchance, understanding.

Deely notes that the *species expressa* 'was also called a concept, *conceptus*, because it is born or brought forth within the mind precisely as the mind is fecundated or specified through the action of a *species impressa*, as we have seen.' Objects of awareness are brought forth by the concept and exist independently of physical interactions (thus, a purely physical interaction will never make one aware of a national 'flag'; and reading this text with any understanding requires more than a physical interaction). Objects of awareness may be the things of a prejacent physical environment, but they may also be incorporeal or fictional beings. However, the critical point for a semiotic analysis is that the concept and its object differ in the same way as that which represents differs from that which is represented. This brings us back to the scholastic terminology of *formal sign* introduced at the beginning of this chapter and to Poinsot's development of an ontology of relations into a doctrine of signs.

Formal Signs

As we have noted, although it is uncertain exactly when this terminology arose, by the fourteenth century the division of signs into instrumental and formal had already been established. In opposition to Augustine's definition of the sign as something sense-perceptible, something that *on being perceived* brought something else into awareness, formal signs are posited to account for the function of 'ideas' or 'concepts' as being, not sense-perceptible, but rather factors which nevertheless bring into awareness something other than themselves, something suprasubjective. I am aware *not* of the idea or concept but rather of that which it represents – its object. The concept is a formal sign that *disappears* before its object. The formal sign (concept) is a *pure relation*, not something that would first be known. As the Latins said, the concept as a formal sign is that by which – or rather, that *on the basis of which* – we know (*id in quo*); it is not that which we know (*id quod*). So, the contrast: the *species impressa* is that 'by which' (*id quo*) we are determined (or 'specified') so as to become aware of this rather than that environmental aspect; the *species expressa* (*id in quo*) is that 'on the basis of which' the environmental stimulus is experienced as an object; while in both cases the object itself (*id quod*) is distinct from the *species*, just as a terminus is distinct from the foundation of a relation. We will come to see that the *species expressae* is functioning as a Peircian *interpretant*,[16] 'the proper significate outcome' (*which need not be an interpreter or mental idea*) in the triadic relation that a sign consists in (sign-vehicle, object, interpretant). However, before elaborating on the interpretant and Deely's remarkable synthesis of Poinsot and Peirce (which Guattari perhaps would have appreciated), I want to offer a few more observations concerning the earlier Thomist and Scotist approaches to the question of concepts and signs in order to clarify the important notion of *objective being*. In fact, clarifying this notion is central to a semiotic approach to cognition and experience.

As we have seen, the critical factor in Thomist and Scotist theories of cognition is the relation between knower and known. The term 'objective being' appears to have arisen in the fourteenth-century debate about the nature of the *species*. Scotus used the term as a qualification of the more general expression '*esse intelligible*,' already used by Thomas. Now in the Thomist/Poinsot synthesis, as we have briefly noted, the concept is understood as a formal sign whose entire function as a sign is to refer to something other than itself before it would, itself, be known by a reflexive act. For traditional Thomism, 'objective being,' 'objective reality,' or 'being-an-object' indicated the status of something 'as known' in relation to a knower. Something was 'objective' to the extent that it was felt or known. Any 'thing' is 'objective' to the extent that it is known, whereas unknown the thing rests in its subjectivity. This is not the modern sense of objectivity, as reality in binary opposition to subjectivity. In the scholastic tradition there are 'subjects' considered in themselves –

that is, apart from being known (whether people or things). These subjects may become 'objects' of an act of perception. With the modern shift from ontology to epistemology (typified by Descartes), 'subjective' has come to mean the perception of a 'psychological subject,' and 'objective' to mean the formal object of perception 'in itself.' Thus the meaning of the terms has been reversed. In fact, Descartes[17] applied the notion of 'objective being' by placing it within the idea, such that objective being became a reflection or representation of the thing in the mind (and it was this reflection that was directly known as an object), whereas for the Thomists the 'objective reality of the thing in the mind' signified a *relation* or interface that united them. The mind was not a container that held things 'inside' itself. Objective being was not an obstacle or 'third thing' positioning itself between the mind and the thing, like a screen.[18] Modern philosophy began once the idea came to be considered the immediate object of knowledge rather than an interface, or relation, or formal sign (which is the same thing). However, although this modern position is traditionally associated with Descartes, its innocent germ can be found in a particular understanding of the Scotist theory of objective being. This makes the black hole of medieval philosophy incredibly complex, because *Poinsot treaded a tightrope between Scotism and canonical realist Thomism*[19] by allowing for a semiotic representational theory based on the ontological particularity of relations *not* as being inherent accidents of substances but rather as having a suprasubjective and potentially 'intersubjective' being. Poinsot sought to conserve the possibility of an adequate 'correspondence' or coherence between thought and thing, but he also laid the semiotic foundation for an image of thought that could not be reduced to this perspective. Relations are truly *between* things: rhizomes or *interbeings*, to use Deleuze and Guattari's terms, or the 'Being of the Between,' to use Heidegger's characterization of Dasein.[20]

Scotist and Thomist Accounts

Does Scotism differ from Thomism in its treatment of cognition and signs? Responding to this question, even briefly, is a demanding but valuable exercise, as it will highlight the particularity of Poinsot's synthesis:

> This last source [the work of Poinsot] is particulary interesting. It purifies the philosophy that assumes the Thomist synthesis, in showing the purely Aristotelian origins and in opposing the deformations to which Thomism

was subjected by Nominalist theologians, from Duns Scotus to Suárez. Thus, in a work published in Spain, during the 17th century, between 1631 and 1635, the historian discovers the Thomist refutation of the main metaphysical and critical theses that constitute the foundation of modern philosophy. Muralt 1985, quoted in Beuchot (1994, 295)[21]

One difference between Scotism and Thomism might be this: Scotus treated the concept like an instrumental sign, whereas Thomism treated the concept as a formal sign. Eric Alliez makes this observation in *Capital Times: Tales from the Conquest of Time* (1996, 211).[22] In a section titled '1300: The Capture of Being,' he takes up Duns Scotus' doctrine of the univocity of being (as indifferent to the finite and the infinite) and his account of cognition. Alliez argues that Scotus broke with the idea of an intentional identity between subject and object and gave priority to the 'autonomy of the intelligible order' (ibid., 208). The intellect is endowed with a power of production independently of the sensory realm. Alliez contends that Duns Scotus was not trying to grant the intellect complete independence, but was attempting to 'substitute an a-priori order of cognition for its formal-sensible definition (in Thomism).' According to Alliez, this produced the modern conception of the object. For Scotus – and for Descartes, and for modernity – the being of the object of thought (its 'objective being) is no longer defined on the basis of things but as a *concept, as a representation* in the intellect that apprehends it. Objective being has become a 'distinct' entity in thought rather than a set of pure relations. From now on, objective being in thought is known *before the thing is known*. The objective being in thought is separated from the thing. Objective being is what is distinctly represented in the mind; it is not the thing itself. *Direct* relation to an independent reality has been elided, because knowledge now only bears on the intellect, the 'cogitatum of the cogito' (Husserl). As Muralt (1991, 45) notes, this particular doctrine of objective being 'is triumphant from Scotus to Frege.' The mind, having been freed from the sensible, concrete object, and 'eliding' intentionality, begins to privilege the *esse objectivum* as constituted by the mind itself (a subjective *a priori*). As Alliez (1996, 211) argues: 'This is where the Scotist enterprise *masters* the primary sense of the *esse objectivum*: that something presents itself as an object of cognition: which it represents in the sense of establishing a logic of the "instrumental sign."'[23]

In a footnote to this claim, Alliez refers us to Maritain's *Distinguish to Unite* (1959) as cited by Solère (1989), where Maritain (an ultimately 'cyclopean,' realist Thomist), clearly inspired by his knowledge of Poinsot, argues that for Thomism the *species expressa*, or concept, is a formal sign rather than an instrumental sign. In fact, such a distinction is based on Maritain's reading of Poinsot; earlier Thomists would have tended to express the matter in terms of intentionality. As Maritain's work is largely forgotten in the contemporary Anglo-American academy, I will quote the passage in its entirety (1959, 119–20):

> Thomists distinguish between two kinds of essentially different *signs*: what they call *instrumental sign*, and what they call *formal sign*. An instrumental sign is anything that being itself first known [i.e. as sense-perceptible] makes some other thing known consecutively: a streak of smoke we see rising into the sky, a portrait painted on canvas that we see in a gallery – both are the objects upon which our knowledge first bears, only to pass from thence to other objects that are known thanks to them – to the fire of which the smoke is the effect, to the sitter of whom the image is the portrait and sign.
>
> A formal sign is a sign whose whole essence is to signify. It is not an object which, having, first, its proper value for us as an object, is found, besides, to signify another object. Rather it is anything that *makes known*, before being itself a known object. More exactly, let us say it is something that, before being known as object by a reflexive act, is known only by the very knowledge that brings the mind to the object through its mediation. In other words, it is not by 'appearing' as object but by 'disappearing' in face of the object, for its very essence is to bear the mind to something other than itself.

Maritain specifically distinguishes this Thomist view from 'various scholastic deviations' such as 'the Scotist notion of *esse objectivum*' in which the concept is claimed to be an instrumental sign, an image, or a portrait of the thing in us, a closed world, rather than a 'living relation.' According to Maritain, the Scotist position sowed the seeds that led to modern idealism, be it that of Berkeley or Hume – *behind this idea-thing there is nothing* – or the Kantian 'solution' – *behind this idea-thing there is something, but we can know nothing of it.*[24]

Muralt (1991) presents a similar argument concerning the idealist element in the Scotist *esse objectivum* and shows that it was Poinsot who, with his doctrine of the formal sign, provided the most original attempt to combat the notion of an entitative immanence of the *species* in the mind. Nevertheless, he also claims that Poinsot's doctrine of signs has a

Scotist influence, and this is relevant to Deely's interpretation of objective being. We need to be careful of the extreme reactions against Scotism by orthodox Aristotelian Thomists. Poinsot, with his semiotic subalternation of 'moderate realism,' goes beyond canonical realist Thomism while seeking to conserve its essential elements by establishing through sign relations the possible correspondence between the objects of experience and the things of a physical environment.

As Muralt (1991, 95) notes, the early Thomist term 'intentional being' suggests that the immanent presence of a species ensures that a cognitive power is led to its object. This can suggest *two* objects: the intentional being as a representation of a 'real' object. But this immanence is not an entitative existence 'in' a physical subject. It is a suprasubjective ontological relation. For Muralt (ibid., 97),[25] it was Poinsot who achieved the most sophisticated interpretation with his doctrine of the *species expressa* as a formal sign. The time has now come to present Poinsot's terse prose as translated by Deely. The most relevant passages that Maritain and Muralt refer to are from Book II of TDS – specifically, in 'Question 2: Whether the Concept is a Formal Sign':

> First Conclusion. A concept or specifying form expressed by the understanding is most properly a formal sign ... And the foundation of the conclusion is taken from the fact that an intelligible concept directly represents another than itself to the cognitive power, as, for example, a man or a stone, because it is a natural similitude of those things, and through its information the concept renders the understanding knowing in act by a cognition terminated *by the cognition of [the man or the stone] itself*, and not from a *preexisting cognition of* [a representation of the man or the stone] itself. (TDS, 247/11-21)
>
> A concept is not said to represent as something first known in the mode of an extrinsic object, so that the qualification 'known' would be an extrinsic denomination; a concept is said to represent as something *intrinsic* known, that is, as the terminus of the knowledge *within* the power. But because it is *not the terminus in which the cognition finally stops*, but one by whose mediation the power is borne to the knowing of an outside object ... And so, by the essentially same cognition, concept and thing conceived are attained, but the cognition of the thing is not arrived at *from* the cognition of the concept. (TDS, 250/7-39)

For now (the details will slowly emerge), let us note that in TDS, Poinsot is distinguishing between *representation* and *signification*. The concept represents – that is, it brings into awareness something other than itself. The concept, treated in its capacity as a sign, founds a 'relation to another,' and it is that 'other' that is directly known. Signs are not objects; they disappear before their objects (which objects may also become signs). The concept (as an object of awareness) is actually 'known' through a reflexive turn. This semiotic avoids the aporias of representational idealism and frees the mind from closed interiority.

Now does Duns Scotus really turn concepts into instrumental signs, as Alliez claims, influenced by a reading of traditional Thomist criticism? And is Scotus so far from Poinsot's synthesis? Following Muralt's analysis (1991, 108–10), it would seem that Poinsot's and Scotus' semiotics concur more than they differ. Both have a representative theory that distinguishes between representation and signification. Muralt claims that for Scotus, the object represented by the *species expressae* is both an *absolute term,* since the act of intellection terminates there; and *an intentional term* (a sign relation), since it is the representative being in intrinsic denomination of the object in itself in its proper existence as cognized or known. There is a formal identity and correspondence between objective being and real being (*esse reale*) that is analogous to canonical Thomism's intentional union of knower and known in act. It is also very close to Poinsot's semiotic as presented in the above extract from TDS. Muralt (ibid., 151) also notes an equivalence between Gregory of Rimini's doctrine of the *complexe significabile*[26] (referred to by Deleuze in LS and DR) and Poinsot's distinction between enunciative and judicative propositions, which I will not discuss here.

Before returning to Deely's development of Poinsot's semiotic, I want to mention one other account of Duns Scotus' theory of signification – one that shows it is an error to dismiss Duns Scotus in the way that traditional Thomists (including Maritain) have done. Scotus' approach to signification is compatible with that of Poinsot, although less developed. Poinsot had the advantage of writing more than three hundred years later, at a time when theories of signification were being widely discussed; and he provided in TDS the first thematic treatment of signs as having a general and univocal being as ontological relations over and above the status of their foundations as instrumental or formal. Furthermore, Peirce was strongly influenced by Scotus, and Deely's own work involves a fascinating synthesis of Poinsot, Peirce, and Scotus without being reducible to these sources.

Dominik Perler, in his valuable essay 'Duns Scotus on Signification' (1993), engages with the controversy that occupied Scotus' contemporaries: Does a spoken word signify a concept or a thing? Perler quotes Scotus: 'In short, I grant that what is properly signified is a thing.' This was a revision of the then dominant doctrine that a word signified a concept. Scotus argued, following Thomism, that an *expressed species*, or concept, is necessary for understanding or signifying. He distinguished between the ontological status of the *species* and its function: the *species* can be understood as an accident affecting the soul, *and* as a sign signifying the thing. Scotus argued that the function of the *species* as a sign was to direct the intellect to something other than itself (the same applied to the spoken word). He distinguished between the concept or *species* as the *immediate significate* of a word, and the thing as its *mediate significate*. As Perler (1993, 104) notes: 'The distinction of two significates enables Scotus to say that by uttering a word we speak about the thing itself, and not merely about our intelligible species of the thing, although it is the intelligible species that is immediately signified.' In the same way as Thomism, Scotus argued that the intelligible species was only through a reflexive second intention a significate in itself, or an object of awareness.

Duns Scotus also replied to the objection that we do not always use a word to signify an extra-mental, existing physical thing, in the following way: The thing is signified not as it exists but insofar as it is an object of the intellect – insofar as it is known or understood, that is, as a concept. This is Duns Scotus' objective being. Now is this 'thing as it is understood' the intelligible or expressed species? Perler notes that Scotus does not give a detailed answer to this question, but offers the following account based on his distinction between existence and essence: There is a 'formal' distinction between existence and essence, and 'the thing as understood' is the *essence* of the thing. This essence, although not separable from the thing, is formally distinct, without being a real distinction or distinction of reason.[27] The essence is not produced by the intellect; rather, it is a potency or prospective intelligibility that is known by thought, but not dependent on it.

Perler concludes by noting that Scotus claims that a spoken word directly signifies the essence of a thing (the thing as understood) by way of a metaphysical distinction (between essence and existence). This is because Scotus 'wants to preserve an immediate relationship between language and reality *and* the possibility to signify non-existing things.' Three hundred years later, Poinsot would give a more accessible and semiotically satisfying account of the same problematic based on the particular ontology of relations as univocal and indifferent to the mind-dependent/mind-independent distinction. Furthermore, the distinction between formal and instrumental signs becomes derivative (as does intentionality) from an analysis of relative being as either transcendental or ontological. There are relative beings (or subjectivities/substances) *and* there are the ontological ('external') relations they are involved in. Signs as univocal ontological relations can refer to existent or non-existent objects with equal facility, and our 'objective' experience, being a semiotic web of objective sign relations, is an admixture of both. Semiosis does not require the physical existence of the object of awareness. It can be 'purely' objective (such as a dead relative, or a purely fictional being). Experience is a pattern of inherently imperceptible, univocal, objective relations (i.e., relations as understood in awareness) that exhibits the so-called '*essences*' of things, whether these things are considered real or fictional, or no longer existent, or yet to appear. Scientific practice is based on the critical control of this permeable 'objectivity' in seeking to determine (with more or less success) whether these relations of experience coincide with the actual relations that sustain and realize the existence or becoming of a presumed mind-independent 'thing' (e.g., a neutrino). To become is to be in relation – only as a logical abstraction could there be a non-relative empty structure of being, 'by-itself.' To understand a being is to understand the field of relations that sustains it in its being-in-a-world:

> Human understanding must account first of all and in the final analysis for the objectively real, not just for the physically real, and not just for what the prejudices of a given time label as 'real.' 'Reality' is not the physically given, it is the semiosic total of which physical being forms a part. The Mississipi River physically is not the boundary between Iowa and Illinois, but it is so objectively [as known]. Ronald Reagan physically is not President of the United States, but he is so objectively. (Deely 1986b, 270).

This is objective being – which, also intersects with the the concept of the 'truth of the relative,' to use Deleuze and Guattari's term (WIP, 130). The 'Truth of the relative' is not a relativism but a 'constructivism'; it is neither idealist nor realist.

Objective Being as *Umwelt*

In order to make the notion of objective being more concrete, let us now turn to Jacob von Uexküll's concept of *Umwelt* or 'species-specific objective world.' Deely (1986b, 267–8) writes:

> Deeply rooted in Classical German Philosophy – that is to say, Kant – von Uexküll had a lively sense of the role of mental construction in our experience of any 'reality.' But, unlike Kant and fortunately for us, von Uexküll was a remarkably attentive observer of the world of plants and other than human animals. Out of these two preoccupations von Uexküll forged some of the most remarkable and semiotically fruitful notions available to us for understanding the phenomenon of semiosis.

So let us now take a stroll with von Uexküll through the worlds of animals and men.

4 Umwelten

It would be foolish if we attempted to impute or ascribe philosophical inadequacy to Uexküll's interpretations, instead of recognizing the engagement with concrete investigations like this is one of the most fruitful things that philosophy can learn from contemporary biology.

Heidegger (1995, 263)

Uexküll, one of the main founders of ethology, is a Spinozist when first he defines the melodic lines or contrapuntal relations that correspond to each thing, and then he describes a symphony as an immanent higher unity that takes on a breadth and fullness ('natural composition').

Deleuze (1988a, 126)

What busy inquirers into verbal semantics – linguists, logicians – have probed and profited from Uexküll's masterful *Bedeutungslehre*?[1]

Sebeok (1976, x)

Jakob von Uexküll and *Umwelten*

To understand who von Uexküll was and what *Umwelten* are and their relevance for semiotics, I first introduce von Uexküll's work and then move on to its interpretation by Deely. This involves the not unfamiliar manoeuvre of creeping up behind a thinker and producing something new and interesting that both retains essential elements of his thought and places it in an entirely different framework. Here it will be the shift from von Uexküll's understandably German idealism/constructivism ('All reality is subjective appearance'; von Uexküll 1926, xv) towards a semiotic 'constructivism' that is *objective*, but not as the binary opposite of subjective in the classical modern sense. *Objective* in the semiotic sense (with its roots in Dans Scotus and Poinsot) can include aspects of the physical and psychical in a labile interface but remains irreducible to either category (just like being-as-first-known). This requires a certain mental agility for even the most subtly agile critical thinker. A paradigm shift into a *post*modernism worth the name – at least that is Deely's challenge. Whether we retain the term postmodern or opt for Latour's (1999a, 21) *nonmodern*[2] matters little. Whatever the term, it will indicate something different from modernism and *current* accounts of 'postmodernism.'

I will also seek to elaborate the critical distinction between the animal and human *Umwelten* – or species-specific objective worlds as Deely presents it. This distinction is timely, because although it has similarities with Heidegger's treatment of exactly the same question, I will claim that Deely provides a more articulate and nuanced analysis. Those who are shocked by and criticize Heidegger's 'abyss' between man and animal (e.g., Krell 1992; Derrida 1989, 1991) might find this approach of value, even if only to distinguish themselves from it. The ultimate issue is this: To what extent it can be said that a non-languaging, non-human animal[3] apprehends its *Umwelt* or milieu/environing world *as* a world at all?[4] Deely's distinction between zoosemiosis and anthroposemiosis intersects with Wittgenstein's approach to forms of life and expressive capacities that can only exist in language: 'We say a dog is afraid his master will beat him; but not, he is afraid his master will beat him tomorrow. Why not?' (Wittgenstein 1967, §650). What would be the expressive behavioural manifestation of this fear about a future event? To what extent is it intelligible to say that a tick feels pain, or has an opinion, or lives in a 'world' at all? These distinctions might force themselves between us and become interesting. The concept of objective being introduced in the preceding chapter (i.e., as something existing only insofar as it exists within awareness) will be seen as providing the relational network for the fabrication of species-specific objective worlds or *Umwelten*. Deely (1986b, 269) writes:

> If we now translate *Umwelt* as *objective world*, we are also in a fair position to see the significance of this notion for the understanding of semiosis as a unique process in nature. An *Umwelt*, von Uexküll tells us, is the physical environment as filtered or transformed by the given organism according to what is important or 'significant' to it. Elements of the physical environ-

ment are networked objectively, i.e., so as to establish the sphere of experience as something superordinate to and strictly transcending, all the while containing partially and resting upon aspects of, the physical environment in its 'natural' or 'mind-independent' being. *Umwelten* are thus species-specific: No two types of organisms live in the same objective worlds, even though they share the same physical environment. What the bat seeks (nourishment) the moth avoids (providing nourishment for bats), and conversely.

Von Uexküll is better known today than in 1976, when Sebeok asked who had benefited from his *Bedeutungslehre* (theory of meaning). In fact, Deely (1990, 120) once characterized von Uexküll as 'one of the greatest cryptosemioticians of the century.' What did von Uexküll do to attract the attention of Heidegger, Merleau-Ponty, Deleuze and Guattari, and (especially) contemporary semioticians (e.g., Sebeok, Deely) and biosemioticians and biologists (e.g., Hoffmeyer, Maturana, Bateson)?

I will rely principally on Jakob von Uexküll's son, Thure, for a preparatory account of his father's work. Specifically, I will be summoning two works by the son: his introduction to his father's *Bedeutungslehre* (1982), and 'Jakob von Uexküll's *Umwelt* Theory' (1989). Once I have presented the father's essential notions, I will begin a shift to Deely's semiotic interpretation, which liberates von Uexküll from his own somewhat counterproductive reliance on post-Kantian idealism (i.e., objects conform to cognition, *never* can cognition conform to objects – the closed bubble of the representational sphere).[5] Thure also appears to ultimately rely on an orthodox Kantian perspective, although he realizes that 'the epistemological premise of Jacob von Uexküll's theory is neither objectivistic nor subjectivist but – as one would describe it today – "systemic"' (or as we might also say, 'a semiotic reality').

Jakob Von Uexküll was born in 1864 in Keblas, Estonia. He originally studied zoology, and his later work was concerned with how living beings perceive their environment. He originated a method of research he called *Umweltforschung* (*Umwelt* studies) and in 1926 founded the Institut für *Umweltforschung* at the University of Hamburg.[6] As Deleuze notes in our chapter epigram, von Uexküll was one of the founders of ethology. His primary interest was the role played by sign processes in living organisms. His starting point was that living organisms respond to signs rather than to causal impulses. Organisms are selective *interpreters*; they are perceiving and acting subjects that do not respond to external effects in a causal-mechanical way, but rather with specific, autonomous responses.[7] Von Uexküll gives the now philosophically notorious example of the tick's activity to illustrate his *Umwelt* theory.[8]

The Tick as an Interpreter – The Functional Cycle

In his remarkable *A Stroll through the Worlds of Animals and Men* (1957), von Uexküll assumes that anyone who lives in the country will know what a tick is. But given that for many people this is not the case, let us note that a tick is a small insect (*Ixodinae*), related to mites, that lives off the warm blood of mammals. Paraphrasing von Uexküll's account (1957: 6–13), the life of the *tick as interpreter* unfolds in the following way:

The blind and deaf tick needs to eat, so it climbs to the end of some twig or branch, where it may fall or be brushed off onto a passing mammal. The tick climbs towards light because its skin is photo-sensitive. It can detect an approaching mammal with its sense of smell (i.e, the mammal has a specific odour caused by its sweat glands). When the tick senses the odour (or sign) of the passing mammal, it drops (with luck) onto it and latches on. The tick is sensitive to temperature and seeks out a warm, hairless spot (e.g., an armpit), where it will pump itself full of blood, becoming the size of a garden pea.

For von Uexküll, the point of this scenario is that 'what we are dealing with is not with an exchange of forces between two objects, but the relations between a living subject and its object' (1957, 11). There are certainly physical and chemical stimuli, but to stop at this purely physiological observation is to have missed something important! A traditional physiological account would describe the tick's behaviour as a 'reflex arc' elicited by physical and chemical stimuli (e.g., butyric acid, temperature, tactile response). A reflex arc simply transmits, by way of the activity of the nervous system, purely physical effects of motion between sensory receptors and the muscles of the effectors. The entire process involves a transfer of *motion* (like a mechanism) without any interpretive or perceptual activity that cannot be reduced to purely physical terms. Von Uexküll certainly recognizes physical or chemical stimuli, but he also argues that this approach misses the point: 'We are not concerned with the chemical stimulus of butyric acid, any more than with the mechanical stimulus (released by the hairs), or the temperature stimulus of the skin. We are concerned solely with the fact that, out of the hundreds of stimuli radiating from the qualities of the mammal's body, only three become the bearers of receptor cues for the tick. Why just these three and no others?' (ibid.)

The answer for von Uexküll is that living organisms respond to perceptual *signs* (*Merkzeichen*) or 'meaning' (*Bedeutung*),[9] not to causal impulses.[10] Physical, chemical, or thermal changes to the receptor organs are interpreted as signs of the (not yet perceptible) 'perceptual cues' of an object, as a counterpart for a specific behaviour. Von Uexküll argues that the 'subject' (tick) and 'object' (mammal) dovetail into each other and constitute a systematic whole or *functional cycle*. The organism or interpreter receives signs from its environment, and these perceptual signs trigger specific action impulses or operation signs (*Wirkzeichen*). The whole cycle is a process made not of static objects but rather of sign relations – a semiosis. For example, with the tick there are three functional cycles, which follow each other in processual succession: (1) The mammal's skin glands are the sites of perceptual meaning in the first cycle: the butyric acid triggers perceptual signs in the tick that induce the tick to let go of the twig and fall onto the passing mammal. (2) The mammal's hair now produces perceptual signs that trigger the tick to move around until a warm, bare patch of skin is found. (3) The temperature of the mammal's bare skin triggers perceptual signs in the tick that initiate the piercing process with the tick's proboscis.[11]

In this functional cycle the mammal (object) is a connecting link between the tick's effectors and receptors, which metaphorically 'grasp' the object like the two jaws of a pair of pincers. The 'perceptual jaw' gives perceptual meaning to the object, and the 'operational jaw' gives an effector meaning. For von Uexküll there is a counterpoint or *contrapuntal relation* between the organism as a 'meaning-utilizer' or interpretant, and the perceptual cues or 'meaning-factors' of the object – *Nature as music*.[12] Living beings develop in a kind of natural contrapuntal 'harmony' or refrain, with one another and with their environment.[13] Von Uexküll (J. 1982, 53) gives the example of the *octopus*, designated *as the subject* in its relation to *seawater as the meaning carrier*. In this scenario, the fact that water cannot be compressed is the precondition for the construction of the octopus's muscular swim bag. The pumping movement of the swim bag on the non-compressible water propels the animal backwards. Von Uexküll claims that the rule that governs the properties of seawater acts on the protoplasm of the octopus, thereby shaping the melody of the development of the octopus form to express the properties of seawater. *The rule of meaning that joins point and counterpoint is expressed in the action of swimming* – an energetic interpretant.

So the *Umwelt* is a model of a species' *significant* surroundings. The essential claim is that organisms interpret their environment and are not merely the passive objects of natural selection, as emphasized by much contemporary Darwinian evolutionary biology. The *Umwelt* consists of significant sign relationships. However, von Uexküll, in the prevailing context of Kantian idealism, presented *Umwelten* as subjective appearances or phenomena, and he thought of his *Umwelt* research as a confirmation of a Kantian philosophy of mind:

> *All reality is subjective appearance.* This must constitute the great, fundamental admission even of biology. It is utterly in vain to go seeking through the world for causes that are independent of the subject; we always come up against objects which owe their construction to the subject. When we admit that objects are appearances that owe their construction to a subject, we tread on firm and ancient ground, especially prepared by Kant to bear the edifice of the whole of natural science. Kant set the subject, man, over against objects, and discovered the fundamental principles according to which objects are built up from the mind. (1926: xv)

Before examining the contemporary value and semiotic use of the concept of *Umwelt*, freed from a needlessly unsemiotic Kantian philosophy of mind, I will give a brief account of Deleuze and Guattari's appropriation of von Uexküll's work.

Deleuze and Guattari's Appropriation

The key is the concept of the univocity of being. In his 1974 Vincennes seminar 'Anti Oedipe et mille plateaux,'[14] Deleuze articulates von Uexküll's work by moving from the concept of the univocity of being to a Spinozist interpretation of von Uexküll's nascent biosemiotics. For Deleuze, Duns Scotus only *thought* univocal being, whereas Spinoza affirms it with one Nature for all individuals,[15] and von Uexküll's *Umwelt* theory is an expression of the univocity of being. How does this truly creative and remarkable proposition work (not unlike Poinsot grasping the formal sign as an ontological relation in 1632 – the year Spinoza was born), and in what way might it be further articulated with the being of ontological relations?

In the 1974 Vincennes seminar, Deleuze makes (as does this book) a 'terminological detour' through the Middle Ages and seventeenth century (the philosophical black hole of the 'between times'). This trajectory is, in fact, obligatory, as one has to go back this far to rediscover *ontology* and its relevance to an ontology of signs. For Deleuze, this detour concerns the problem of the nature of being, which was discussed by the scholastic seminarians in terms of *equivocity, analogy,* and *univocity*. He emphasizes that these scholastic discussions still have concrete relevance for us because we continue to think with these terms even if we are not aware of them.

To state that 'being is equivocal' means that *'being is said in several senses of that which it is said'* (my italics). For example, being is said in a different way of God, animals, and tables. They have different kinds of being, and there is no common measure between these equivocal senses of being.

To state that 'being is analogical' means that *'being is said in several senses of that which it is said, but these senses are not without common measure: they are governed by relations of analogy'* (my italics). This is the canonical interpretation of Aquinas, and it is intimately linked to the concept of the categories (e.g. substance, quantity, relation) and to the categorial thinking of Aristotle and Kant. The categories are the concepts that are said of every possible object of experience – in other words, the categories are that which is said of the different senses of the word 'being.' Deleuze gives the example of the 'object' lion, which is not a category because one cannot say 'lion' of every object of experience (one of course can do this at the risk of being placed in a mental asylum). Thus categorial thought is analogical because the categories are applied to the different senses of the word 'being.'

Deleuze defines the univocity of being thus: univocal being *'has only one sense and is said in one and the same sense of everything of which it is said'* (my italics). This is the thesis of Duns Scotus. Deleuze understands this as a 'pre-categorial' and pre-analogical thought – '*a mad thought*' (my italics) – which will become an experimentation with relations as the violent and repugnant 'hallucination point of thought.' How can we say that God and ticks, trees and stones, imaginary worlds and impossible objects (e.g., a square circle), have *one sense*, or univocal being?

Now it is possible at this point to sense that we are beginning to drown in a set of sterile debates that have absolutely no relevance to our experience. I have no mastery of scholasticism nor of the history of philosophy, but there is something interesting happening here that I would like to focus on.[16]

Duns Scotus is not seeking to completely eliminate analogy from the concept of being, but to show that it cannot be *exclusively* analogous. He does not exclude analogy, but rather allows for its possibility. His fundamental point is that unless there is a univocal concept of being common to the analogous ones, they will not be analogous but equivocal. In fact, he affirms that although being is metaphysically or logically univocal, in the order of entitative physical being it is analogical. Deleuze (Seminar, 14 January 1974) notes that without this distinction univocity would become heresy and lead to unpleasant consequences at the stake: 'If I say being is univocal, this means: there is no categorial difference between the assumed senses of the word 'being' and being is said in one and the same sense of everything which is. In a certain manner this means that the tick is God; there is no difference of category, there is no difference of substance, there is no difference of form. It becomes a mad thought.' Scotus did not go this far; his motives were to safeguard the possibility of our knowledge of God and to give metaphysics its proper object in a univocal concept of being. He thought this would distinguish metaphysics (as a science of being qua being) from physics portrayed as concerned with the reality of singular physical existents (*entia realia*).

Now Scotus argues, following Avicenna, that if being is univocal it follows that being is the primary object of the intellect, preceding any particular notion of being as applied to God or creatures (e.g., infinite or finite – being-as-first-known is neither infinite nor finite). The intellect or understanding has its own proper object or *primum intelligibile*, just as sound is to hearing (*primum audibile*) or light to seeing (*primum visibile*). The object of the intellect or understanding is *ens primum cognitum*, being-as-first-known. Avicenna had made being the primary object of the intellect, in contradistinction to either God or substance, the proper subject of metaphysics. Scotus adopted this position with his own nuances, which I will not attempt to pursue here.

Contemporary Value and Semiotic Use

So what? Deely will claim that Poinsot's conception of the coinciding univocal being of relations in objective existence (i.e., as known), whether mind-dependent or mind-independent (ontological relations are truly relations and distinct or 'external' to their terms, whether posited as mind-dependent or mind-independent), is grounded in the univocity of the primary object of the intellect, *ens primum cognitum*, as understood by Avicenna. The ontological rationale of relation is univocal, neither physical nor psychical, although capable of being either depending on the particular circumstances. Relations are transversal; they can pass freely between what we consider mind-dependent and mind-independent. Relations in their univocal being as 'objective' relations are neither 'real' nor 'ideal,' although at any given here and now they will be one or the other – the ultimate abstract machine. For Deely it is this univocity that allows for both semiosis (the action of signs) as the being proper to experience and the consequent fluid intermixing of 'nature' and 'culture' in our experience as constituted through ontological sign relations in anthroposemiosis – the human use of signs.

Of particular interest is that both Deleuze and Poinsot emphasize that there is something about univocal being which is *pre-categorial*. As Heidegger (1962, 23) puts it: the 'problem of the unity of Being as over against the multiplicity of categories applied to things.' Poinsot's doctrine of signs is a more *fundamental ontology* in that the action of signs as the medium of communication is presupposed by any system of categories and it is semiosis – the action of signs – that allows for the subsequent construction of categorial schemas. Traditional Aristotelian natural philosophy was concerned with the structure of *ens reale*, or mind-independent existence understood in terms of *substances* or units of independent existence and their *accidents* or properties and characteristics. Poinsot's genius was that he undercut this categorial approach by showing that it is from within an expanded notion of experience that being is divided up between the mind-dependent (*ens rationis*) and mind-independent (*ens reale*) *and that these two kinds of being come together in the sign understood as an ontological relation*. Poinsot realized that the formal sign is an ontological relation, 'external' to its terms. It is existentially inseparable from its foundation but nevertheless distinct from it. A doctrine of signs or semiotic is not restricted to one side of the division – it is as 'realist' as it is 'idealist.' We can genuinely encounter the mind-independent existence of things (rather than simply affirm their existence, as in Kant's philosophy) because the ontology of the sign relation is univocal. The ontological relation is neutral or indifferent to its realization, whether in nature or thought. Ontological relation is contrasted with the transcendental 'relation,' or rather the relativity of relative (i.e., finite) beings. A transcendental relation is *not* a relation, but rather the fact that individual existents or subjects are *not* relations, but *relative beings*. All being is 'relative,' but this relativity is twofold – transcendental and ontological. That is to say, within experience we find that as soon as we wish to explain or understand some individual existent we are obliged to take account of what those individuals are not – namely, their relations and dependencies on things other than themselves (their ontological relations). For example: the eye or visual system is not a *relation*, but as soon as we wish to discourse about the eye we are forced by its manner of being to consider its relation to light. I am not my mother, but I am related to my mother – that relation is an ontological relation 'over and above' my transcendentally relative being, my being as an individual being dependent on many factors other than my actual instantiation.[17]

Poinsot's semiotic approach is pre-categorial because the sign 'as the medium of communication functions by *distinguishing connections* within experience, and so is not only presupposed to any system of categories, but is also the instrument of their establishment' (Poinsot, 1985: TDS, 476). What needs to be emphasized is that the sign is univocal in its being as an ontological relation and that this univocity is 'grounded' in the univocity of being-as-first-known, the primary object of the understanding.

In other words: univocal, semiotic reality – the reality of experience – is not reducible to the mind's own workings (e.g., as in the Kantian synthesis) nor is it to that of a prejacent external physical world in which the mind has no part. It is a limitless interface where the line between what is and what is not, independent of interpretative activity, is a constantly shifting semiotic process. As Deely observes so well in numerous articles,[18] what comes first in experience is neither *ens reale* nor *ens rationis*. It is in our experience that being divides into what is not independent of understanding (*ens rationis*) and what is independent of my understanding (*ens reale*). Thus there is a 'prederivative' sense of being, and this 'sense' of being, 'whatever it be, is prior to being in either of the derived senses; and it is this prior being – the being proper to experience – that semiotic takes as its province' (Deely 1988b, 73). This priority of univocal being is not a linear temporality that would be left behind; it is intrinsic to the possibility of being able to predicate anything at all (e.g., 'what is that?'). Univocal being is a 'unique' or singular notion, *sui generis*. As we have noted, Scotus is inspired by Avicenna in his understanding of univocal being, as is Deleuze, who understands 'sense' in terms of Avicenna's univocity. For Deleuze it is the univocity of sense that allows the escape from the circle of the proposition. We are established 'from the outset' within sense as that which allows for the articulation of the difference between things and propositions. Sense, or univocity, is presupposed and is that which allows for the distinction between the particular and the general. For Avicenna univocity is the third state of essence, essence as sense, the 'pure event,' indifferent to all opposites.[19] For Deely (1988a, 8), this Persian doctor and metaphysician (Ibn Sina) was a critically important and somewhat neglected figure: 'In fact, we are able to see in hindsight that what Avicenna had given a name to was nothing less than the *materia prima* of anthroposemiosis. The *primum cognitum* of medieval thought turns out to be precisely what the linguistic sign informs in enabling us through discourse to argue about what is and what is not in nature as about how experience is and is not rightly to be interpreted in any given context of discourse, including the metaphysical.'

Deely will argue (with some reference to Heidegger) that this apprehension of univocal being by the understanding or intellect is only available to animals operating in language (currently human animals), because language entails the grasping of relations of signification as such, rather than only perceptible aspects of things. Non-languaging animals are aware of their surroundings and of relative beings but *not of the relations themselves*, because relations themselves are not sense-perceptible. Univocal being requires an understanding of something that is *not* perceptible and that can only be expressed through linguistic means. In such an incorporeal scenario, this would be what differentiates human animal communication from animal communication. We will inevitably return to this 'problematic' proposition.

Let us recapitulate: There is a pre-categorial, 'pre-derivative' understanding of being (or sense) as univocal. It acts as the permeable, osmotic interface or articulation between the orders of being and non-being, or the mind-dependent and mind-independent as they are distinguished by experience. It allows for the communion between thought and being. It is superior to any categorial standpoint in that it allows for categorial interconnections by distinguishing connections or relations within experience. Says Deely (1988b, 80): 'The thesis is that relation, rather than substance or accident, is to serve as the basis for all *semiotic* explanation, and that the ontological explanation in the traditional categories of substance and accident, to whatever extent it is valid, is subordinate to the standpoint of semiotic by reason of being assimilable to (and subsequently analytically derivable from) transcendental relation and ontological relation generally.'

Thus, as Deely often observes, semiotic is 'an integral philosophy of experience' that goes beyond both Aristotelian and Kantian categorial thought. Aristotelian realist categories are concerned with nature as it is supposed to exist independently of human thought. Kantian idealism takes the opposite view, contending that the order of beings as existing in themselves is forever hidden from human understanding. The Kantian categories represent universal forms or structures that are presupposed to any judgments about the world of appearances or *phenomena*, not to things in themselves. Deely argues throughout his work that although Poinsot recognizes the inadequacy of the Aristotelian categorial schema for the perspective of semiotic which understands experience as a product of sign relations, it is Peirce's semiotic categorial scheme (Firstness, Secondness, Thirdness – which are three classes of relations – monadic, dyadic, triadic) that begins to truly develop this realization of the interpenetration within experience of a living tissue of sign relations that does not preclude mind-independent elements from experience. This interpenetration within experience of 'nature' and 'culture' is possible because of the univocal being of the ontological sign relation (Peirce's thirdness as triadic relation), in which nature and culture come together. Deely does indicate that in Hegel's *Logic* ('Being, as the immediate indeterminate, is in fact nothing') there is a confused recognition that not all relations are the work of the mind, but he adds that Hegel never clearly articulates their interrelation in experience, nor does he adequately isolate the ontological rationale of the univocity of relation.[20]

Furthermore, Deely will argue that it is Peirce's 'semiotic categories' that account for the transformation of the species-specific objective world of the animal *Umwelt* into the species-specific objective world of the human *Lebenswelt*, within which it is realized that the human *Umwelt* (or *Lebenswelt*) is *different* from, and not coextensive with, the sense-perceptible physical surroundings, and by reason of including understanding the imperceptible relation of signification as such. The 'animal' remains captured by its *Umwelt*, which never becomes present to it *as* an *Umwelt* – although the animal is clearly aware of sense-perceptible aspects of its surroundings. (Heidegger would say that the animal is 'benumbed'). Although Heidegger's analysis in FCM is 'violent and awkward' (Derrida 1991, 111), it is obvious that Heidegger is struggling to differentiate zoosemiosis (as common to animals) from anthroposemiosis (as unique to linguistic animals) without the necessary semiotic tools. The approach taken by Deely is neither anthropomorphic (in fact, it precisely avoids misplaced linguistic anthropomorphism) nor bad biology; it 'simply' distinguishes among different uses of sign relations – to wit, physiosemiosis, phytosemiosis, zoosemiosis, and anthroposemiosis. Animals use signs and communicate, but they do not live *in* language and do not grasp imperceptible sign relations as such. Their apprehension terminates in sense-perceptible aspects of the physical environment. Or to be more reserved, we can say that currently we have no knowledge of a non-human *linguistic* animal that *ipso facto* grasps (or rather understands) the incorporeal sign relation as distinct from its terms. The species-specific human *Lebenswelt* arises with the awareness of the distinction between the relation and the things it relates; this is what allows for the arbitrary systems of communication that we designate as languages – and as a consequence for textuality and the infinite (in principle) malleability of the *Lebenswelt*. Eugen Baer succinctly states the matter:

> Semiotics [the human study of semiosis] begins ontogenetically as 'a moment of anthroposemiosis' with the insight that experience depends on the action of signs. Once signs are recognized as imperceptible ontological relations which correlate objects and/or things, we are at the threshhold of what for Deely is specifically anthroposemiotic, the ability to introduce into objects the dimension of stipulability. This underlies the capacity for language and renders semiosis in principle unlimited. The stipulable sign is the characteristic trait of what Deely calls 'text.' And it is this capacity to produce texts that distinguishes anthroposemiosis from zoosemiosis. It is species-specific for human semiosis.
>
> What exactly is textuality? Texts are strings of signs that are in principle exchangeable (substitutable) with other signs in accordance with a given code. Texts are thus transformable from one set of objects to another, precisely because their 'being' resides not in things or objects, but 'in-between' them. (1992: 355–6)

Both Henri Bergson and Raymond Ruyer (who are major influences on Deleuze and Guattari) make a similar distinction – albeit less analytically nuanced – between the animal and human animal use of signs. In *Germinal Life: The Difference and Repetition of Deleuze*, Keith Ansell-Pearson (1999, 54) reminds us that for Bergson, in *Creative Evolution*, the instinctive signs that characterize the language of insects are limited and attached to specific objects: 'The sign is adherent to the thing signified' (Bergson 1975, 174). What characterizes human language is the ability of signs to be transferred from one object to another; they become infinitely 'mobile' rather than 'adherent' – '*the intelligent sign is mobile*' (ibid., 175; Bergson's italics). There is a difference in *kind* between the human and animal use of signs (moreover, animals don't know they are using signs). The main insight of Bergson is that without language – as the awareness of the relation of signification, which allows the sign to be 'mobile' – the animal is 'riveted' to materially present sense-perceptible objects. The animal is captured or riveted to an *Umwelt*, whereas the human animal lives with the understanding of being-in-an-*Umwelt* and can play with the relations that constitute it, and thereby enjoys the possibility, among others, of developing and discussing philosophies of life and semiotics.

In *L'animal, l'homme, la fonction symbolique*, Ruyer (1964: 98–9) makes essentially the same observation when discussing the well-known case of Helen Keller, who was blind and deaf. He discusses the matter in terms of the difference between the animal's use of *stimulus-signals* and the human's grasp of *sign-symbols*, the difference being that the human animal grasps the relation of signification as such:

> To understand a signal as a signal, following a conditioning process, is not at all to understand it as a symbol. On the contrary the signal-function blocks the symbol function. The decisive point for Helen Keller is that 'water' wasn't necessarily a sign-signal by which water was requested or expected, but was 'the name of the substance whereby it could be mentioned, conceived, remembered, celebrated.' At that moment, the meaning, for her, of the word 'water' could not be interpreted as the last phase of a conditioning. *As long as one attempted to condition Helen Keller to a word, one in fact prevented her from understanding what language was.* It was necessary that she suddenly realized that the word *had* a meaning. A discovery that leads to the discovery that everything has a name, and that every name had a meaning. From now on she was no longer in an animal *Umwelt*, but in the world.[21]

Deleuze and Guattari make a related observation in ATP when they refer to the well-known example of the bees' dance studied by Karl von Frisch[22] as taken up by Emile Benveniste. Deleuze and Guattari are claiming that the first determination of language is not trope or metaphor but *indirect discourse.* The bee 'has no language because it can communicate what it has seen but not transmit what has been communicated to it. A bee that has seen a food source can communicate the message to bees that did not see it, but a bee that has not seen it cannot transmit the message to others that did not see it.' (ATP, 77). For Deleuze and Guattari, language must be able to go from a second to a third party, neither of whom has seen. Language is deterritorialized and can be passed on *ad infinitum*. As Maritain notes,[23] commenting on von Frisch's work, this means that bees use signs but do not know they are using signs. The bees' dance is no more a language than the fact of a dog sitting when his owner says 'sit.'[24]

Deleuze and Guattari will argue, following Spinoza's medieval ethics and proto-ethology, that things, animals, or persons are defined by movements and rests, speeds, and slownesses, and by affects. These assemblages are individuations not of an already individuated object or person, but rather of relational events that can include, for example, a time of day, a season, or anything at all ... a text, a social body.

Deleuze and Guattari contend that beings are distinguished not analogically in terms of genus or species, but rather by their degrees of 'power,' which correspond to a certain capacity to be *affected*. They construct a univocal Spinozist ethology or cartography of affective capacities. The univocity of being is expressed through one determining factor: What are the affections or relations that a being can enter into – what assemblages can it participate in – what are its *becomings*? From the perspective of univocal being, the only difference is the different relations that a being can enter into. Univocity for Deleuze 'is said' of completely different, equivocal beings (boy, table, girl, train, god): 'a single and same voice for the whole thousand-voiced multiple' (DR, 304). This is a conception no longer of genera and species, but rather of the assemblages into which each being is capable of entering. In other words, a being is defined by the relations and assemblages it can enter into – tell me what relations you can enter into, and I will tell you who you are. These relations, as the relations of relative beings, are *Univocal* in their being as relations. And this gives us precisely the distinction in our experience between relative beings and their relations prior to a categorial schema. In *Spinoza: Practical Philosophy*, Deleuze puts it thus: 'So an animal, a thing is never separable from its relations with the world' (1988a, 125). Gregory Bateson and many other biologists make the same observation – for Bateson, the 'unit of 'survival' was organism + environment.

In ATP (*the* book of subjectless events and becomings) this approach is illustrated with (among many other striking and creative examples) Jacob von Uexküll's notorious tick. The tick is viewed in terms of its affective capacities or relations rather than in terms of physiology. As Ansell-Pearson (GL, 187) notes in a brief but insightful encounter with the work of Deely,[25] this is a 'semiotics of affect' in which von Uexküll's *Umwelt* theory and concept of organism can be understood in terms of the scholastic notion of '*species*' rather than in Darwinian terms of relations of descent. The organism does indeed inhabit a 'species-specific objective word' (the expression is Deely's) in that its world is specific to its biological type; *but also* in that its '*species*,' whether impressed or expressed, is what makes its 'world.' And as we have already noted at some length, scholastic expressed 'species' are formal signs or interpretants that are not 'subjective' in the modern classical sense. Their whole being as ontological relations is in 'being-toward.' This is what makes *Umwelten* 'objective' or open worlds rather than 'subjective' closed worlds. Objective worlds are not in binary opposition with the modern sense of subjective. Objective worlds as experienced include a shifting amalgam of mind-dependent and mind-independent aspects (or the 'psychical' and 'physical') through the univocal being of sign relations. This dynamic is what allows for the enterprise of constructive scientific relative realism, through the critical control of objectification, and through the possibility that some theories remain purely objective fictions (i.e., with no physical lining) or return to the status of fictions (e.g., the ether, phlogiston) whereas others become 'objective' testimonies to nature's subjective being (i.e., the being nature has independently of its being known). For example, the earth's tectonic plates now drift and collide, over and above our thinking that they do, although for many years such a 'fiction' was ridiculed. Some things are not reducible to our experience of them, but paradoxically become more substantiated and 'for themselves' the more we are *related* to them, or the more they are 'for us' – 'the truth of the relative' or the truth of relations.[26]

Species-Specific Objective Worlds

A recapitulation: Deely has systematically and continuously argued for the importance of the notion of *Umwelt* or species-specific worlds for understanding the action and being of signs in the constitution of an *objective world* – that is, a world to the extent that it exists in any way as known. As experienced, the physical world is *objective*, it is an object of awareness. The distinction between objects of experience that are *only* objects of experience and those that are *also* physical existents also occurs within experience (which leads some thinkers to a position in which experience is 'subjective' and we can know nothing apart from our 'constructions' or representations). Experience is not locked into realism or idealism; it is neither/nor, for it is univocal in its being, including both the constructions of the mind and elements that are not reducible to the mind's constructive capacity.

Instead of a dichotomy between subjective (observer dependent) and inaccessible objective (observer independent), there is a *trichotomy*, or triadic semiotic relation, including an experiencing organism (or interpretant), the object experienced, and the basis on which the object exists as experienced. I will present an extended quotation from Deely, which I suggest indicates that semiotics has fortunately progressed, in his hands, beyond anything Heidegger's phenomenology was able to articulate:

> That in which experience consists in the being proper to it is the sign relation, or rather, the network of sign relations colorfully called 'the semiotic web' by Thomas Sebeok in a metaphor borrowed from the German biologist Jakob von Uexküll. This web is, on the one side, superordinate to physical nature [...], on the other side, subordinate to the constitution of the knower (the cognitive organism). The being proper to experience is not the being of objects, still less the being of things. It is the being proper to the network of interpretive relations according to which the cognitive organism is inserted in the environment not merely as one physical thing among others (one substance with its accidents among other substances with their accidents), but as a being whose objective world is shot through and constituted by cares and interests species-specifically proper to it according to its biological constitution. Beyond this, in the case of human beings, the objective world is further structured through linguistic relations (a species-unique type of semiotic relation) which convey a cultural heritage linked, not directly, but indirectly only, to a specific biological constitution. 'Being-in-a-world,' that is to say, an objective world as distinct from a merely physical environment, is not something uniquely human, though 'being-in-a-world' that has the texture of linguistic understanding woven into its fabric or perceptual and sensory objects is uniquely human. (1992, 309)

This brings us back to the difference between the animal *Umwelt* and the human animal *Umwelt*, or *Lebenswelt*, as Deely will call it. As we have already noted, this distinction lies in the peculiarity of the human animal's ability to interact and play with pure relations. This is equivalent to the 'emergence' of language and allows for the possibility of inventing an *Umwelt* in ways that are not strictly proportionate to biologically determined positive, negative, or indifferent affects. Deely (NB, 221) gives the example of legal systems, which distribute property not on the basis of species territoriality but 'according to an abstract plan of objective boundaries imposed upon the physical environment as identified with this or that of its features – for example, 'the Mississippi River as separating Iowa from Illinois for a certain stretch.' The essential point here is that the human *Umwelt* is not 'riveted' or 'captured' by its species-specific world, as Bergson would say, but is able, through the human understanding of relations as distinct from related objects, to be restructured *Umwelt* in infinite ways – an unbounded semiosis within anthroposemiosis, a human-becoming-itself in its unlimitedness.

As Deely notes (NB, 218–19), the notion of *Umwelten* or species-specific worlds is now well established in semiotic studies to distinguish between the prejacent physical environment and the objective world of an organism.[27] In *A Stroll through the Worlds of Animals and Men* (1957, 5), Jakob von Uexküll imagined the *Umwelt* as like an invisible bubble surrounding the organism: 'We must first blow, in fancy, a soap bubble around each creature to represent its own world, filled with the perceptions which it alone knows. When we ourselves step into one of these bubbles, the familiar meadow is transformed. Many of its colourful features disappear, others no longer belong together but appear in new relationships. A new world comes into being.'

In the same extraordinary work, von Uexküll also compared the *Umwelt* or world of experience to a spider's web: 'As the spider spins its threads, every subject spins his relations to certain characters of the things around him, and weaves them into a firm web which carries his existence' (ibid., 14). This is what Sebeok designated the semiotic web.

In order to illustrate the constitution of an objective world, Deely (NB, 219) combines these two notions 'into the single model of a kind of geodesic sphere whose interior as well as its surface consists of a series of intersecting lines.' He notes that the spherical image is only analogous, as the surface of the 'sphere' is irregular and determined by the radii relations linking the individual with elements of its physical surroundings (some of which are very close and some 'as far as alien galaxies'). The model is so valuable and interesting that I will quote from Deely's own work, which would be absurd to paraphrase:

> Each intersection is an object, each line a relationship. Lines radiate outwards from the center where each of us stands to the surface of the sphere, and lines extend also crosswise, intersecting the radii. The radii lines represent relations between ideas and objects, the intersecting lines represent relations between objects, and the intersections themselves represent the objects. Thus, the objective world is the sphere of an individual's experi-

ences built up out of relationships, and the internal constitution of this sphere is precisely that of a web the various intersections of whose strands present to us the objects according to the meaning of which we lead our lives. At the center of such a three-dimensional spider's web, by maintaining and elaborating it, we live our lives.

It is crucial to understand that in this model the surface of the geodesic sphere of experience is a 'virtual intersection or interface between nature and culture.' The external senses guarantee that elements of the physical surroundings are objectified in experience in interaction with our bodies. Now this model of experience is further (and infinitely) complexified by memory and imagination, which add new radii and further intersections. Thus there are incorporated into this web of experience elements that do not correspond to actual physical environmental influences. Now, as von Uexküll and Deely note, this web of experience is determined by the biological constitution of the organism or species – it is a species-specific objective world. As we have already had occasion to observe, human animals understand the relational strands themselves, which structure sense-perceptible objects and which can now be used to restructure the *Umwelt*, starting with the realization that it *is* an *Umwelt*, and then perhaps wondering what other *Umwelten* are like – which, as Deely claims (1990, 123), is *a priori* impossible in the *original* Kantian scheme: 'Either *Umweltenforschung* is a form of transcendental illusion, or, if, for example, von Frisch really did interpret with some exactness the bee's dance or von Uexküll the toad's search image – then von Uexküll, in extending Kant's ideas to biology, was doing something more, something that the Kantian paradigm did not allow for, namely, achieving objectively and grasping as such an intersubjective correspondence between subjectivities attained through the sign relation.'

Deely argues that von Uexküll is going beyond the Kantian paradigm in spite of himself. Von Uexküll saw the *Umwelt* as a 'subjective' or phenomenal world distinct from an 'objective' world, but the semiotic approach to experience cannot be completely assimilated to Kantian idealism any more than it can be to simple realism. Semiotic reality is an interpenetration of the mind's own constructs with aspects of a mind-independent environment woven seamlessly together in the ontological univocity of the sign relation. Semiotic objectivity (*esse objectivum*/objective being), as we have had much occasion to note, is not assimilable to the modern opposition between subjective and objective. It is 'the truth of the relative.' Objectivity in this sense is opposed to both subjectivity and objectivity as understood in classical modern idealism. As Deely notes (ibid., 122), the reappropriation of the scholastic notion of objectivity (particularly as formulated by Poinsot – and implicitly developed by Peirce) is 'necessary to make sense of the very title von Uexküll gives to a main section in one of his key essays (1957: 73), "The Same Subject as an Object in Different *Umwelten.*"'

This kind of objectivity is engendered by Peirce's interpretant or proper significate outcome of a sign, which makes present an object other than itself to some third in a mediated semiotic interaction that cannot be reduced to a dyadic physical interaction. In *Chaosmosis* (1995, 22), Guattari suggests that we place the concept of an enlarged definition of 'subjectivity' within this relational perspective:

> So we are proposing to decentre the question of the subject onto the question of subjectivity. Traditionally, the subject was conceived as the ultimate essence of individuation, as a pure, empty, prereflexive apprehension of the world, a nucleus of sensibility, of expressivity – the unifier of states of consciousness. With subjectivity we place the emphasis instead on the founding instance of intentionality. This involves taking the relation between subject and object by the middle and foregrounding the expressive instance (or the interpretant of the Peirceian triad).

For Guattari, it was imperative to enlarge the definition of subjectivity beyond the classical opposition between individual subject and society. All his work involved developing a more 'transversalist' or 'schizoanalytic' approach to subjectivity, one that recognized the importance of non-linguistic elements irreducible to the linguistic analysis of the Saussurian tradition. Guattari always affirmed the value and importance of Peirce's semiotics over and above European semiology. It should also be noted that part of Deely's contribution to the commonwealth of ideas lies in his being one of the most astute contemporary readers and innovators of a post-Peirceian semiotics capable of doing justice to our experience, rather than simply engaging in elaborate feats of explaining it away.

Heideggerian *Umwelten*

In *The Fundamental Concepts of Metaphysics: World, Finitude, Solitude* (1995), Heidegger, in some of his most relentless and stunningly benumbing reflections, presents the thesis that '*the animal is poor in world*' (Heidegger's italics).[28] I will not attempt here to give a complete account of Heidegger's 1929–30 biology lectures,[29] but will simply attempt to indicate the relation between Heidegger, Peirce, and Deely and thereby demonstrate the contemporary relevance of a semiotic appropriation and reformulation of Jakob von Uexküll's *Umwelt* theory.[30]

For Heidegger (and for many others in their own way) what is peculiar to the animal is the way it is captivated by its environment and is thus 'poor in world.' What might this perhaps troubling and problematic expression mean?

As a possible theme for a *fundamental problem of metaphysics*, Heidegger asks this question: 'What is world?' And as a strategy for answering this question, he undertakes a comparative examination of three theses: 'the stone is worldless,' 'the animal is poor in world,' and 'man is world forming.' He starts from the middle by asking what it means to say that the animal is poor in world. He quickly notes (FCM, 192) that at first sight this thesis appears 'to run directly counter to the most penetrating fundamental reflections in biology and zoology, when we consider that ever since J. von Uexküll we have all become accustomed to talking about the *environmental world of the animal*.' How does Heidegger deal with this apparent contradiction? His thesis unfolds in the following way.

Being poor in world implies poverty in the sense of possessing less. But less of what? (FCM, 193). Heidegger, taking most of his examples from von Uexküll, starts with the proposition that the animal has fewer relationships than human Dasein has at its disposal. For example, the bee, the frog, and the chaffinch all operate within their strictly limited domains of relations. But there is something more crucial than this. Heidegger contends that the manner in which an animal can 'penetrate' whatever is accessible to it is also limited. His fundamental claim, which he will constantly rework and examine, is that the animal does not know things *as* things. As a first approximation, the animal lacks the structure of the *apophantic as*. This is in fact strikingly close to Deleuze and Guattari's analysis in ATP (especially in the plateau 'The Geology of Morals'). A threshold of deterritorialization is crossed wherein 'the scientific world (*Welt*, as opposed to the *Umwelt* of the animal) [allows for] the translation of all the flows, particles, codes, and territorialities of the other strata into a sufficiently deterritorialized system of signs, in other words into an overcoding specific to language' (ATP, 62).

The worker bee is familiar with the colour and scent of the blossoms it frequents but does not know the stamens of these blossoms *as* stamens.

Nor does it know of the number of leaves or of the roots of the plant. Heidegger will (FCM, 193) argue that compared to the world of animals, the world of man is more extensive, both in its penetrability 'and in respect to the manner in which we can penetrate ever more deeply in this penetrability.' This is why man is characterized as *world forming*. Heidegger emphasizes that at this point in the analysis, there is no question of claiming some hierarchical evaluation or superiority for man and incompleteness for the animal.

To get closer to understanding the sense of the word 'poverty,' Heidegger in his comparative examination turns to the stone, which is *worldless*. The stone lies on the path but does not touch the path. Everything around the stone is *inaccessible* to the stone itself (FCM, 197). The stone is not deprived of anything (it is not poor in world) because it has no access to the beings among which it turns up. Thus there is a distinction emerging between the *specific manner of being* pertaining to animals, and the *specific manner of being* pertaining to a material thing. The rock is given *in some way* to the lizard but not *as* a rock – the rock is not accessible to the lizard *as a being*. The blade of grass is a 'beetle path' for the beetle, but it is not a blade of grass. Heidegger will argue that the metaphysical significance of the specific relationships of animals with their environments has never been fully appreciated. If the animal has some access to the beings around it in a way that the stone does not, the animal is not deprived of world, but has world.

Heidegger frankly admits that the preliminary results of his comparative examination are perplexing and apparently logically impossible: 'The animal reveals itself as a being which *both has and does not have world*' (Heidegger's italics). He argues that the concept of world must therefore need further clarification.

I will pass over the discussion of solipsistic, modern idealism (Descartes, Kant, Hegel) in which man is initially understood as subject and consciousness, existing in its own isolated 'ego-sphere,' and take the story up with Heidegger's clarification of the '*proper being or proper peculiarity as the manner of being specific to the animal and its way of being proper to itself* [*Sich-zu-eigen-sein*] (FCM, 231). In distinguishing the organism from a machine, Heidegger (like many others) notes that the 'peculiar' character of the organism lies in its 'capacity' for *self*-production, or *self*-preservation.[31]

The capacity for molecular *self*-production indicates a kind of bootstrapping or circular production in which the capacity of the organism to produce itself '*does not leave itself behind*' (FCM, 233) or escape itself. To use Heidegger's novel terminology, the capacity for *self*-production remains *proper to itself* without any *self-consciousness* or *reflection*. The essential being of this *self*-productive capacity is *properly peculiar* [*Eigentümlichkeit*]. Heidegger reserves the expression 'self' and selfhood for the *specifically human peculiarity* of possessing reflection and consciousness beyond the *proper peculiarity* of *self*-production or autopoiesis proper to all organisms, including human animals.³² The proper being of the animal or of animality lies in this *proper peculiarity* of *self*-production and possession, which does not lose itself but rather remains 'its self' in this autopoietic drive or capacity. This drive has a self-reserve and circular production that is not reflective. Thus, for Heidegger, neither the animal's mode of being nor its behaviour directs itself towards beings *as such*.

The essential lesson of this analysis is that ultimately, for Heidegger (and Deely), the environing world (*Umgebung*), or *Umwelt* of the animal, is ready to hand but not present at hand. The animal is open to its surroundings, but not *as* a world that is not coextensive or reducible to the prejacent environment. Heidegger gives detailed accounts of experiments on bees (among other examples), drawn from the work of von Uexküll, to illustrate the thesis that the behaviour of the animal (in this case the bee) is not determined by the presence or absence of honey or flowers but rather by a play of inhibited and released drives. The bee is captured by the sun and does not grasp the sun *as such* – it does not *view* the sun. The animal is encircled by a ring of drives within which it is both open and captivated – it *is incapable of ever properly attending to something as such* (FCM, 248). Heidegger is distinguishing this approach from that of von Uexküll, who suggests that the animal lives an *Umwelt as* an *Umwelt*. It will be in anthroposemiosis that this realization occurs. However, Heidegger moderates the analysis:

> This question now leads us toward the distinction we tried to express by talking of man's *world-forming* and the animal's *poverty in world*, a poverty which, roughly put, is nonetheless a kind of wealth. The difficulty of the problem lies in the fact that in our questioning we always and inevitably interpret the poverty in world and the peculiar encirclement proper to the animal in such a way that we end up talking as if that which the animal relates to and the manner in which it does so were some being, and as if the relation involved were an ontological relation that is manifest to the animal. The fact that this is not the case forces us to claim that the *essence of life can become accessible only if we consider it in a deconstructive* [*abbauenden*] *fashion*. But this does not mean that life represents something inferior or

some kind of lower level in comparison with human Dasein. On the contrary, life is a domain which possesses a wealth of openness with which the human world may have nothing to compare. (FCM 255)

Deely contends that although Heidegger makes use of the term 'ontological relation,' he does not have the univocal concept of it as developed by Poinsot.[33] The ontological relation is not manifest to the animal because it is *imperceptible* and in its proper univocal being is neither mind-dependent nor mind-independent (although it will be one or the other at any given *hic* and *nunc*). Animals can be aware of 'absent signifieds' (objects that are not actually present), but these absent objects would always have some physical instantiation. Relations, by contrast, occur as the 'incorporeal vapour' (Deleuze) or as the 'ethereal *linkage itself between* the terms' (Deely), which can be understood but not seen or touched. As Deely emphasizes, non-human animals see related things *but not the relations* (which can only be understood, not perceived). The human animal, by distinguishing things from objects (and the relations from both) within anthroposemiosis, can use those relations to create the systems of communication we call languages. As we shall see in the following chapter on autopoiesis, Maturana will argue in a similar way, claiming that animals do not live in language, although he will suggest that some animals can begin to enter into language (as a coordination of a coordination of acts) *when living with languaging human animals*. However, Deely will claim that although animals can enter into coordinations of coordinations of acts – as long as these coordinations terminate in sense-perceptible objects – they have not attained language in its species-specific human sense. Animals communicate and are aware of their surroundings, but not of their surroundings *as* surroundings, of their *Umwelt* as an *Umwelt* or objective world grasped as a whole in relation to itself; this requires a distinction of objects from things and relations from both. This, as Deleuze and Guattari observe, is what transforms an *Umwelt* into a *Welt* or – to use Husserl and Deely's term – a *Lebenswelt*. It is a question of thresholds. The fact of Guattarian 'non-human enunciation,' 'proto-subjectivity,' 'ontological intensities,' 'specific enunciative consistencies,' or a 'non-human for-itself' does not gainsay a distinction between human and non-human enunciation.[34] What is remarkable in Guattari's 'fractal ontology' and 'transversalist' enlargement of enunciation is the refusal to accept the couplet Being-being as an ontological binary digit and to replace it rather with polyphonic Being and processes of deterritorialization deploying particular relations of alterity.[35] Emphasis is no longer placed on Being but on the *manner* of being, the machination producing the existent (1995, 108–9).

Deleuze and Guattari's appropriation of Ruyer's work in WIP gives us one line of approach to the question of whether a robot (as these currently exist) has an *Umwelt*.[36] To the extent that the robot is not a *primary true form*' – that is, is not self-producing and does not have the 'proper peculiarity' of autopoietic systems – it cannot even have 'poverty in world,' never mind an *Umwelt*.[37] In *Chaosmosis*, developing an approach already proposed by Stafford Beer, Guattari seeks to expand the concept of autopoiesis, arguing that when one thinks in terms of the machinic *assemblages* that machines constitute *with human beings*, 'they become ipso facto autopoietic' (1995, 40). This coupling between the biosphere and the mechanosphere (and reworking of the concept of autopiesis) allows for a more complex approach to questions of non-human enunciation and 'a-signifying semiotics' – an approach that will not be developed further at this point.

The Transformation of *Umwelt* into *Lebenswelt*

As we indicated earlier, Deely (1998, 217) calls 'Peirce's "new list of categories" his "semiotic categories," or "categories of experience," because precisely what they do is account for the transformation of the animal *Umwelt* into the human *Lebenswelt*.' I will conclude this chapter with a short summary of Deely's argument.

The fundamental argument is that Peirce's category of *Firstness* – which is for Deely equivalent to Avicenna's univocal being, or Aquinas' 'being-as-first-known' (*primum intelligibile*), or (within the context of this book) Deleuze's 'sense,' or Heidegger's prelogical apprehension of beings as a whole – provides for the intelligibility of the objective world (*Umwelt*) presented in perception, apprehended in relation to itself. As Deely notes (ibid., 220): 'Here, however, at the level of *primum intelligibile*, it is not a question of any given object of perception being cognized in relation to itself. It is rather a question of the objective world as such, the *Umwelt* as the totality of objectification at any given moment, being grasped in relation to itself.'

For Deely this is Peirce's category of 'Firstness,' 'the conception of being or existing independently of anything else' (CP, 6.32);[38] 'the present in general' (ibid., 1:547). It is the apprehension of the imperceptible 'relation to itself' that transforms the *Umwelt* into a *Welt* or *Lebenswelt* over and above the naturally biologically determined *Umwelt* of zoosemiosis. For Deely it is at this point that *Umwelt* becomes present at hand rather than ready to hand. Firstness as a species-specifically human mode of apprehension establishes the possibility of asking the question, 'What is that?' Deely (1998, 226) writes:

> The animal aware of its objective world [*Umwelt*] in such a fashion is alone positioned to form the conception along with reality, and of a piece with it, of *otherness*. Otherness (present-at-handness, in contrast to the ready-to-handness which reduces the environment within objectivity to the level of that extension of organismic dispositions which is the essence of an *Umwelt* proportioned to the biological nature of the cognizing organism) arises precisely within experience through 'brute actions of one subject or substance on another, regardless of law or of any third subject' (CP 5.469). It is 'the conception of being relative to, the conception of reaction with, something else' (CP 6.32). It is, in a word, the conception of 'something other,' of one thing different from another thing within the play of objects of awareness. The experience of otherness within firstness is the motivation of every question of the form 'What is that?'

Deely concludes his account of the relevance of Peirce's 'semiotic categories' (which unlike Aristotle's or Kant's are designed to express the interweaving of mind-dependent and mind-independent relations in the univocal being of the sign relation as an ontological relation) by claiming that although Heidegger does not have the clarity of Peirce's thought on sign relations and their manner of being, what Heidegger does contribute is an extraordinary analysis of the distinction within human experience between objects and things subsumed within the concept of being-as-first-known.

One might conclude by suggesting that Deleuze's 'logic of sense' should not be ignored in any attempt to understand 'things' as signs, and their 'external' relations on a univocal plane of immanence.[39] Language, understood as the relation between a proposition and thing, is possible because of the incorporeality of univocal sense attributed to bodies, but distinguished from them. It is the 'event' of sense that allows for language to be in relation with things. The question of the truth or falsity of a proposition requires this primary univocity of sense and relation. Even a false proposition has a sense. Deleuze thought that everything he wrote constituted a *theory of signs*, and both Deleuze and Guattari saw Peirce as the modern inventor of semiotics, a semiotics they complexify for their own peculiar purposes.

5 Autopoiesis and Languaging

> Creation and self-positing mutually imply each other because what is truly created, from the living being to the work of art, thereby enjoys a self-positing of itself, or an autopoietic characteristic by which it is recognized.
>
> Deleuze and Guattari (WIP, 11)

> The decisive threshold constituting this new aesthetic paradigm lies in the aptitude of these processes of creation to auto-affirm themselves as existential nuclei, autopoietic machines.
>
> Guattari (1995, 106)

The concept of autopoiesis, as already noted, has significant relations with the concept of an *Umwelt*. The purpose of this chapter is to give some account of Humberto Maturana and Francisco Varela's theory of autopoiesis, particularly in relation to language or 'languaging,' and to determine whether, with some modifications (not unlike those applied to Jakob von Uexküll's work by Deely), that theory is compatible with a doctrine of signs that affirms ontological relations and interbeing – or the being of the between – and escapes from the realist/idealist opposition into a mutual specification or codetermination between living beings and their worlds.[1]

Background and Context

Maturana and Varela's field of study originates in biology and neurophysiology and is concerned primarily with how biological processes are related to the phenomena of cognition and language. It would be fair to say that contemporary philosophy and scientific discourse remain largely ignorant of their work (outside of a few specialized fields); yet their research has profound consequences for our understanding of mind, information, evolution, causality, and autonomy.

To the extent that Maturana's work is known at all to non-specialists, it is for his co-authorship (with Letvin and McCulloch) of the classic 1959 paper 'What the Frog's Eye Tells the Frog's Brain'[2] and for his later work with Varela.

Guattari, in his most recent work, *Chaosmosis* (1995), appropriates and develops Maturana and Varela's concept of autopoiesis, arguing that it is a useful conceptual tool for analysing unconscious formations and the aesthetic/autopoietic generation of novel and affirmative subjectivities.

Maturana and Varela published *Autopoiesis and Cognition* (1980) and *The Tree of Knowledge* (1987). The Centre for Philosophy and History of Science at Boston University described *Autopoiesis and Cognition* 'as among the most original attempts at a systematic biology in decades, and as a profoundly philosophical work' in which Maturana and Varela construct a theoretical biology that defines living systems *not* as the represented objects of observation and description, but rather as self-contained entities whose only reference is to themselves.[3]

For Maturana and Varela this requires that a distinction be maintained between our *descriptions* of living systems and their *actual operations*. They remind us that 'everything that is said is said by someone' – that is, by an observer (and participant) in language. The 'observer' is constructed in and by language. They argue that it is essential not to confuse the operation of the living system with descriptions made from the 'outside' by an observer. This distinction is ignored when elements of our descriptions are incorporated into an explanatory conceptual system. Valid descriptions of a system's actual operations ought to be concerned with the system's internal dynamics, not with referring these dynamics (its autopoiesis) to some external encompassing context. For example, 'purpose' and 'aims' are not features of the organization of any machine, living or otherwise. These terms arise in the domain of external descriptions and '*have no explanatory value* in the phenomenological domain they pretend to illuminate, because they do not refer to processes indeed operating in the generation of any of its phenomenon' (Maturana and Varela 1980, 86).

As an illustration of this, they offer the example of the navigator who has always lived in a submarine. The navigator is to be understood as the nervous system, not the 'outside' observer of the nervous system (Maturana and Varela 1987, 137). All that exists for the navigator are indicator readings. It is only for an observer 'outside' that relationships are distinguished between the submarine's movements and its environment. The dynamics of the submarine's different states, with its navigator who does not know the outside world, never occur with representations of the world the 'outside observer' sees. There are no entities such as 'beaches' or 'reefs' for the submarine or navigator, only correlations between indicator readings. Maturana and Varela argue that this analogy is valid for all living systems. The 'observer' is also generated by a living system, of which he or she cannot be an 'outside' observer.

Observers can generate different descriptions of the activities of living systems, depending on the distinctions they make. A system can be seen in the domain of its internal states (or milieu), wherein the 'environment' is bracketed. Or a system can be described in terms of its interactions with an environment (i.e., its exterior or annexed milieu).

Given the crucial role of the observer in generating distinctions among domains or milieux, Maturana and Varela propose an account of the self-referential dynamics of living systems and their interactions that explains the emergence of language, and within language the further generation of the experience of self-consciousness (i.e., the observer). At this point I shall simply emphasize that for Maturana and Varela, language, mind, and consciousness are not 'in' the brain, rather, they are phenomena of the networks of social interactions (or 'structural couplings') that constitute language. Deleuze and Guattari develop the social (rather than individual) character of enunciation with the concept of 'collective assemblages' (q.v. ATP, 'Postulates of Linguistics').

First I will explain Maturana and Varela's basic concepts. Their shift in perspective requires us to stop importing the descriptive elements of an 'outside observer' of the sort that produce the standard characterizations of living systems such as species and genus – that is, classifications produced in terms of function or purpose, or of observed organism-environment relations, or of causal interactions with an external world. The latter, for instance, are semantic descriptions that do not apply in the domain of the operations of the nervous system itself, which has neither purpose nor interaction with an environment. These can only be interactions from the perspective of an outside observer. A living system responds to its own changes of state, which are determined by its structure (i.e., the *actual* components, and the *actual* relations between them that constitute an organism or a composite unity of any kind).

Purposes or aims are not features of the 'organization' of any machine, living or otherwise. These notions belong to the domain of discourse about our actions. '"*organization*" denotes those relations that must exist among the components of a system for it to be a member of a particular class. "*Structure*" [what Deleuze and Guattari call strata or stratification] denotes the components and relations that actually constitute a particular unity and make its organisation real' (Maturana and Varela 1987, 47). 'Organization,' in this sense, is like a plan implying or referring to relations that must exist for a unity to continue to exist as a member of a particular class. Maturana and Varela emphasize that 'organization' is not to be understood in a transcendent or mystical sense, as having some explanatory value of its own. Organization implies a particular set of relations. For example, in an autopoietic system, organization refers to the network of processes and relations that realize the system. The 'structure' of a living system is in constant transformation (whereas its organization or abstract machine remains invariant). In a non-living system (such as a toilet) the 'organization' consists in the assemblage of relations between an apparatus capable of detecting the water level and another apparatus capable of stopping the inflow of water. The specific structure could be changed by using wood instead of plastic components, but there would still be a toilet organization.

Maturana and Varela define a living system, in contrast to this, as an 'autopoietic machine' that at the most fundamental level produces itself. This is to be distinguished from allopoietic machines, which produce something different from themselves. An autopoietic machine regenerates its cellular structure (albeit not indefinitely). *The product is the same as the network of processes involved in production.* A car is produced by processes independent of the organization of the car, and its 'product' (i.e., transport) is not part of its organization.

Thus an autopoietic system maintains its organization and defines its boundaries through the continuous production of its components. If the autopoietic process is interrupted, the system's organization (i.e., its identity as a particular kind of unity) is lost, and the system disintegrates (perishes/dies). From this perspective, autopoietic machines are, first of all, *autonomous*: 'That is, they subordinate all changes to the maintenance of their own organization.' Second, they 'have individuality; that is by keeping their organisation as an invariant through its continuous production they maintain an identity which is independent of their interactions with an observer. Allopoietic machines have an identity that depends on the observer and is not determined through their operation, because its product is different from itself; allopoietic machines do not have individuality' (Maturana and Varela 1980, 80).

The self-referential character of Maturana and Varela's (autopoietic) systems that have no 'outside' was described by the editors of *Autopoiesis and Cognition* as 'Leibnizian for our day.' Leibniz asserted that unities or 'monads' are absolutely independent of one another and do not 'act' on or 'cause' change in other unities. God has established a harmony between unities such that they 'express' one another. This reference to Leibniz is also found in Thure von Uexküll's introduction to Jakob von Uexküll's *Theory of Meaning* (discussed briefly below). These connections are made at this point simply to illustrate the complementarity and intertwining of ideas to be found in the varied theses within both the humanities and the sciences we are examining here. The purpose is not to construct a grand unified theory, but rather to point to a crisis across all knowledge disciplines in the mechanized and instrumental theories of the body, mind, language, and society that have been the product of a positivist approach to science. All of these thinkers are searching for a non-mechanized comprehension of the world, albeit in different fields of knowledge.

An organism presupposes an 'organization' or abstract machine – that is, processes and relations *between* components – *not* the properties of components themselves. This distinguishes the approach of the thinkers discussed above from traditional mechanistic theories, which are concerned with components rather than relations (e.g., explaining living systems in terms of genetic structure and thereby obscuring the autonomous 'organization' or abstract machine of living systems). Each of the above-mentioned thinkers will be discussed briefly in relation to Maturana and Varela.

Leibniz's concept of monad[4] refers to his conception of the world as made up of an infinite number of simple unities or 'monads,' which do not act on one another. For Leibniz, these monads 'have no windows by which anything could come in or go out' (Monadology, para. 7). Athough no monad really acts on any other, God has established a harmony among the states of all monads. In the language of Leibniz, God has created substances such that each one 'expresses' all others.

Leibniz argues that although monads can only have a perspective on the universe, there is in fact a 'single universe,' which monads perceive from their different positions. In theory, the real nature of the world can be described neutrally – that is, outside of any particular perspective.

Nietzsche radically develops Leibniz's 'perspectivism,' arguing that there is nothing apart from perspectives and that the idea of the world or universe 'in itself' is a fiction: 'As if the world would still remain after one had deducted the perspective' (1968, 567).

To make any claim about the world in itself would require going beyond any particular perspective – to 'the view from nowhere,' or God's view. This should not be understood in the sense that there are only 'mere interpretations.' There are nothing but interpretations. Maturana contends that reality as a universe of independent entities is a fiction of the descriptive domain and that the notion of reality should be applied to this domain of descriptions in which we, the describing system, interact with our descriptions *as if* with independent entities. He argues, furthermore, that this is 'a constitutive human cognitive condition, not a circumstantial limitation' (Maturana 1988, 80).

Maturana and Varela are seen as 'Leibnizians for our day' because they develop the notion of structure-determined self-referential unities that do not have 'inputs' or 'outputs' (such as in the computer model of the brain). However, in their conceptual system they forgo Leibniz's *a priori* reliance on 'the will of God.'

Maturana and Varela stress that both the proposition of a phenomenon to be explained (e.g., cognition) and the proposition of an ad hoc generative mechanism (e.g., autopoiesis) are brought forth *a priori* in the praxis (experience) of living of the observer. From this perspective, scientific explanations are creations of the human mind and explain human experience and *not* an independent world.

Here we can begin to see that Maturana and Varela oscillate between realist claims about the nature of the individuality of autopoietic systems independent of an observer and idealist and phenomenological claims wherein thought is not able to have a real relation with something other than itself. Ideas have become Berkeleyian descriptions rather than signs that are capable – given the necessary conditions – of relating to a mind-independent world. In other words, there is no univocal ontological relation in the modern and nominalist post-Kantian tradition with which Maturana and Varela align themselves, no possibility of escape from interiority or 'transcendental subjectivity' or the phenomenal structure of Dasein.

Looking back over the development of the concept of autopoiesis, Varela (1996, 407) expresses himself thus:

The tendency to which I refer, stated briefly, is the disappearance of the intellectual and social space which makes cognition a mentalist representation and the human being a rational agent. It is the disappearance of what Heidegger calls the period of the image of the world and what could also be referred to as Cartesianism. If autopoiesis has been influential it is because it was able to align itself with another project which focuses on the *interpretive capacity of the living being* and conceives of the human as an agent which doesn't discover the world, but rather constitutes it. It is what we could call the ontological turn of modernity.

A complex set of themes is unfolding here, which only slowly will become digestible. Varela in recent years has distanced himself from Maturana's 'constitutive ontology' or 'ontology of observing' and is seeking to develop a 'naturalized phenomenology' or 'generative neurophenomenology.' But without the concept of univocal ontological relation, Varela might remain enmeshed in the same kinds of problems that have befallen Heidegger who, while grasping the importance of univocity, or an order of being that is neither 'subjective' nor 'objective,' never completely abandons a phenomenological method, even when he seeks to do so. Maturana contends that Heidegger (presumably in his later work) seeks to conserve the 'objectivity' of the being that shows up in a distinction, *and that in doing so Heidegger is mistaken.*

For the present I will argue that Maturana and Varela, like Heidegger, recognize the importance of the interpretive capacities of human beings; but without an understanding of signs as ontological relations they always slip into an idealism based on the primacy of consciousness in the constitution or bringing-forth of the world. These approaches are bedevilled by a lack of awareness of the univocal action of sign relations of the sort that allow for a genuine communion and shifting interface between mind and nature. They encounter the same problem as von Uexküll with his Kantian *Umwelt* theory.[5]

The reference to Leibniz's 'monads' will appear also in the introduction to Jakob von Uexküll's 'The Theory of Meaning' (1982). Von Uexküll's term *Umwelt* has often been translated in a Kantian sense as a phenomenal or self-world, and his son Thure (1982, 3) offers this description:

> Reality, to which all things must yield and from which everything must derive, is not 'outside' in infinite space that has neither beginning nor end and that is filled with a cloud of elementary particles. Nor is it 'inside,'

within ourselves in the indistinct, distorted images of this 'outside' that our minds create. It reveals itself in the worlds (Jakob von Uexküll calls them *Umwelten*) with which sensual perception surrounds all living beings as if with bubbles that are sharply delineated but invisible to the outside observer. These 'bubbles of self-worlds' are like Leibniz's 'monads' the bricks and mortar of reality.[6]

We have sketched briefly the background and context of Maturana and Varela's work. Its content now demands articulation, particularly with regard to their understanding of cognition.

Maturana and Varela introduce complex terminology that can be extremely difficult to grasp on a first reading (partly due to the unfamiliar syntax and vocabulary). Because their ideas are so interdependent, the basic concepts must be clearly understood so that an appreciation of their hypothesis is possible.[7]

Maturana and Varela's definition of cognition is central to their theory of autopoiesis and will now be examined.[8]

Cognitive Systems

> A cognitive system is a system whose organisation defines a domain of interactions in which it can act with relevance to the maintenance of itself, and the process of cognition is the actual (inductive) acting or behaving in this domain. *Living systems are cognitive systems, and living as a process is a process of cognition.* This statement is valid for all organisms, with and without a nervous system. (Maturana 1980, 13)

Cognition, in this reformulation, is not the acquisition of knowledge by a 'knowing subject,' or an epiphenomenal by-product of neuronal activity in the brain, but rather the organizing activity of living systems (i.e., their autopoiesis). This activity manifests itself from the dynamics of the individual cell all the way up to the self-regulatory capacities of the planet.

An organism 'knows how' to live – it is displaying *effective or adequate action* that enables it to continue its existence in an environment. This reformulation of cognition as effective action demands a fundamental conceptual change in our contemporary understanding of cognition, in that it does not assume objects of knowledge, representations in the 'mind' or 'information processing' and 'storage.' As Maturana (1990, 36) expresses it: 'Cognition as a biological phenomena ... has no content and is not 'about' anything. Therefore when we say that we know *some-thing* we are not connoting what happens in the mechanism of the phenomenon of cognition as a biological phenomena; we are reflecting in language on what we do.'

From within the system there is only 'know how.' Knowledge as traditionally understood (i.e., as an embodiment of 'truth' that reflects the world 'in itself,' independent of the 'knower') exists from the point of view of an observer. Our 'knowledge' of 'the world' reflects *a cut made within experience* between what we call 'ourselves' and what we call 'the world.' For Maturana, knowledge as something independent of us is a fiction of description in which the describing system interacts with descriptions as if they were separate entities.

Maturana and Varela argue that adequate behaviour or action is the only criterion we have for assessing cognition. They are not saying what cognition *is*, but rather how we, as observers, recognize it. Evaluations of whether or not there is 'knowledge' are always made in a relational context. 'Knowing is doing.' We expect a demonstration of effective behaviour in a context that we specify with a question. For example, the only way a person's piano-playing ability can be assessed is through his or her playing of the piano. However, whether or not adequate behaviour is demonstrated depends on the presupposition of the questioner.

Maturana and Varela are proposing that living systems are cognitive systems in that they display effective action or behaviour in the activity of autopoiesis (living). The ability of a living system to maintain its autopoiesis will, they argue, necessarily generate further recursive couplings with its medium and with other living systems, which may under certain conditions (to be described hereafter) further generate language and the observer capable of describing himself or herself in language. From this perspective the nervous system does not function with representations or 'take in' an environment. Such terms only exist in the descriptive realm of organisms capable of language.

For Maturana, mental terms such as 'knowledge' cannot *meaningfully* be taken as descriptions of state or structure. To say that 'the animal knows X' is not a statement about a static state but refers rather to actions (past or projected).

Maturana and Varela propose a scientific explanation of cognition as effective action. This explanation must take into account four requirements:

1. *The specification of a phenomenon to be explained as a feature of the experience of an observer through the description of what he or she must do to experience*

it. The phenomenon to be explained is the effective action of a living being in its environment, how it conserves its organization (identity).
2. *The proposition of a mechanism that would give rise to the experience of the phenomenon to be explained.* The explanatory generative mechanism is autopoiesis, the autonomous organization of living beings.
3. *The deduction, from the mechanism proposed in 2, of other phenomena.* Deducing from 2. other phenomena, such as behavioural coordination in interactions recurring between living beings.
4. *The experience by an observer of the additional phenomena deduced in 3.* Further observations; social phenomena, language, and self-consciousness, obtained from 3, and explaining how these arise.

In other words, Maturana and Varela propose a conceptual system that seeks to demonstrate how cognition as effective action can produce living beings that, like ourselves, are capable of making descriptions and reflecting on them.

Note well that Maturana and Varela's scientific explanation makes no claims to objectivity and does not require it. Remember, too, that they argue that the notion of objectivity is a fiction. Scientific explanations explain an observer's experience, not an independent world. They also argue that this is the intrinsic character of *all* scientific explanations, regardless of the preconceptions that certain scientists and philosophers may entertain about the objectivity of science.

Cognition as effective action includes the cellular level and deals with the relevance of action to the maintenance of autopoiesis. Deleuze and Guattari affirm that in the economy of the cell there are molecular perceptions no less than molecular reactions. This can be seen in 'the property of regulatory agents to "recognise" only one or two kinds of chemicals in a very diverse milieu of exteriority' (ATP, 51). The cell is displaying cognition in its effective action and ability to 'recognize' – although this doesn't imply perception in the sense of image or representation.

The term 'autopoiesis' was foreshadowed in the preceding pages. To ensure clarity, we again emphasize that autopoiesis means self-production, *not reproduction*. The formal definition is as follows:

> An autopoietic machine is a machine organised (defined as a unity) as a network of processes of production (transformation and destruction) of components that produces the components which: (i) through their interaction and transformations continuously regenerate and realise the net-

work of processes (relations) that produced them; and (ii) constitute it (the machine) as a concrete unity in the space in which they (the components) exist by specifying the topological domain of its realisation as a network.' (Maturana and Varela 1980, 79).

Such a machinic conception also arises in Deleuze and Guattari's portrayal of desiring production in *Anti-Oedipus* 1983, 1): 'Everywhere *it* is machines – real ones not figurative ones: machines driving other machines, machines being driven by other machines, with all the necessary couplings and connections ... The breast is a machine that produces milk and the mouth is a machine coupled to it.'

Reproduction assumes the prior existence of an autopoietic unity that is capable of reproduction, and consequently reproduction is not a defining characteristic of the living. A mule is capable of living without reproducing itself – as are old trees, young and older people, and so on.

Living Systems

To understand Maturana and Varela's theory of living systems requires the exposition of three critical concepts that form the basis of their explanation: (1) operational closure, (2) structure determinism, and (3) structural coupling.

Operational Closure

This term refers to the activity of the nervous system for which there is no 'inside' or 'outside' but only the maintenance of correlations that continuously change.

Through his research on perception and colour vision, Maturana concluded that perception should not be viewed as the grasping of an external reality but rather as the generator of phenomena. It is possible to illustrate this with a number of quite simple perceptual experiments (see Maturana and Varela 1987, 18,19, 20). For example, Maturana and Varela describe an experiment on the phenomenon of coloured shadows, noted by Otto von Gueriche in 1672 and first explained in physiological terms by Goethe.

If one looks at the two shadows of an object that simultaneously partially intercepts the paths of two different lights, one white and one red, it is apparent that the area of the shadow from the red light that receives white light looks blue-green. This is surprising, but nevertheless an incontrovertible experiential fact. The area of the shadow from the red light 'should' look white or grey, because it receives only white light. If an instrument is used to measure the light composition in this example, it will be found that there is no predominance of wavelengths called green or blue in the shadow seen as bluish green, but only the normal distribution occurring in white light.

Maturana and Varela emphasize that this is not an isolated situation that can be classified as an 'illusion': 'Our experience of a world of coloured objects is literally independent of the wavelength composition of the light coming from any scene we look at ... If I take an orange from my room to the patio, the orange will seem to be the same color; however, the inside of the house was illuminated by fluorescent light, which has a greater number of so called blue (or short) wavelengths, whereas the sun has mostly so-called red (or long) wavelengths' (ibid. 1987, 22). The essential argument they are demonstrating is that the experience of colour is not determined by the light received from an object but rather 'corresponds to a specific pattern of states which the structure of the organism determines.' They further argue that this is true for all dimensions of visual experience (such as movement, texture, and form) and in fact also for any other mode of perception (such as touch and hearing).[9] Von Uexküll, inspired by Kantian philosophy, was perhaps the first scientist clearly to anchor perception in biology. In this critical biology the world known through the senses – the *Umwelt* – can only be a phenomenal world, not an objectively known world of things in themselves. Von Uexküll claims that each living organism, because of its own properties, determines an individual environment. Only an independent being that does not experience the world but knows it unconditionally could speak of an 'objective' world: 'A semiotic that is biologically uninformed is sheer amateurishness,' asserted von Uexküll.[10] (As noted in the previous chapter, von Uexküll's – and Maturana's – attachment to Kantian phenomenology does not allow the potential of semiotic to fully develop into a semiotic that is neither realist nor idealist, but capable of incorporating elements from both positions.)

Maturana contends that these experiences demonstrate that we cannot experientially distinguish 'perception,' 'illusion,' and 'hallucination' in the actual living of these experiences, but only after the fact, *a posteriori*. As a consequence, the notion of objectivity – that is, the ability to perceive the features of a world independent of the observer – is *biologically impossible*. Any theory that does not question the properties of the observer assumes the independent existence of what is known (be it matter, energy, ideas, God, mind, spirit, ... or reality).

For many, this seems to contradict common sense. However, for Maturana and Varela, the proposition that 'reality' is constructed (commensurate with our biological and social history) rather than received as an impression of 'objective reality' can be practically demonstrated: 'We do not see the "space" of the world; we live our field of vision. We do not see the "colours" of the world; we live our chromatic space' (ibid., 23).

In this approach, structure is dynamic rathen than static. Structure alters with every interaction, particularly with respect to living systems, which are constantly undergoing changes in their components and the relations between these components. Living systems are operationally closed, not thermodynamically closed. Their identity (or autonomy) is specified by a network of dynamic processes whose effects do not leave that network. Maturana and Varela call this dynamism of the nervous system 'structural plasticity.' Deleuze and Guattari draw on insights from molecular biology throughout their work. For example: 'We should speak less of automatism of a higher center than coordinations between centers and of the cellular groupings or molecular populations that perform these couplings' (ATP, 388). They see this behavioral-biological 'machinics' or molecular engineering as a tool for understanding problems of consistency.

Structure Determinism

From their studies in the neurophysiology of perception, Maturana and Varela developed the hypothesis that it is a system's structure (i.e., its actualized components and the relations between them) that determines the behaviour or changes of state the system may undergo. This applies equally to living systems (autopoietic machines) *and* non-living systems (allopoietic machines). The structure of an object determines its behaviour by specifying all the interactions it may undergo. For example, when you press the button on a vending machine this *triggers* the structure to 'give' you an object. The machine is not 'instructed' but rather triggered to act in accordance with its structure. As mentioned in the preceding section on operational closure, structure is not a static thing; rather it alters with interactions. Living systems, however, have an infinitely greater dynamism or 'plasticity' in their structure, especially when nervous systems are developed. In dynamic living systems, the structure is constantly changing. When you move, your structure changes, because the structure is both the components and their relations.

For Maturana and Varela, structural determinism is in fact a necessary prerequisite for a scientific explanation. They argue that the central point of such an explanation is the proposal of a mechanism that generates the phenomenon you choose to explain: in this case cognition, defined as effective action (which, they further argue, may under particular conditions to be examined generate language and self-consciousness).

For something to be a mechanism it must generate the construction of an entity whose structure (the relations and changes of relations of its actual components) determines what happens to it. If the system is not a structure-determined entity, a scientific explanation will not be possible, because scientific explanation requires a mechanistic experimental hypothesis. For example, if your car doesn't start when you turn the ignition key, *you assume there is something wrong with the structure of the car, not your thumb and index finger.*

Nevertheless, Maturana claims that, contrary to the prevailing interpretations of both science and philosophy, scientific explanations are constitutively non-reductionistic. Mechanistic explanations propose a *generative* mechanism that gives rise, as a consequence of its operation, to the phenomenon to be explained, in a different phenomenal domain from the one in which it (the generative mechanism) operates. The phenomenon is intrinsically not reducible to the generative mechanism: 'One domain may generate the elements of another domain, but not its phenomenology which in each domain is specified by the interactions of its elements' (Maturana and Varela 1980, 55).

Maturana argues that phenomena such as language and self-consciousness require an interplay of 'bodyhoods' (bodies) as a generative structure but do not take place in them. This understanding of scientific explanation leads away from transcendental dualism. There is relationship, but not reduction of one phenomenon to another. For example, there is a generative relationship between neurophysiology and behaviour, but they occur in different phenomenal domains. Behaviour consists in actions and coordinations of actions that take place in interactions between organisms and/or their exterior milieu (medium), not in the organisms themselves. This parallels Deleuze and Guattari's understanding of the subject as occurring in interactions, not in the body.

Maturana (1990, 8) further insists that 'scientific statements are consensual statements valid only within the community of standard observers that generates them, and science as the domain of scientific statements does not need an independent objective reality, nor does it reveal one.'[11] This notion of consensual reality will be discussed later in differentiating Maturana and Varela's position from solipsism and objectivity or representationalism. The point to bear in mind is that for Maturana and Varela a scientific hypothesis is necessarily mechanistic but inherently non-reductionistic, because distinctions are made between domains or milieux, and what is appropriate to one cannot be reduced to the other. A phenomenon is not reduced or explained in more fundamental terms; rather, a generative mechanism is proposed that gives rise to phenomena occuring in a different phenomenal domain. This will become clear when we examine Maturana and Varela's analysis of the generation of language. They will claim that although language requires the neurophysiology of the participants, language is not a neurophysiological phenomenon.

Bearing in mind Maturana and Varela's understanding of scientific explanation, their structural determinism thesis requires further examination.

PIAGET'S NOTION OF STRUCTURE

Given the widespread use of the terms structure and structuralism in the humanities (e.g., Levi-Strauss's 'deep structure' of myth, and the Freudian unconscious as deep structure in psychoanalysis), it is important to be clear about the ways in which Maturana and Varela's 'structure' differs from prevailing notions. The psychologist Jean Piaget argued that structure can be observed in an arrangement of entities that embody three ideas: (a) wholeness, (b) transformation, and (c) self-regulation.

(a) *Wholeness* means that the constituent parts of an entity have no independent existence apart from their *relations*, which determine the coherence of such an entity (or unity). This appears to conform to Maturana and Varela's notion that there is no such thing as a 'free-floating' component existing independently of the unity it integrates. Therefore Maturana and Varela's system is strictly 'closed' in its operations.

(b) *Transformation* means that the structure is not static but structuring. The structure must be capable of transformational procedures whereby new material is constantly processed by and through it. This conforms to Maturana and Varela's notion of autopoiesis or self-production through a network of processes of production (transformation and destruction) that produce the components and their relations.

(c) *Self-regulation* means that the structure makes no appeals beyond itself in order to validate its transformational procedures. It is self-referential. This conforms to Maturana and Varela's notion of 'operational closure' and 'structure determinism.'

However, as explained below in the section on 'structural coupling,' Varela emphasizes that *the nervous system is not to be treated as a decoupled monad* constructing any arbitrary 'reality.' The nervous system is triggered by interactions, but these interactions are not 'inputs'; rather, they trigger changes of state that lead only to other changes of state in the system itself. There is an 'operational closure' of its dynamics of state (defined as a relative balance between neural surfaces). For example, 'perception' of colour requires interactions with light, but colour is not a property of light wavelengths. It is the nervous system itself that determines colour perception in its operational closure.

APPLICATION IN MATURANA AND VARELA

Thus there is a fundamental concordance between Piaget's notion of structure and that of Maturana and Varela. However, there are important differences between these theorists in their actual application and use of the term structure (although Varela credits Piaget as an important precursor).

Piaget's interpretation of structure as a closed system seems to prevent him from developing the notion of coupling through interactions that would, in Maturana and Varela's perspective, generate language and a world of 'objects.' Piaget (and Levi-Strauss) appear to confuse the brain (biological entity) with language and mind. The 'self' = the 'body.' Maturana and Varela (1987, 234) argue that 'the locus of the dynamics of mind and consciousness belong to the realm of social coupling.' Social coupling may be necessary for the generation of language, but it is not sufficient in itself – the social coupling of many animal worlds does not produce language. The specific couplings that Maturana and Varela contend would produce language will be introduced in a later section.

The notion of structural coupling developed by Maturana and Varela is thus crucial to understanding their divergence from traditional notions of structuralism.

Structural Coupling

Structural coupling is Maturana and Varela's description of the relationship between two or more structure-determined entities and the medium in which they exist: 'We speak of structural coupling whenever there is a history of recurrent interactions leading to the structural congruence between two (or more) systems' (ibid., 75).

The interactions between two or more unities and their medium or environment consist of reciprocal perturbations that only *trigger* structural changes in the two unities respectively – that is, it does not specify or direct them. Vice versa for the environment. The term 'medium' is used to emphasize the relational character – there is no separation or space between an organism (or unity) and its 'environment.' To be more precise, Maturana distinguishes *niche* as the part of the medium operationally defined moment by moment in a unity's encounter with a medium in structural coupling. A unity specifies the space in which it exists. An autopoietic system (i.e., one with a dynamic, changing structure) inevitably evolves in such a way that its structure is effectively coupled to its medium – otherwise it would disintegrate (die). That which is not structurally coupled to the world in which it exists cannot exist. This may seem obvious, but structural coupling is necessary for what Maturana and Varela term cognition – namely, adequate or effective behaviour. As Maturana says, 'the teacher that determines this *fundamental adequate conduct* for us is life. If we remain alive, we have adequate conduct – whichever way we manage to remain alive.' The most fundamental cognition is 'knowing' how to exist.

A structurally plastic autopoietic system endowed with a complex nervous system, such as that of human animals, has a greatly expanded realm of interactions available to it. These interactions, which are mutually triggering between organisms and their environment, generate new phenomena by allowing new dimensions of structural coupling. Maturana and Varela argue that it is structural coupling which forms the basis of all human and animal systems. If the environment contains other structurally plastic systems, they will become coupled to one another as a necessary consequence of their interactions in mutually triggering changes of state.

Among most social insects, the mechanism of structural coupling occurs through a chemical coupling called trophallaxis (from the Greek 'flow of foods'). 'There is a continuous flow of secretions between the members of an ant colony through sharing of stomach contents each time they meet' (ibid., 186). However, such coupling in organisms can take place through any form of interaction – chemical, visual, auditory, and so on .

These couplings or interactions form a network of coordinations of actions, which generate phenomena that an isolated organism could not generate (e.g., communication and possibly language).

The essence of Maturana's hypothesis is that human beings develop language collectively in a social domain through recursive coordinations of coordinations of actions (distinctions about distinctions): 'Words are nodes in a network of coordinations of actions between bodyhoods.' 'Language is not an abstract activity but takes place in the domain of relations between organisms.' 'Language and bodyhoods are coupled through the structural interactions that take place in language.' (For all these expressions and arguments, see in particular Maturana 1988, 1990.)

Maturana and Varela have coined the term 'linguallaxis' (a linguistic trophallaxis) to refer to the coupling in language that is specific to human beings.[12]

What is of particular importance is first, that Maturana and Varela stress that self-consciousness takes place in language in the social domain: 'In the network of linguistic interactions in which we move, we maintain an ongoing descriptive recursion which we call the "I." It enables us to conserve our linguistic operational coherence and our adaptation in the domain of language' (1987, 231).

Second, we exist as human beings in a consensual domain that is neither objective nor subjective, but brought forth through our interactions. Solipsism is negated as a problem once we understand that language is a consensual system of interactions and that objectivity is constitutively impossible for us as biological creatures bound to our world of experience. The problem here is that experience seems to become a collective bubble and that the phenomenological transcendental subject has simply been replaced by the needs and prejudices of a Wittgensteinian community or 'form of life.' One of the strengths of Poinsot and Deely's (and Peirce's) semiotic approach is that in recognizing ontological relations, they do allow for an interface between language and things outside language. For Maturana, there are 'no-things' outside language. Language is a closed domain of recursive consensual coordinations of actions, and the distinctions we make in language (such as objects or relations) do not apply outside it. There can never be a genuine relation or conformity between the objects of experience and the things of a prejacent physical environment. As with Kant, the 'epistemologically' necessary substratum of our experience is radically unknowable, and one can say nothing about it (even saying 'it' is to bring 'it' into language). The excesses of 'savage' deconstruction and 'radical' constructivism surely lie in this tradition. All these excessive positions arise because of a lack of awareness of the univocal being of relations.[13]

Maturana and Varela effectively deny the possibility of objectivity or truth claims in their analysis. In a consensual or codependent reality there is no fixed point of reference independent of ourselves that can give certainty to our descriptions of the world. Maturana, in a manner similar to Deleuze and Guattari's notion of 'order-words,' asserts that a claim to objectivity is an operation in the realm of discourse as well as a demand for obedience. Any claim to objectivity leads the observer to require a transcendental referent as the ground or source of validation for the explanations he or she accepts (Maturana 1988, 29).

A more nuanced approach will be suggested in this book whereby there is a Deleuzo-Guattarian 'truth of the relative' rather than a 'relativity of truth.' There is as much nature in culture as culture in nature, and a paradoxical double-individuation of subjects and objects wherein an autonomous reality forces human animals to describe it in particular ways. Through such an approach, although we are related to the environment by way of a species-specific objective world or *Umwelt*, we really do know something about things (like neutrinos) that are irreducible to phenomenal appearances – they are not just *for us* but also *for themselves* by way of an ontological birelativity or reciprocity or coemergence. Deely claims that such an approach is already outlined in the work of Aquinas, Duns Scotus, and particularly Poinsot through the foregrounding of signs as univocal relations that can shift unchanged between the orders of natural and cultural being.

One most striking convergence is between Maturana and Varela's and Deleuze's conception of Nature as an Individual, composed of all modes of interaction.[14] The environment is not a reservoir of information but a 'plane of consistency' on which individuals (organisms) interact and are 'coupled' together.

Languaging

We are never signifier or signified. We are stratified.
                                            Deleuze and Guattari (ATP, 67)

This section focuses on the analyses of language implied by the work of Maturana and Varela and Deleuze and Guattari, based on the primacy these thinkers give to multiplicity and its social/cultural stratifications, and especially in relation to their notions of 'consistency' arising within multiplicities. Maturana and Varela's theory concerning the generation of language, and Deleuze and Guattari's criticism of the 'Postulates of Linguistics,' will be discussed in particular. It will be argued that there is a striking commensurability between all four men – most importantly, in their claims that language is directly related to actions in social domains.

Pragmatics and context become the foundations of language together with, for example, ethological, ecological, corporeal, and incorporeal dimensions that cannot be reduced to signifier/signified or cybernetic informational models, with their emission and reception of signs or messages. The question for Deleuze and Guattari and Maturana and Varela is this: How were these 'signs' and their significations generated?

A primary focus of Deleuze and Guattari's work is the analysis of signifying systems or 'regimes of signs,' and how their emergent autonomy determines the social place and identity of the 'subjects' or participants. For Varela, the study of emergent properties or self-organization is crucial to an appreciation of the 'manipulative' as well as creative power of language. An emergent property such as language appears as transcendent to the agents that participate in it; yet the agents themselves, through their interactions, bring forth this emergent property (Varela 1987).

Deleuze and Guattari and Maturana and Varela emphasize the *act* of language rather than its representational or symbolic role. They analyse language in terms of actions that produce transformations, rather than in terms of words and things or signifiers and signifieds. These notions (signifier/signified) occur in the descriptive realm of language and do not explain, but rather obscure, the nature of language as sets of enunciations and of statements generated in a social field. Deleuze and Guattari argue that few linguists have paid attention to the social character of enunciation (exceptions would be William Labov, Mikhail Bakhtin, Michel Foucault, and the speech act theorists). Maturana and Varela argue in like fashion that language is generated in a social field through coordinations of coordinations of consensual interactions. Deleuze and Guattari would add that many – perhaps most – of these coordinations of coordinations of actions are not consensual in this simple sense, but are a product of social/cultural *forces* to which a speaker has to submit.

Compare this with their claim that all language consists of 'order-words' in two senses: (1) they produce a social order – in this sense they are like Maturana and Varela's 'consensual' *but*; and (2) they demand obedience – they are like commands.

Terry Winograd and Fernando Flores, in their pioneering text on the design of computer technology (1988), have also drawn attention to the convergence between speech act theorists and the work of Maturana and Varela. In the research programs of our four theorists (Deleuze and Guattari, Maturana and Varela) there is a revisioning of the nature and function of communication and language. For Maturana and Varela, notions such as 'universal grammar' and 'signals' and information exist in the descriptive realm of an observer; they do not refer to actual processes taking place in the interaction between an organism and its medium. They argue that signs in the domain of living organisms presuppose an emitter, a receiver (a message 'transmitted' between them), and interpretation (coding/decoding); thus the notion of a sign or message exists in a system's exterior, descriptive realm in language. That is to say, it is this that needs to be explained: who determines the accuracy of the message? Of course, an observer is necessary for any description, but notions pertaining to the descriptive realm itself (signs, coding, information, and so on) are not valid when imported into the phenomenal domain of the structural dynamics of the nervous system.

Deleuze and Guattari also argue that the notion of signs could be, 'at the limit,' forgone entirely (ATP, 67). They offer the example of a genetic code, which can be described without referring to signs. Drawing on the work of the biologist François Jacob,[15] they argue that the genetic 'code' 'has neither emitter, receiver, comprehension nor translation' (ATP, 62). For related but distinct reasons, Maturana and Varela argue that genes do not contain 'information' that could specify a living being. It is the network of interactions of the whole cell that constitutes its provisional totality. The DNA is part of an autopoietic network. Thus Maturana argues that notions of information transfer or coding, currently used in relation to cellular reproduction and heredity, do not correspond to any particular process taking place in a cell as an autopoietic unity.

To recapitulate: For Maturana, the term information (the transmission of a message from point A to point B), even in the strictly technical sense of coding, emission, reception, decoding (i.e.: divested of meaning or signification), does not apply in the biology of living systems because the initial conditions (A) and the so-called end point (B) do not exist as fixed entities but are constantly subjected to structural modification. These notions exist in a descriptive realm in language, but only to describe fixed systems – for example telecommunications.

Furthermore, the metaphorical sense of information (as meaning) is also descriptive and requires an evaluation made by an observer in language from a perspective exterior to the system (interacting organisms) in question. Maturana argues that these notions *presuppose* an organizational and structural complementarity, if not identity, between systems that would make the stability of the signal connoted by the term information (or signal) possible.

In engineered systems, such as in telecommunications and computer design, the structure/organization complimentarity is designed by a human agent. In biological systems this, of course, is not the case. Any structure/organization complementarity that exists between organisms would arise in evolution through a history of consensual interactions (epigenesis). Information theories as well as signifier theories in linguistic science are descriptive of certain domains but never explanatory. They do not provide a generative mechanism for the observed regularities of behaviour among organisms: 'In biological systems such a situation is the result of phylogenic and ontogenic histories of interactions in which the selective mutual triggering of structural changes with the conservation of the mutual structural coupling (mutual adaptation) of the involved organisms (or systems) is the mechanism for its origin. Informational descriptions do not grasp this.' (Maturana 1983, 155).

Maturana and Varela's Conception of Language

Maturana and Varela propose that the structural coupling of living organisms with one another and with the medium (external milieu) in which they exist is the generative mechanism that gives rise to phenomena such as communication and language, which *isolated* organisms cannot produce.

Interactions among organisms tend to take on a recursive pattern, both through sexual reproduction and as a consequence of their existence in the same milieu.

Maturana and Varela refer to the classic example of social insects (ants, termites, wasps, and the like) to illustrate structural coupling involving an entire colony of organisms. The mechanism of coupling among most social insects occurs through a chemical coupling called trophallaxis (food sharing), whereby stomach contents are shared. This results in the distribution throughout the colony of substances (e.g., hormones) that determine the differentiation and specification of roles. For example, the queen is only a queen as long as she is fed in a certain way. This is also the case for 'barren females,' 'worker females,' 'males,' and so on.

In organisms with larger, more complex nervous systems such as mammals, interactions include visual and auditory modes, which allow for greater flexibility in the behavioural couplings they can engage in. For example (Maturana and Varela 1987, 190), a wolf pack, whose members coordinate their behaviour by adopting different postures, can hunt and kill a large moose; a single wolf could not do this.

The important point is that these interactions generate phenomena that isolated individuals cannot produce. Maturana and Varela term this recurrent coordination of actions 'communication,' which occurs in a domain of *social interactions*. Maturana refers to the domain of social interactions as a 'consensual' or 'linguistic' domain. This linguistic domain is the basis of language but not yet identifiable with it.

Their extension of the term 'linguistic' to include any mutually generated, consensual domain of interactions needs to be clearly understood. When two or more organisms interact recurrently, they generate a social coupling in which they are reciprocally involved in maintaining their respective autopoiesis. The coordinated conduct or behaviour that can be observed among organisms involved in social couplings is the precise sense that Maturana and Varela give to the term 'communication.' Thus communication exists in a social field in a flow of interactions, not 'in' an individual agent.

'Communication' can be instinctive, or it can be acquired in the individual life history of an organism (its ontogeny). This acquired or learned behaviour, they argue, *can* be described in semantic terms of 'signalling' or meaning, and Maturana and Varela refer to such acquired behaviour as a 'linguistic domain.' They specifically extend the term beyond its conventional usage to emphasize that for them, 'human linguistic behaviours are in fact behaviours in a domain of reciprocal ontogenic structural coupling which we human beings establish as a result of our collective ontogenies' (Maturana and Varela 1987, 208).

As in the reformulation of cognition or cognitive acts, their purpose is to define the notion of communication in terms of adequate or effective behaviour or actions in the maintenance of autopoiesis, rather than in terms of symbolic or logical abstractions. The following examples of acquired 'linguistic' (consensual) behaviour will clarify Maturana and

Varela's reformulation of this term and lead to their distinction between linguistic behaviour and language.

Example 1 of a 'linguistic' behaviour (i.e., acquired behaviour that can be described in semantic terms).

When my cat comes to the bedroom door each morning, meows, and runs down to the food bowl, it is possible to describe this behaviour in semantic terms as the cat 'signalling' to me its desire to eat (i.e., the metaphoric sense of information). In other words, it is possible to imagine that the 'meaning' of the behaviour determined the behaviour. Maturana and Varela argue that this semantic description obscures the mutual coupling of structures that generates the behaviour (and ultimately its explanation by an observer in language).

Example 2: A human observer can describe the barking of sheepdogs as the conveying of meaning to one another while they are controlling a flock of sheep. Again, the behaviour can be explained in terms of the structural coupling of dogs and sheep. The notion of meaning is a reflective description of behaviour and takes place in language.

In the above two examples the notion of information in its technical sense remains within the descriptive realm of an observer.

Maturana and Varela argue that the operational coherence or consistency in the above interactions – and in animal communication generally (e.g., the 'mating' calls or duets of birds) – is based on mutual structural coupling (the conservation of autopoiesis and mutual adaptation) through structural interactions. For Varela (1979, 268), 'animal communication is a network of interactions that has no basis except in its history of coupling and is relative to that history. The signals exchanged during, say, courtship among birds reflect nothing except the possibility of the emergence of those coherences.'

What, then, is the distinction between these consensual or 'linguistic' interactions and the domain of language?

The essence of Maturana and Varela's theory is that in the flow of recurrent social interactions generated in small groups (fifteen to twenty members) of bipedal primates moving through the savannah three million years ago, language began to emerge when the operations in a 'linguistic domain' resulted in coordinations of actions pertaining to the linguistic domain itself. That is, language itself is a *coordinations of coordinations of actions*. In this process, 'objects' also arise as linguistic distinctions of linguistic distinctions that *obscure* the acts they coordinate. Furthermore, the observer arises as a 'languaging entity'[16] by operating in language with other observers, and generates the 'self' as a linguistic distinction of its participation in a linguistic domain (i.e., a consensual domain of interactions). For Maturana and Varela, the self is generated as a fourth order recursive distinction. Basic coordinations are a first-order linguistic domain (i.e., a domain of coordinations of actions). 'Observing' and 'languaging' are constituted as a second-order recursion in consensual coordinations of actions. The self (fourth-order recursion) arises through a coordination of a coordination of a coordination of a coordination of actions. The observer, (third-order) arises with the distinction of the operational realization of observing in a bodyhood. Thus, fourth-order recursion is 'I am observing.'

For Maturana and Varela, the self is a secondary, *generated*, not generating, phenomenon of language. Thus, this recursive system entails the following: basic coordinations (first order), observing (second order), observer (third order, observing observing), and self-consciousness (fourth order) – that is, 'the observer distinguishes his or her bodyhood as a node in a network of recursive distinctions.'[17]

What, then, in Maturana and Varela's theory, are coordinations of coordinations of actions (i.e., second-order recursion)?

The following two examples will illustrate this:

(1) Imagine a dog and his owner out for a walk. They arrive at an intersection, and the dog crosses over to the other side ahead. The owner whistles to the dog and points to his side; the dog crosses back over the road, and the dog and owner continue walking in the new direction.

This is a coordination of coordination of actions. The dog and its owner have coordinated their actions and moved off in a new direction. This coordination takes place in the *flow of interactions* between the participants, not in them individually. There is sufficient intimacy and recurrence of interactions between dog and owner for them to coordinate their actions. For the dog, this is the beginning of a participation in 'languaging'; but the dog does not come to live in language. For human animals it is possible to become coupled in recursions in consensual behaviour.

(2) Imagine a person waiting for a taxi. The taxis are passing in the opposite direction on the other side of the road. In order to hail a taxi the person makes a circular movement with his arm, the taxi does a U-turn and pulls up next to the prospective passenger, who gets in.

This is a coordination of coordination of actions.

Maturana and Varela also contend that objects arise as linguistic distinctions of linguistic distinctions that obscure the acts they coordinate. The following two examples will illustrate this:

(1) The word 'table' is about all the various acts that we may do in relation to a flat surface that we can put things on. 'Thus, the word "table" coordinates our actions with respect to the actions we perform with a "table," obscuring the actions that (as operations of distinction) constitute the table by bringing it forth' (Maturana and Varela 1987, 210). The essential point here is that we do not just put something on the table; we can also say 'I am putting something on the table.' The language act (linguistic distinction) obscures the domain of acts that the language acts are about.

The notion of pragmatics and speech act theory, which are in fundamental accord with Maturana and Varela's conception of language, is also developed by Deleuze and Guattari: 'Pragmatics becomes the presupposition behind all of the other dimensions and insinuates itself into everything' (ATP, 78). 'A statement is the redundant accompaniment of the act it accomplishes' (Lecercle 1985, 187).[18]

(2) 'Chalk' (i.e., the distinction of a piece of chalk) is constituted by the action involved in the use of chalk – that is, writing on a blackboard, or 'chalking.' 'When I say this is a chalk I coordinate my behaviour with you in a manner which obscures chalking. Please pass me the chalk – i.e., pass me chalking' (Maturana, Melbourne seminar, 1991).

Maturana is emphasizing (as does speech act theory),[19] that language is a form of social action directed towards what he calls 'mutual orientation.' This orientation is not grounded in a correspondence between 'language' and 'the world,' but exists as a 'consensual domain' – as a flow of interlinked patterns of activity. In the same way, Maturana and Varela view 'cognition' not as some abstract activity in a mental realm, but as a pattern of behaviour relevant to the functioning of the person or organism in its world.[20] 'Notions such as transmission of information, symbolization, denotation, meaning or syntax, are secondary to the constitution of the phenomenon of languaging in the living of the living systems that live it. Such notions arise as reflections in language upon what takes place in languaging' (Maturana 1990, 39).

Maturana and Varela argue that this recursive coordination of coordinations of actions that constitutes language is specific to human beings and originated as a result of a particular 'manner of living,' which they characterize as follows.

Early hominids (approximately three and a half million years ago) lived in small groups that included males, females, and children. They were bipedal, and this freed the hands to carry food (besides increasing tool-making abilities). Food sharing and social bonding (influenced by the shift to non-seasonal or 'regular' menstrual cycles), together with 'a more intimate sensual co-existence,' facilitated a manner of living that provided fertile ground for increased cooperative behaviour (i.e., recurrent interactions), to the point that language arose as a coordination of a coordination of acts. Maturana and Varela suggest from anthropological evidence that all of this could have arisen around two and a half million years ago. Concomitant with this intimate manner of living in small groups would be the development of a biology of languaging through evolution, epigenesis, and the selective advantage of a cooperative manner of living. Maturana argues that transformations to the face and larynx (among other characteristics) could have occurred in the last three and a half million years. This brief outline should not be taken to mean that the genetic code, through 'random' mutation, determines selective advantage. For Maturana and Varela, the transgenerational conservation of a particular structural feature is not determined uniquely by the genetic code, but rather by the autopoietic network in its entirety. They argue that molecular genetics overemphasizes the role of 'genes.' On a separate note, current research indicates that genetic structure may be directly affected by environmental factors (see *The New Scientist*, 21 September 1991, 20–5).

Maturana and Varela have coined the term 'linguallaxis' (linguistic trophallaxis – i.e., linguistic 'food sharing') to describe the linguistic couplings in human societies. In social insects, for example, communication requires constant physical interaction and mixing of stomach contents; whereas in human animals the recursive potential of language commonly allows for communication without constant physical (corporeal) interaction. This emergent recursive autonomy of language, which Varela argues 'is not a mere linear addition' of each agent's acts, is described by Deleuze and Guattari as 'the superlinearity of language.'[21]

The essential feature to be grasped in Maturana and Varela's approach is that although language requires the neurophysiology of the participants, it is not a neurophysiological phenomenon. Language takes place in the flow of consensual coordinations of actions, not in the bodily materiality of the participants. Maturana emphasizes that physiology (i.e., the internal dynamics of the organism) and behaviour (i.e., interactions with the milieu or other organisms) occupy different phenomenal domains. Nevertheless, the flow of actions will trigger structural changes in the bodyhoods of the participants, and vice versa. In other words, changes in our bodyhoods result in changes in our interactions, and changes in our interactions result in changes in our bodyhoods. Conversations affect bodies, and bodies affect conversations.

Thus Maturana argues that phenomena like language, mind, and ego, and psychic and spiritual phenomena in general, depend on the operation of our bodyhoods but do not take place 'in' them. They are, rather, distinctions that an observer makes of the different networks of conversations – that is, recursive behavioural and physiological couplings in which he or she lives – most importantly, the language networks he or she is *born into* and has to take place within.

These different networks of conversations, in which our bodies are nodes of operational intersection and words are 'nodes in coordinations of actions in languaging,' imply what Maturana calls 'multiplicity of domains of existence.' The 'identity' of a human animal is constituted as it is realized in his or her participation in a particular network of conversations. Thus each human being exists as a configuration of many different temporary 'identities,' which intersect in their realization in his or her bodyhood. The notion of multiplicity as used by Deleuze and Guattari is more appropriate than the notion of identity, which suggests a continuity of sameness as a first principle from which deviations and changes have to be accounted for. The concept of identity is developed in a language game. This resonates well with Maturana's multiplicity of domains of existence.

'Objects' (a term that usually implies this notion of self-identity) are to be understood in Maturana's theory of language as tokens for the coordinations of actions that they (qua identical 'objects') obscure. Objects as self-identity representations arise in language as consensual coordinations of actions in the recursion of consensual coordinations of actions that is languaging. The consequence of this analysis is that 'for living systems that do not operate in language there are no objects, or in other words objects are not part of their "cognitive domains"' (Maturana 1990, 38). This is to say that organisms not operating in language in their domain of adequate actions do not distinguish or operate in a world of objects, but rather are operating in a domain of effector-sensor correlations that do not operate with a 'representation' of an 'environment' (Maturana 1980, 26):

> The 'visual handling' of an environment is no handling of an environment, but the establishment of a set of correlations between effector (muscular) and receptor (proprioceptor and visual) surfaces, such that a particular state in the receptor surfaces may cause a particular state in the effector

surfaces that brings forth a new state in the receptor surfaces ... and so on. Behaviour is like an instrumental flight in which the effectors (engines, flaps, etc.) vary their state to maintain constant, or to change, the readings of the sensing instruments according to a specified sequence of variations, which either is fixed (specified through evolution) or can be varied during the flight as a result of the state of the flight (learning).

Deleuze, in his extraordinary braiding of Spinozist philosophy and ethology, invokes von Uexküll's illustration of the tick's behaviour as one example of viewing animal bodies in this way. A body (e.g., a tick) is defined in terms of its capacity to affect and be affected. The tick operates not with objects but rather with affective capacities, of which it has only three: sense of smell, sense of light, and sense of heat (warmth). The tick 'climbs up a branch' towards the light (it is affected by light), drops onto a 'passing mammal' that it has recognized by smell, finds a hairless warm area, and feeds.

For Maturana and Varela and Deleuze and Guattari, this perceptive, sensing ability does not operate with representations. The tick, like any organism/animal operating prior to language, does not 'view' anything in the sense of self-conscious 'imagery.' This is the logical conclusion of Maturana and Varela's analysis. Yet mainstream biology (as well as most natural history television programs) continue, to operate on the assumption that an animal 'views' (consciously) a phenomenal world. For example, it is assumed that a snake views humans as red objects.[22] However, if the snake is not an observer – that is, not existing in language – it does not 'view' anything. Eyes are sensing, affective organs, but the possession of eyes does not imply 'viewing' a world. Roger Sperry's research[23] on 'split brain' patients confirms this. Without language, the right brain is not self-conscious of what it 'sees' and cannot describe what affected it. Maturana cites Sperry's earlier work and his own experiments to argue that, for example, a frog is not 'aiming' at a fly when it sticks out its tongue.

For example, an observer notes that a frog shoots out its tongue in the direction of a fly, and can make the anthropomorphic presumption that the frog is looking and aiming at that a fly. It is possible to rotate the eye of a tadpole 180 degrees (keeping intact the optic nerve) and allow the animal to complete its development. Subsequently, if the rotated eye is covered and the frog is shown a fly, its tongue goes out and captures it. However, when the normal eye is covered and the prey is shown to the rotated eye, the frog shoots out its tongue with a deviation of 180 degrees. That is, if the prey is below and in front of the animal, the frog will now shoot out its tongue backwards and up. This deviation is never corrected by the animal.

This experiment[24] demonstrates that for the frog there is no up, down, front, or back in reference to an outside world as it exists for the observer. There is only an internal sensory motor correlation between a perturbation to the retina and the muscular contractions that move the frog's body. This is an example of the operational closure of the nervous system. Maturana argues that such experiments rotate the world of the observer with respect to the operated animal and that the animal is not committing a mistake even if it starves to death as a result of never catching another fly:

> Animals that do not live in language cannot be conscious or aware in the same mannner in which we are conscious or aware when we speak or our consciousness or awareness as languaging animals. If we speak of body awareness as we refer to the operation of handling their bodies performed by non-languaging animals (as the self-cleaning of a wasp), then we also exhibit a comparable body awareness when we accommodate our position and movements to the circumstances of our interactions and relations, when we are not attending (in language) to our doings and we say afterwards that we acted unconsciously. I claim that animals that do not live in language do all that they do as we do what we do unconsciously. And I claim that this is so because they do not have the operationality of language which makes self-consciousness possible. (1995, 166–7)[25]

This claim is remarkably close to Heidegger and Deely's approach to language and 'animality.' The non-languaging animal lives in *Umwelt* but does not distinguish it *as* an *Umwelt*. The *Umwelt* is ready to hand but never present to hand. What is specific to human animal language, as opposed to animal communication, is the awareness of the external or ontological relation, *as such*, 'between' a sign-vehicle and an object signified. Deely does not go as far as Maturana in denying animals a world of objects; he does however, argue that they do not grasp the relation of signification as such that allows for the infinite recursivity, or unlimited semiosis, that is distinctive of human animal language. The non-languaging animal is using relations but is not aware of them *as* relations.

Why is there a fly there when the frog sticks out its tongue? This question is answered by Maturana and Varela in accordance with their theory of structural coupling. The frog and the fly belong to the same history of congruent changes through millions of years, and become one eating the other in the process of becoming frog and fly. For Maturana and Varela the nervous system does not compute information from an environment; rather, it performs internal correlations that are triggered by perturbations from its external milieu, or by its own changes of state. The nervous system is therefore operationally closed – its current affective ability is determined by a history of interactions. Bergson calls this habitual recognition 'sensory-motor determinism'; but insofar as there is a brain, and depending on the 'complexity' of that brain, there is an increasing interval between the perceptual stimulation and the motor response. In human animals the affects and memory or recollection images operate in this gap and alter the response in undetermined ways. Deleuze gives an account of Bergson's theory in *Cinema I: The Movement Image* (1996).

From an observer's perspective, the action of the fly may not appear as adequate in conserving its autopoiesis; but if the fly and the frog are coupled with the biosphere, conceived of as an organism (Gaia) or second-order, metacellular, autopoietic system, this apparent paradox is resolved. That is, as observers, we can distinguish the substantial multiplicity of which the components (organisms or cells) are a part. When we isolate things in themselves – such as flies – we obscure the multiplicity they constitute with other components in their interactions. As Bateson insisted, the unit of evolution is the organism-and-its-environment.

All living bodies can be viewed in terms of their capacity to be affected and the affects of which they are capable. In the case of human animals, these affective capacities are not known in advance. We do not know what a body is capable of (Spinoza). This perspective avoids the notion of the organism as a set of preordained functions and opens bodies up to be understood as the multiplicities they in fact are. What needs to be investigated are the consistencies or assemblages or relational domains such bodies can enter.

For a living system not operating in language (e.g., a tick), there is no inside or outside. Such a distinction arises in language as a particular consensual coordination of actions in which the participants are recursively brought forth as distinctions of systems of distinctions. It follows from this argument that the individual (observing, the observer, self-consciousness) arises in language: 'Furthermore, it also follows from this that since language as a domain of consensual coordination of actions is a *social* phenomenon, self-consciousness is a social phenomenon, and as such it does not take place within the anatomical confines of the bodyhood of the living systems that generate it; on the contrary, it is external to them and pertains to their domain of interactions as a manner of co-existence' (ibid., 39).

For Maturana (as already noted), the term 'consensual' has a technical meaning that does not presuppose a conscious prior agreement about conduct. Consensual coordinations of actions refer to the mutually triggering interlocked conducts that occur when two or more organisms interact recursively, each becoming a medium for the autopoiesis of the other. Maturana argues that from the perspective of an observer, such a domain of recursive interactions is indistinguishable from a consensual domain in which the conduct of the structurally coupled organisms is established during the history of their interactions and through their interactions (co-ontogeny).

Maturana argues further that the interactions of the organisms (e.g., the coordinations of conduct among birds through producing a common song, the melody of which is specific to each couple) can be described in strictly operational terms without recourse to function or meaning: 'Yet, when an observer communicates with another observer, he or she defines a metadomain from the perspective of which a consensual domain appears as an interlocked domain of distinctions, indications, or descriptions, according to how the observer refers to the observed behaviour' (Maturana 1978, 48).

Confusion arises if the observer assumes that the consensual domain operates as a descriptive system intrinsic to the organisms, giving them information to compute the ad hoc status needed to operate in the *described* environment. That is, the observer can assume that the nervous system of an organism interacts with internal representations (descriptions) of the circumstances of its interactions, as if the changes of state were determined by the semantic value of these representations: 'Yet all that takes place in the operation of the nervous system is the structure-determined dynamics of changing relations of relative neuronal activity proper to a closed neuronal network' (ibid., 49).

For Maturana the key feature of languaging is that it enables those who operate in it to describe themselves, thereby generating the self and its circumstances as linguistic distinctions of the self's participation in a linguistic domain – that is, a domain of recursive consensual coordinations of actions. Meaning arises as a relationship of linguistic distinctions. Thus, words are distinctions of consensual coordinations of actions in the flow of consensual coordinations of actions – they are *not* symbolic entities – and meaning and languaging become part of the medium in which the participants exist contingent on the conservation of the social system.

This is why the term 'consensual' can be misleading if we do not understand it in its technical use by Maturana as interlocked patterns of conduct (without prior conscious agreement). Maturana emphasized in his later work (e.g., Maturana 1988) that social systems are conservative systems in which power relations operate through obedience:

> The normal interactions of a human being in a social system to which he or she belongs are confirmatory of it and of his or her membership in it, and contribute to the production of members that confirm it. Social systems are constitutively conservative systems; due to this, human social systems can only change if their members have experiences that trigger in them changes in bodyhood that result in them no longer participating in its constitutive network of conversations. For this to happen in any particular human social system, its members must have experiences outside the network of conversations that constitutes it. (ibid., 69–70)

We are born into a society or collective assemblage in which change can only occur through acts which are not confirmatory of it – that is to say, through dissonant non-consensual acts. It is dissensus,[26] not consensuality, that generates change: 'This is why social creativity, as the generation of novel social relations, always entails interactions operationally outside the society, and necessarily leads to the generation, by the creative individuals, of modes of conduct that either change the defining relations of the society as a particular social system, or separate them from it. Social creativity is necessarily antisocial in the social domain in which it takes place' (Maturana 1980, xxvii–xxviii).

For Maturana, language is a social phenomenon, and the significance or meaning of any given behaviour does not occur in the nervous system or any aspect of the behaviour itself but rather in the ongoing social process in which it arises. Nietzsche, Foucault, Deleuze, and others have shown that social processes are always operations of power relations. A force will always overcome, be overcome, or merge with another force; there is no equilibrium; consensus is achieved through the operations of diffuse power relations. We are constrained to consent by regimes of signs, among other things.

From this perspective, human beings as languaging creatures are immersed in a network of interactions and language; this network orients our actions and does not present to us an independent, objective world. In language, worlds are brought forth *with others* (objects arise in our cognitive domain) through recursive coordinations of actions that obscure the acts they coordinate. Reality arises in language as an explanation of the distinction between self and non-self in the praxis of living of the observer: 'Nature, the world, society, science, religion, the physical space, atoms, molecules, trees [...] indeed all things are cognitive entities, explanations of the praxis or happening of living of the observer [...] Every *thing* is human responsibility' (Maturana 1990, 51).

Varela, in particular, has drawn attention to the similarity between postmodern philosophy and the consequences of Maturana and Varela's understanding of cognition.[27] Reality, from this perspective, cannot be understood as given, assuming a starting point outside first. Nor is it constructed by us in an arbitrary fashion, assuming a starting point inside first. There is no fixed point of reference or foundation to which we can anchor our perceptions, no transcendental reality in which to ground our beliefs. For Maturana and Varela this view has important ethical consequences: 'Everything that we do becomes part of the world that we live as we bring it forth as social entities in language' (ibid., 51). We are 'autopoietic machines' *producing* a world together, not *representing* one.

How has the experience of '*self dialogue*' arise? Maturana's theory would answer this question as follows: A nervous system (such as that of human animals) is capable of generating language and the observer as the distinction of the operational realization of observing in a bodyhood. This should not be interpreted as overprivileging sight perception. The recursive operations invoked in generating the 'observer' apply to the recognition of *all* our affective capacities. Congenitally blind people are excellent observers. If observers can orient themselves towards themselves describing themselves, they can recursively describe themselves describing themselves endlessly. (In a geometric sense, this could be likened to the recursive symmetry in a fractal). Language can occur in the operation of a single human being because 'its structure in that moment is the result of its participation in a history of languaging with other organisms' (Maturana 1988, 47). Your language belongs to an implicit domain of consensual coordinations of actions in which internal dialogue is, as Varela argues, always in reference to the network of others that has given rise to you. Or as Maturana puts it: 'What is peculiar to us is that due to our manner of living in language the distinction of relations of relations that take place in the flow of languaging makes it possible that our nervous system should operate inside itself in the recursive distinctions of relations that constitute the operation in language and self-consciousness in solitude' (1995, 169).

This does not mean that self-consciousness as a recursive distinction of relations of relations has now been reduced to a neurophysiological activity. Once the nervous system has become a recursive languaging brain, it can generate through its internal dynamics, as a closed network, 'sensory/effector correlations that pertain to the flow of languaging even when the organism that it integrates is alone, or doing nothing apparent to an external observer' (Maturana, Mpodozis, and Letelier 1995, 24).[28] Thus dreams, reflections in solitude, and logical operations become 'unavoidable possibilities.'

This approach intersects with Deely's argument that ideas as semiotically conceived – that is, as signs or relations – cannot be states of the nervous system. Neural states are in principle sense-perceptible, but relations are not. The relational domain or *Umwelt* is 'suprasubjective' and potentially intersubjective.

The fundamental difference between Deely and Maturana is that for Maturana an animal such as the gorilla 'Koko' (q.v. Paterson and Linden 1981) has the possibility of entering into a languaging relational domain *with* human animals (not alone), and can do all the fundamental operations we do in languaging (i.e., coordinations of coordinations of behaviour). Deely (1982, 203) contends that coordinations of this kind *never* constitute what is fundamental to human animal language as distinct from animal communication (i.e., the awareness of relations as distinguished from their terms or fundamentals):

> Take the case of civil government. Consider the notion of a president – the president of this country. If I were the Premacks, I would teach my chimpanzee each time, say, Richard Nixon walked into the room, to put on the board plastic symbols indicating 'Here comes the President.' Now, if I were the Premacks, I would forthwith claim that I had taught Sarah or Washoe or whichever chimp the meaning of the word 'president.' But the fact of the matter is that the animal doesn't see a *president*. Indeed, a president, *as such*, never appears *to the eyes*. The chimp doesn't have a clue one as to what is referred to by the term 'president' as it designates something distinct and distinguishable from the given concrete individual. When the chimp associates the word 'president' with R.M. Nixon, and when a human being says, 'Richard M. Nixon was the President of the United States,' the materi-

ally same sound or symbolic marker for 'president' is functioning in a completely different sense, once above the linguistic interface as well as below it, the other time below it only.

One of the main focuses of most mystical, shamanic, meditative paths or 'lines of flight' is to stop or move tangentially to the endless recursive looping, descriptive, and interpreting process. I, I, I. Deleuze and Guattari cite Castaneda's books as of 'profound interest' in demonstrating how to combat – with drugs or other experiences, (e.g., meditative ones or extreme physical ones – the mechanisms of interpretation: by 'stopping' the internal dialogue. It hardly needs to be emphasized that such experiences are to be undertaken with caution, lest total self-destruction occur – drug addiction, paranoia, pathological obsession with Nirvana or mystical 'union' (as something to be acquired/possessed). It is said in the Ratnavali (an ancient Buddhist text): 'A foolish and intellectually conceited person, because he misunderstands devoidness, destroys his own person by rejecting it and plunges headfirst into the hell of Avici.'[29] In more contemporary language, Maurice Blanchot, in commenting on Foucault, has stated that it is not a question of eliminating the subject but of putting into question its 'overdetermined' unity.

What remains extraordinary is that such a putting into question or 'decentring' of the subject should be considered radical or a purely contemporary strategy. This demonstrates the extraordinary power of the constraints to consensus as well as their fragility.

A human being reared in complete isolation does not develop language (q.v. Maclean 1977). Likewise, the isolation of a 'languaging adult' (e.g., Robinson Crusoe) over an extended period will tend to produce a deterioration in the ability to operate in language – unless substitutes for social interaction are invented. Thus Crusoe throws himself into work and order, schedules, time keeping, and so on, in a search for substitutes for social interactions. (See Deleuze 1990, 301–21, for a commentary on Michel Tournier's novel *Friday*. Tournier's novel is inspired by the Crusoe story but develops a 'perverse world without others.') In a striking analysis, Deleuze argues that the perceptual field could not function as it does without the Other, understood as an organizing principle rather than as an individual subject. That is to say, laws affecting the constitution of objects (e.g., form background), depend on the Other as a structure, not as a particular form inside a perceptual field: 'The part of the object that I do not see I posit as visible to Others, so that when I will have walked around to reach this hidden part, I will have joined the Others behind the object ... As for the objects behind my back, I sense them coming together and forming a world, precisely because they are visible to, and are seen by Others. When one complains about the meanness of Others, one forgets this other and even more frightening meanness – namely the meanness of things were there no Other (ibid., 305–6).

Deleuze and Guattari's Conception of Language

Recursivity of actions is necessary for language, and this in turn requires affective capacity – an ability to affect and be affected – to act and be acted upon: 'The phenomena of self-referentiality cannot account for the performative. The opposite is the case; it is "the fact that certain statements are socially devoted to the accomplishment of certain actions" that explains self-referentiality' (ATP, 78). This is in agreement with Maturana and Varela's thesis, outlined earlier.

An essential feature of Maturana and Varela's analysis of language is that symbols do not pre-exist language but arise after it, and in it, as distinctions made by an observer of consensual relations of coordinations of coordinations of actions. They argue that the understanding of language as a denotative symbolic system for the transmission of information requires the pre-existence of the function of denotation, *but that this function is the very one whose evolutionary origin should be explained.*[30]

Deleuze and Guattari, elaborating partly on Austin's[31] speech act theory, begin their criticism of linguistics from similar observations: 'Austin's famous theses that there are intrinsic relations between speech and certain actions that are accomplished by *saying* them – e.g., *the performative*: I swear by saying "I swear"! The utterance constitutes an act. The *illocutionary*: I ask a question by saying "Is..."?' These non-discursive immanent relations between statements and acts have, for Deleuze and Guattari, three important consequences:

> (1) [They] made it impossible to conceive of language as a code, since a code is the condition of possibility for all explanation. [Deleuze and Guattari substitute Forms of Expressions and Forms of Content.]
> (2) [They] made it impossible to define semantics, syntactics, or even phonematics ... independently of *pragmatics*.
> (3) [They] made it impossible to maintain the distinction between language (la langue) and speech (la parole) ... The meaning and syntax of

language can no longer be defined independently of the speech acts they presuppose. (ATP, 77)

The relation between Maturana's conception of language and Deleuze and Guattari's extension of speech act theory is not delineated in order to develop a unified theory but rather to emphasize the elements of the tradition they criticize. The major criticism of traditional linguistics is that it ignores the *act* of language and concentrates on its syntax and semantics, thus closing language in upon itself and making pragmatics a 'residue': 'Signifier enthusiasts take an oversimplified situation as their implicit model: word and thing. From the word they extract the signifier, and from the thing a signified in conformity with the word and therefore subjugated to the signifier. They operate in a sphere interior to and homogeneous with language' (ATP, 6).

For Deleuze and Guattari (as for Maturana and Varela), language is derived from interactions on a 'plane of consistency' that links autonomous elements, (e.g., organisms). The consistency of the plane is *in the relations or interactions, not in subjects or forms* (in the traditional sense). Multiplicities are not reducible to unities. In Maturana's terms, language occurs in the coupling or *flow* of consensual coordinations of actions, not in the bodily materiality of the participants. Observing, the observer, and self-consciousness arise as respectively second-, third-, and fourth-order recursions in coordinations of actions.

The challenge and difficulty in engaging with Deleuze and Guattari's analysis of language theories is that it is embodied within a text (ATP) whose style and manner of construction seeks to express a way of thinking that abandons all traditional academic divisions and linear, step-by-step explanations. They invent and multiply concepts in an attempt to convey a real feeling for the multidimensional complexities, coherences, and consistencies among what they call the 'strata' of the earth. These strata correspond, basically, to the physicochemical, organic, and anthropomorphic (human) levels. Deleuze and Guattari characterize and examine the interrelationships of these 'strata' in a unique way that they describe as rhizomatic or nomadic. In a technical sense, rhizomes are underground root systems that grow in a horizontal rather than an arborescent, vertical manner. The shoots that do push through the surface are not independent of this maze of underground 'plagiotropic' (running at a slant to the plant) growth.[32] This is playfully in contrast to the tree model so beloved of Chomsky and many other linguists. Deleuze and Guattari use this image of the rhizome to connote a manner of investigation that recognizes the fundamental importance of interconnections and couplings. They argue that there is no language in itself, nor is there a functional separation between syntax and semantics and the social field from which these emerge.

This examination of Deleuze and Guattari's criticisms of linguistics and their complementarity and consistency with Maturana and Varela's conception of language presumes to do no more than indicate to the reader the extraordinary depth and richness of *A Thousand Plateaus*. As indicated, its manner of construction does not facilitate conventional manners of exegesis, and with that consideration borne in mind let us attempt to stroll through the strata, focusing on the emergent autonomy of language and its constraining and creative power in the human world:

> The same Professor Challenger who made the earth scream with his pain machine, as described by Arthur Conan Doyle, gave a lecture after mixing several textbooks on geology and biology in a fashion befitting his simian disposition. He explained that the earth – the Deterritorialized, the Glacial, the giant Molecule – is a body without organs. This body without organs [or plane of consistency] is permeated by informed, unstable matters, by flows, in all directions, by free intensities or nomadic singularities, by mad or transitory particles. (ATP, 40)

Strata occur on this body without organs (e.g., through dissipative structures and autopoiesis), giving form to matter and organizing molecules into molar aggregates. The organic and anthropomorphic strata are the concern of this section. Using the terms 'content' and 'expression' taken from the linguist Louis Hjelmslev (as an alternative to the signifier/signified model in structural linguistics), Deleuze and Guattari's analysis proceeds to examine the organization of matter (the unformed, non-stratified plane of consistency) through its 'double articulation' of content and expression. For Deleuze and Guattari this approach has the advantage of breaking with the form-content duality. There is a form of content, and there is a form of expression. Furthermore, there is a substance of content and expression. Consider an example.[33]

The *substance of content* of a high school is the students. The *form of content* is the school itself, its architecture, and so on. The *form of expression* is the administrative rules and traditions that determine how the school is laid out and what it does (teaches/inspires/moulds). The *substance of expression* is the phonemes and letters embodying those functions. The crucial issue is 'who' determines what happens in the school (its form of expression)? It will become apparent that the subject of this expression is the interactions among people rather than anything 'in' one person's 'mind.' That is (using Deleuze and Guattari's terminology), the subject consists in a collective assemblage of 'enunciation' operating in a social field. Deleuze and Guattari argue that these terms (content/expression) offer a richer understanding than can be provided by signifier/signified relationships or form and substance. Whereas form and substance are not really distinct, content and expression can have an autonomy in their double articulation in the organic stratum. How can this autonomy of expression be characterized?

In the organic stratum, expression becomes linear rather than voluminous. The essential thing is the linearity of the nucleic sequence.

Thus, for example, in the crystalline stratum, the crystal form expresses a microscopic structure. However, the distinction is only 'formal,' as between scales or orders of magnitude. In the organic stratum the distinction between content and expression becomes 'real' rather than formal. The linearity of the nucleic sequence is not that of an order of magnitude (or three-dimensionality); rather, it is 'unidimensional,' and expression develops an autonomy (or 'deterritorialization') from content with the consequence that there is now a mechanism for reproduction: 'The crystal's subjection to three dimensionality, in other words, its index of territoriality, makes the structure incapable of formally reproducing and expressing itself; only the accessible surface can reproduce itself, since it is the only deterritorializable part' (ibid., 60).

In the anthropomorphic or human stratum, form of expression 'becomes linguistic rather than genetic' and achieves a further deterritorialization: 'Vocal signs have temporal linearity, and it is this superlinearity that constitutes their specific deterritorialization and differentiates them from genetic linearity' (ibid., 62). The phenomenon of translation (from one language to another) becomes possible, as form of expression is now independent from substance of expression. Deleuze and Guattari contend that independence of form of expression from its substance does not occur on the other strata. They draw on a staggering range of anthropological and biological works to characterize the manner of living and changing biology that would facilitate this 'superlinearity' or 'deterritorialization' and development of language.

The substance of expression in language (phonemes) affects the whole configuration of the face (as Maturana argues), and neotenic birth (requiring extended nursing) facilitates language learning: 'The steppe, once more seems to have exerted strong pressure for selection: the 'supple larynx' is a development corresponding to the free hand and could have arisen only in a deforested milieu' (ibid., 62).

Comparative Assessment

Thus, both in Maturana and Varela and in Deleuze and Guattari the biological/social conditions that could generate language are given due emphasis without this being a reductive hypothesis. The phenomenon of language arises in the phenomenal domain of interactions, not in the body. However, the body is affected by these interactions due to the recursive coupling of behaviour and neurophysiology.

The 'superlinearity' of language corresponds to the second-order recursion in coordinations of coordinations of acts. Maturana and Varela argue that this arose somewhere between two and three-and-a-half million years ago as a result of a manner of living involving 'intimate sensual coexistence' and a recurrence of social interactions and bonding such that this recursion in coordinations was liable to occur. The period noted here is based on fossil remains indicating that the structural features of present-day human animals (e.g., bipedalism, opposing thumb, omnivorous feeding habits) cannot be recognized prior to this period. Furthermore, Maturana and Varela argue that such a manner of living implies mutual acceptance of others in coexistence, and that without this mutual acceptance there can be no social process and increasing recurrence of interactions. They argue that this mutual acceptance is generated by the emotion of 'love' as a 'biological phenomenon:' 'When I speak of love I do not speak of a sentiment, nor do I speak of goodness, nor recommend kindness. When I speak of love I speak of a biological phenomenon, I speak of the domain of actions in which living systems coordinate their actions in a manner that entails mutual acceptance, and I claim that such operations constitute social phenomena' (Maturana 1988, 56).

Maturana and Varela are claiming that man is fundamentally an ethical animal and that anything which blocks or destroys this mutual acceptance, such as ideological or religious convictions, destroys social phenomena. Furthermore, they argue that since language is generated in a social context through interactions with others in coexistence, and since our 'reality' or 'world' is constructed by the distinctions we make in language, every languaging act has an ethical meaning because it constitutes or 'brings forth' a world. In his preface, Michel Foucault described Deleuze and Guattari's *Anti-Oedipus* as a book of ethics concerned with an art of living that would counteract fascism: – 'The fascism in us all, in our heads and in our everyday behaviour, the fascism that causes us to love power, to desire the very thing that dominates and exploits us.' There is thus an ethical foundation to the work of all four of these thinkers.

Until recently, Maturana and Varela focused their research on the biological origins of cognition, perception, and language and paid little attention to the constraining power of language as a form of expression generated in a social field. Theorists in the humanities such as Foucault and Deleuze and Guattari have offered highly detailed accounts of the constraining force of language, within which we are born.[34] Nevertheless, Maturana is today studying culture (defined by him as a particular network of conversations and the actions or doings implicit in them) – specifically, the rise of patriarchy as a culture of oppression. In the humanities, the term 'discourse' (or 'episteme,' after Foucault) corresponds to Maturana's network of conversations. He sees this network as intimately connected with the transition from a nomadic to a pastoral (herding) lifestyle during which defence and appropriation, beginning with the restriction of mobility of animals and their enclosure, led to a more general change in the manner of living. This change was characterized fundamentally by the importance given to procreation in the herd and by the displacement of the notion of fertility onto that of procreation. This work will not be further examined here, except to note Maturana's involvement in 'cultural' questions concerning the relationship between the state and nomadic lifestyles, which are also a central concern of *A Thousand Plateaus*. These issues, which are intrinsically bound up in languaging and discourse, are the subject of a highly original and complex treatment by Deleuze and Guattari, which, again, will not be further examined here (see ATP, 'Treatise on Nomadology – The War Machine').

The critical point for Deleuze and Guattari is that few linguists have studied the social character of enunciation. They argue that statements are individuated only to the extent that an 'impersonal collective assemblage' requires it. They extend pragmatics by arguing that the subject is not the origin, but only the mouthpiece for an utterance. One's speech is always an instance of indirect speech: 'Direct discourse is a detached fragment of a mass and is born of the collective assemblage, but the collective assemblage is always like a murmur from which I take my proper name, the constellation of voices, concordant or not from which I draw my voice' (ibid., 84).

For the Deleuze and Guattari of ATP, the elementary unit of language is the 'order-word' – the relation of every word or statement to implicit presuppositions (speech acts) that are accomplished in the statement (e.g., I swear by saying 'I swear'). They extend the theory of the performative sphere developed in speech act theory by viewing the subject, 'I,' as derived from collective assemblages. The 'subject' becomes a symbiotic node within social interactions.

Order-words are social in origin; they are expressed words but not reducible to them. They are concerned not merely with commands, but with every statement that entails some kind of social obligation (e.g., promises, affirmations, negations – 'You are no longer a child').

These order-words (or 'statement-acts') do not arise from 'intersubjectivity,' as subjectivity presupposes the coupling of bodies in a social field, which itself generates subjectivity (Maturana and Varela's consensual or linguistic domain). Deleuze and Guattari analyze this coupling as already foreshadowed, in terms of content and expression as applied to collective assemblages that take two basic forms: a 'machinic assemblage,' which couples bodies, actions, and passions (content); and a 'collective assemblage of enunciation or regime of signs' (expression). Bodies are coupled through a machinic assemblage (not unlike Maturana and Varela's structural coupling) that generates corporeal or structural changes in the bodies of the assemblage; and 'instantaneous incorporeal transformations' are generated through the collective assemblage of enunciation in its speech- or statement-acts. Examples include the judge's verdict, which instantaneously transforms the 'accused' into 'guilty'; the 'I do' of marriage; and the awarding of a diploma at a graduation ceremony. All are instantaneous incorporeal transformations. These incorporeal transformations effectuated through speech acts generate structural changes in the bodies of the participants. The 'meanings' or 'significations' or 'expressed' of statement-acts can dramatically affect bodyhoods. They are instantaneous, and they trigger changes in physiology as a result of the coupling between the domain of language acts and the bodyhoods of the participants. 'Words' can kill, depress, or inspire.

All of this conceptual innovation highlights the inadequacy of signifier/signified or word/thing relationships. Collective assemblages operate through a complex interrelationship between states of things and statement-acts (which are not reducible to words).

This understanding leads Deleuze and Guattari to argue that language is neither informational nor communicational; rather, it effectuates *acts* (e.g., ordering, questioning, promising, affirming).

Using different strategies, all of these thinkers affirm that language is not fundamentally informational. For Maturana, notions such as information arise in language as reflections and are secondary to what takes place in languaging (i.e., coordinations of acts). Interactions do not take place in a domain of abstractions, but in what Deleuze would call the 'co-functioning' or symbiosis of 'bodies,' which may be physical or social or verbal.

Maturana contends that the traditional view of language as a denotative symbolic system for transmitting information concerning independent entities has obscured the fact that such a conception assumes the pre-existence of the function of denotation, whereas denotation is the very function that requires explanation in *an evolutionary theory of natural languages*. For Maturana, language must arise as a result of something that does not require denotation. Denotation requires consensus, and for him it is the process of structural coupling that generates a consensual domain of interactions. He argues that language is connotative, orienting the orientee within his cognitive domain (i.e., domain of adequate or effective behaviour).[35] Thus there is no transmission of information between organisms except in a metadomain as an *a posteriori* commentary made by an observer. In other words, notions such as information and the rules of syntax and generative grammar (Chomsky) are descriptions within the cognitive realm of the observer and have no explanatory value when it comes to the actual machinic operation of living autopoietic systems.

Autopoietic systems parallel Deleuze and Guattari's notion of abstract machines and their concrete realization in machinic assemblages: 'It is still the same abstract animal that is realized throughout the stratum, only to varying degrees, in varying modes ... only autonomous realisations of the same abstract relations' (ibid., 46). Maturana and Varela define the 'organization' of a machine as relations between components regardless of the components themselves. These relations (not the components) constitute the 'abstract machine,'[36] which is effectuated or embodied in 'machinic assemblages' (Maturana and Varela's structure): 'An assemblage is necessary for organisms to be caught within and permeated by a social field that utilises them' (ibid., 71).

To recapitulate: the unformed (although not 'chaotic') plane of consistency becomes 'stratified' through the action of an abstract machine, which actualizes its abstract relations on a specific stratum through particular machinic assemblages: 'Thus there is no vital matter specific to the organic stratum, matter is the same on all the strata. But the organic stratum does have a specific unity of composition, a single abstract Animal, a single machine embedded in the stratum, and presents everywhere the same molecular materials, the same elements or anatomical components of organs, the same formal connections' (ibid., 45).

Maturana and Varela likewise insist that the organic stratum is defined by a particular organization (i.e., in terms of relations, not component properties) rather than by some 'vital' force. Paradoxically, reductionistic explanations (e.g., in terms of genetic structure) are, according to Maturana and Varela, vitalistic, in that they confer all the properties of the living onto one or some of its components. Thus molecular genetics (à la Jacques Monod) becomes a vitalistic explanation of living systems, emphasizing one component rather than relationships. Jacques Monod, one of the most influential contemporary cellular biochemists, argues that the properties of a living system can be reduced to the properties of the amino acid sequences of polypeptide chains: 'It is at this level of chemical organisation that in a very real sense lies, if there is any, the secret of life' (Monod 1971, 94).

Maturana and Varela emphasize that autopoiesis, the organizing principle of living systems, is not a transcendent notion but refers to the specific relations that define an autopoietic system. Yet, these relations do not identify particular mechanisms in the organism. The organization of autopoiesis is actualized in a particular living system, on a plane of consistency that is pre-individual but not transcendent.

Autopoietic living machines (abstract animals) are coupled through their recurrent interactions on this plane. In fact, Deleuze and Guattari's notion of consistency is influenced by the work of Eugene Dupréel (1968), a virtually unknown French philosopher who sought to develop a philosophy of biology in the 1930s and 1940s based in part on the notions of 'consolidation' and 'consistency' (q.v. ATP, 328–9): 'The consistency of a being is the capacity to conserve its identity throughout the vicissitudes that result from its relationships with other beings' (Dupréel 1968, 18).

Maturana and Varela (1987, 74) state this principle as follows: 'Ontogeny is the history of structural change in a unity without loss of organisation (identity) in that unity.'

Organisms become bound up with one another through the 'consolidation' of their coexistence in what Deleuze and Guattari call a *machinic opera* (ATP, 330), and what Maturana and Varela call 'a structural dance in the choreography of co-existence' (Maturana and Varela 1987, 248).

For the abstract machine (autopoietic system) to endure, it must be coupled in congruent recurrent interactions with a medium in which it retains its autonomy (through changes of state/structure which conserve its organization, that is, through structural coupling). If these interactions are not congruent, the autonomy of the autopoietic machine disintegrates.

The plane of consistency (or abstract machine) becomes 'stratified' by the actualization of machinic arrangements that express 'consistency' through their own autonomous functioning as well as through congruent couplings in which consistency is conserved. In fact, the plane of consistency is simultaneously constituted by the following: unformed elements, intensive affective capacities, and immanent formal relationships, which 'emerge' as autonomous systems through, for example, dissipative structures and autopoietic living machines. If this appears to be 'fuzzy logic,'[37] or complex – it is. The plane of consistency on which these 'consistent' autonomous autopoietic systems are actualized generates consensual worlds (a multiverse rather than a universe) wherein languages (as consensual coordinations of coordinations of actions) develop their own emergent autonomy and wherein 'regimes of signs' become descriptive media that can manipulate and transform bodies through signification and incorporeal transformations.

However, this autonomy of languages is also creative, allowing its participants to describe, imagine, and conjure up the past and invent the future. Order-words may constrain and determine subjectivity, in particular as one is born into regimes of signs. *However,* there is always the possibility of unpredictable encounters and novel interactions leading to previously unimagined observations, statement-acts, and networks of conversations:

> If a human being can observe the social system that he creates with his behaviour, he may dislike it and reject it, and thus become a source of change; but if he can only undergo interactions specified by the social system that he integrates, he cannot be an observer of it and his behaviour can only confirm it. Accordingly, all coercive political systems aim, explicitly or implicitly, at reducing creativity and freedom by specifying all social interactions as the best means of suppressing human beings as observers

and thus attaining political permanence. To obtain this ultimate goal, however, the typically human mode of creativity must be completely suppressed, and this, as long as there is any capacity to establish such second-order consensual domains as the use of language requires, is impossible. (Maturana 1978, 62)

The Achilles heel of absolute domination = relations.

Conclusion

Just as an artist borrows from his precursors and contemporaries the traits which suit him, I invite those who read me to take or reject my concepts freely. The important thing is not the final result but the fact that the multicomponential cartographic method can co-exist with the process of subjectivation, and that a reappropriation, an autopoiesis, of the means of production of subjectivity can be made possible.

Guattari (1995, 12–13)

Only logically is being prior to and presupposed by action: existentially, a being is only so long as and through the actions (and resulting relationships) it entertains, both actively and passively, with its surroundings, whether objective or physical. Hence also only logically do structures 'exist' apart from actions. They exist only as virtualities of the action itself which sustains being, and – especially – as the pattern of relations resulting from those virtualities as sustenative.

Deely (1994c, 1)

To fail to recoil at the relational limit is to risk becoming philosophical.

Massumi (2000, 195)

The account of relations that has been presented in the foregoing pages moves inexorably from ontological, to ethological, to semiotic, ethico-aesthetic, and political dimensions. To speak or write about relations is to inevitably have *forced* upon oneself the problem and question of what relations we might wish to be involved in. This is not to suggest that we can simply pick and choose at will, but that there is an ethical imperative to take responsibility for our actions and *experiment* with the kinds of worlds we wish to enter into with others. What kind of cosmopolitics, or manner of coexistence, do we want – and with whom and what creatures, things, and hybrids? Thus a continuum or transversality from theory to practice to action becomes ontologically inevitable.

I claim no special originality for this observation, which forced itself on me while I was engaging with the materials that comprise this book. What is more, this claim is quite explicit in Deleuze and Guattari's work. Guattari especially emphasizes the ethico-aesthetic and political consequences of his 'schizoanalytic cartographies.' He never stops repeating that subjectivity is not a natural given, but has to be constructed – just like a new molecule or entity of any kind – and that the 'three ecologies' of the mental, the environmental, and the social interpenetrate.

As examples, Guattari refers to the most diverse and often low-profile tentatives, such as the manner in which a retirement home is run, or the kitchen in a mental hospital. In fact, there are an infinite number of examples, from education to so-called 'personal relations'; and as Guattari observed through his work as a therapist and activist, this reappropriation of autopoiesis or creative autonomy in one domain can catalyse a recovery of creativity in other, unforeseen domains.

To avoid misunderstanding, I would emphasize that this question of ethico-political practice is not by any means the only one at issue. As I have tried to suggest, the univocal ontology of relations presented to us by Poinsot seems to have extraordinary resonances with Deleuze's logic of sense, in particular the concept of an 'outside' of thought that is not the outside of an external world but rather the externality of relations that allow thought to have a relation with something that does not depend on it. Relations are external to their terms, and the issue is not primarily a relation of thought to the external world but rather the relation of thought to something other than itself.

As Zourabichvili (1996, 31) notes so magnificently, for Deleuze (and Guattari) 'things' involve a concept of force, and things are first of all *signs* that refer (renvoyer) *to something other than themselves* – they refer to the force they manifest or express. Thus things have no traditional essence. The 'essence' becomes a nexus or pattern of relations, and philosophy becomes a semiotic that treats things first of all as signs of relations and forces. A phenomenon is reduced to a thing when it is no longer grasped as a sign. Coupled with this semiotic is the 'truth of the relative' wherein both the subject and the object are involved in a double individuation. The world is not identical to itself, but changing, and we are changing with it (the exit from the Kantian horizon). This involves a perspectivism which is not that of *a point of view on* neutral things (the relativity of truth), but a perspectivism in which the point of view also belongs to the object, and the identity of the object as seen by a seeing subject vanishes into difference, which refers to other differences that differentiate it. Difference replaces identity ... Every object, every thing, must see its own identity swallowed up in difference, each being no more than a difference between differences. 'Difference must be shown *differing*,' (DR 56). In this philosophy there is an absolute exteriority of perspectives beyond the relative exteriority of the represented world to a subject, or the relative exteriority of external things in relation to one other – an absolute 'outside' which is not that of an external world but of the exteriority (and univocity) of relations to their terms. It is this capacity of relations that allows thought to go beyond recognition or representation and encounter the unknown or non-thought – to create a little genuine novelty. And what does thought encounter that forces it to think? Signs (which, as we have seen, are relations). All thought is 'in' or by way of signs.

So what? Or where to from here?

There are a many interesting directions in which this autosemiopoiesis can be taken:

First, the practice of a *generalized ecology*, which includes an ecology of the virtual as much as the visible world, and which seeks to engender new formations and alliances that would allow for mutual flourishing and preservation (à la Spinoza and Deleuze). As Guattari boldly claims (1996, 107) 'these alternative forms of existential reappropriation and self-valorization may in the future become the *reason for living* for human collectivities and individuals who refuse to give in to the deathlike entropy characterizing the period we are passing through.' Of course, it need hardly be mentioned that the living hell that millions of people have had *forced upon them* requires that assistance must often come from others.

The current work of Bruno Latour and Isabelle Stengers provides valuable material and examples of conceptual work with practical and ethical applications. Latour's 'political ecology' and Stenger's 'cosmopolitics' are complementary and raise fundamental ethical and political questions. 'Who or what do you take into account?' 'At what price are you ready to live the good life together?' Latour sometimes refers to this approach as a 'relationism' or 'the truth of relations.' Both these writers, educators, and 'activists' draw significantly on the work of Alfred North Whitehead, a philosopher who has also influenced Deleuze and

Guattari. It is symptomatic of the state of contemporary mainstream academia that Whitehead's work is largely ignored today. This is not to suggest that we should all become 'Whiteheadians,' but rather that a creative use of his concepts (such as 'event,' 'proposition,' and 'actual occasion') provides an ontological breath of fresh air.

For the record, it is worth noting that Latour brilliantly revitalizes Whitehead for his own uses and that Stengers recently published a book on Whitehead's 'philosophy of organism,' *Penser avec Whitehead* (2002), in which she claims that Guattari's twin autopoietic folds, briefly developed in *Chaosmosis* (1995), repeat the Whiteheadian process of actualization.

Now this is interesting, because Whitehead sought to develop a *logic of relations* in which the ultimate entities are complexes of relations or overlapping series of events. Whitehead's 'reformed subjectivist principle' takes an approach quite consonant with that of Poinsot and Deely. He insists that relations are real (although this is not yet to have grasped the *univocal* status of relations), and he specifically engages with the opposition between Bradley and Russell on internal versus external relations. In fact, he argues in his serial pluralism that an actual occasion is internally related to its antecedents through 'prehension,' but that its completed antecedent occasions are not internally related to it. In this approach, external relation seems to denote no relation at all, and it remains unclear to me (and to Ivor Leclerc in *The Nature of Physical Existence* [1972]) whether Whitehead has in this way satisfactorily dealt with the problem of relations. Specifically, to what extent is prehension really a relation? Deely has suggested that Whitehead's prehension is a 'confused' form of transcendental relation – that is, a relative being, but not a relation. What is nevertheless supremely relevant is that relations are a crucial problem for Whitehead (as for the history of philosophy). However, here we are more concerned with the task of *creating new relations* than with clarifying their ontological status.

A most striking avenue for active and activating ethico-aesthetic and political engagement is the extraordinary intersection between the concerns of Poinsot, Deely, and Deleuze and Guattari, and the work of the contemporary Italian philosopher Giorgio Agamben, together with the work of Alliez, Stengers, Latour, and Negri and colleagues (as it now becomes articulated by way of the French journal *Multitudes*).[1]

What is fascinating about Agamben's work as a stimulus to ethico-aesthetic and political action is his progression from an account of medieval logic and scholastic meditations on signification and language to ethico-political conclusions concerning the state and the individual. For example, in *Potentialities* (1999) we find an account of intentionality that corresponds exactly with Deely's approach in *New Beginnings* (1994a). What is more, we find a brilliant essay on Deleuze, Guattari, and the concept of 'absolute immanence'; references to Gregory of Rimini; and, in *The Coming Community* (1993), even a reference to Jakob von Uexküll's *Umwelt* theory concerning the status of the singularity, 'being-thus' or 'being-such,' which is neither a universal nor a particular, Nietzsche's affirmative 'yes' not said of a state of affairs but of its being-*thus*. For Agamben, the State does not want singularities that do not have an identity and cannot be easily controlled.

These reflections arise partly from an analysis of sense and Stoic logic, and the introduction to *Potentialites* by Daniel Heller-Roazen even refers to Gregory of Rimini's *complexe significabile* – the total signification of a proposition, irreducible to the linguistic terms of the proposition or to the objects to which they refer. Muralt (1991, 151) has suggested a relation between Poinsot's theory of enunciation and Gregory of Rimini's *complexe significabile*. For Agamben, as for Deleuze, the Stoic *lekton* refers not to a particular being but to the event of language itself. Agamben's novel procedure is to consider that language *expresses* a capacity of expression and that this leads to a consideration of language as the *existence of potentiality*, or of what it means to be 'capable.' Language is the capacity to signify rather than an actual signification, and what is expressed is communicability itself. For Agamben this leads to a political philosophy by way of a reflection on what it means to be a 'political animal' – that is, the animal that has language. For if language is potentiality, the 'coming community' will not belong to the state but rather will appropriate its own being-in-language, or belonging itself without affirming a representable identity, and exist as absolute potentiality.

In a discussion of Derrida's terminology, Agamben argues that in the semiotic scheme by which *aliquid stat pro aliquo*, A stands for B, the *intentio* must refer to the 'standing for' itself. He remarks that this is the reason for 'the particular "terseness" of Derrida's terminology' (1999, 212), in which one *standing for* stands for another *standing for*. The non-concept of 'trace' is the relation itself. Deely makes a remarkably similar point in the chapter on *renvoi* in *New Beginnings*, where he argues that the classical formulation *aliquid stat pro aliquo* should be reformulated as *aliquid stat pro alio*: a sign is anything that stands for something *other* than itself. This avoids confusing signs with objects; it also foregrounds the relation or *intentio* of renvoi or referral, rather than a thing that refers.

Another recent work that merits attention is Rodolphe Gasché's *Of Minimal Things: Studies on the Notion of Relation* (1999). In the valuable introduction, Gasché notes that, following Aristotle's classical theory of relations, it is in medieval philosophy that the topic of relation first becomes a significant philosophical issue, and he follows the scholastic definition of relation as 'being-towards-another' that has been the central topic of this book. Gasché contends that relation is the essential philosophical topic and that at the same time it exceeds philosophy, in that it is more elemental or 'minimal' in a positive sense than any of philosophy's defining concepts.[2] However, Gasché never seems to establish clearly the relation between signs and relations. The book itself contains important treatments of Heidegger and Derrida, and it is this latter thinker who might also be a subject of interest for those wishing to pursue the relations between deconstructive strategies and the relational semiotic that has been presented in this book – in particular, the question as to whether Derrida's oeuvre in fact contains the concept of ontological relation, or whether *différance* is rather a *relatio secundum dici* (transcendental relation).[3]

I make these brief allusions simply to point to what is as yet largely unexplored terrain. Deely's *Four Ages of Understanding* (2001) provides valuable material for engaging with these themes.[4]

In his essay 'Absolute Immanence,' Agamben (1999) also refers to Deleuze and Guattari's *What Is Philosophy* (1994, 213), where he finds 'one of the most important passages of Deleuze's late philosophy, life as absolute immediacy is defined as "pure contemplation without knowledge."' I take this observation as a final way of indicating an effectively new body of inquiry or emerging corpus of knowledge that may have some life in it. In fact, Agamben contends that the 'coming philosophy' will have to engage with the concept of life that Foucault and Deleuze entertain in their final works, and construct a genealogical inquiry into the term 'life.'

The passage Agamben selects from *What Is Philosophy* is this:

> Vitalism has always had two possible interpretations: that of an Idea that acts but is not – that acts therefore only from the point of view of an external cerebral knowledge (from Kant to Claude Bernard); or that of a force that is but does not act – that is therefore a pure intentional Awareness (from Leibniz to Ruyer). If the second interpretation seems to us to be imperative, it is because the contraction that preserves is always in a state of

detachment in relation to action or even in relation to movement and appears as a pure contemplation without knowledge.

Agamben asks how it is possible to conceive of a desire that remains immanent to itself – an absolute immanence that is immanent not to something else but only to itself. I have written elsewhere (1997) on the work of Raymond Ruyer, and on how Deleuze and Guattari take up his concepts of 'absolute survey' (there is no brain behind the brain), equipotentiality, and 'primary true forms.' Here I want to reaffirm the importance of engaging with these concepts, and concur with Agamben that a genealogical inquiry into the term 'life' remains unavoidable and constitutes an essentially philosophical and political task.

One possible avenue of inquiry that remains unexplored and that offers extraordinary potential for mutual enrichment and distinction between these different thinkers is a virtually unknown Argentinian/German school of neurobiology and philosophy that has developed in Buenos Aires over the past century. It is striking that in the same way that the Hispanic scholastic John Poinsot was largely ignored for 350 years, this Argentinian school remains almost totally unknown to the Anglo-American academic mainstream. I am referring to the work of Alicia Ávila and Mario-Fernando Crocco,[5] which in fact does provide a genealogy of life. What is more, this school is familiar with the work of Raymond Ruyer, the neurophysiologist Karl Lashley (who coined the term 'equipotentiality'), Deleuze, Kant, Poinsot, Heidegger, and Derrida (among many other scientists and philosophers), and constitutes a thousand-page thesis on what it is to be a finite person[6] or psychism (whether human or non-human) whose existentiality is not another's. There is no English term for this 'condition' (i.e., for the fact that one was not born in another body, family, or epoch), and the Spanish neologism 'cadacualtez' ('each-oneness') should be distinguished from Heidegger's subjectivist *Jemeinigkeit* (translated as 'my-own-owness' by J.L. Mehta). Mariela Szirko defines cadacualtez as:

> the constitutive determination of each person to both causally affect and be causally affected by no other portion of nature – namely, such and such a brain and its bodily and outer circumstances – than the portion which, because of this determination, acquired the status that is called 'her': 'this matter to which I am bound,' in Thoreau's words. *Cadacualtez* is one's determination to sustain constitutive causal exchanges with a fixed portion

of nature, rather than one's existentiality having, instead, eclosed to any other constitutive brain or circumstance.[7]

Or, in other words, the fact that as a finite observer, one finds oneself thrown to experience 'one's' corporeal and historical circumstance *instead of another.*

Another striking intersection is the one between Ávila and Crocco's *Sensing* and the recent work of Derrida (1999) on the question of man's relation to animals – specifically, the presumption that animals are inferior, and the denial of suffering and language in animals that can be found in the philosophical tradition from Aristotle to Lacan, a tradition which includes Descartes, Kant, Heidegger, and Levinas. Recall here that Maturana denies suffering and language in animals. Deely, like Maturana, 'denies' animals language (as distinct from communication) and makes no explicit comment on suffering. In his *Four Ages of Understanding*, however, Deely introduces the revolutionary point that the late Latin analysis of ideas as formal signs would apply to psychological states as such, cognitive *and* affective, both of which are found in animals whether or not they are rational. On this interpretation, Deely's view of what the medievals called 'passions of the soul' as formal signs would bring not only cognition but also feeling and emotion under the rubric of semiosis, an action of signs. From this it would plainly follow that all animals are capable of suffering – another sharp departure of semiotics as a postmodern intellectual movement from the main traditions of modern philosophy, which tend to deny feeling to animals other than humans.

Derrida, apparently unaware of Deely's work and its implications for zoosemiosis, notes (1999, 291) that he has never come across any protest by the 'great' philosophers – or by anybody who approaches philosophically as such the so-called animal question – against the singular general term 'the animal.' Derrida goes so far as to declare this homogenous term 'the Animal in general' one of man's greatest stupidities. Particularly interesting is that Derrida notes (ibid., 300) that animality, or 'the life of the living,' is currently defined as 'sensibility, irritability, auto-motricity, spontaneity capable of self-movement [*apte à se mouvoir*], self-affectivity.' He emphasizes that it is this auto-affection and relation to self that is the characteristic of the living and of animality in general. Furthermore, he notes that there appears to be 'an abyss' between this relation to self ('ce Soi, cette ipséite') and the I of 'I think.' What is interesting here (apart from the reflections on language) is that Derrida recognizes the problematic term 'animal in general,' or 'the animal,' which denotes a kind of neutralized group existence, but continues to employ the term 'ipseity' to designate the self-relation of the living. Ávila and Crocco (1996, 501–3) specifically distinguish the Scholastic notion of ipseity from *cadacualtez*. The scholastic ipseity (or 'standard uniqueness') is a

> 'contraction' (in which it is akin to the Jain and Hinduist concepts of ahankara) of postulated pre-existing constitutive principles, viz., ideal classes, sortals, 'Types,' Figures of ontic feasibility, eidoi, forms, 'quiddities,' ontic Formats, possibles, Templates, natures, or essences conferring generic-specific identity to the entities, whereby all identities are only simulated, indeed produced by a deeper play or game as, to study identity, Gilles Deleuze started with in his thesis on *différence et répétition*.

Ipseity cannot do justice to the distinction between 'a' fish or penguin 'species' and 'a' single individual, because all of them are deemed alike, defined as simply the invariant of all its transformations (like autopoiesis). The term ipseity ignores the very quality Derrida seeks to emphasize: that there are 'living beings' whose plurality cannot be grouped together in the term 'animality' as opposed to humanity. 'There is a multiplicity of living beings that can in no-way be homogenized except through violence' (Derrida 1999, 298). For Derrida it is not a question of 'giving speech' to animals but of thinking differently the absence of the word – specifically, as other than a privation. According to Ávila and Crocco, Derrida Deleuze, and Heidegger have not adequately grasped *cadacualtez*, and their work constitutes a unique laboratory of material that deserves further exploration – if only to critique it – especially given the importance of theories of pre-personal individuation for Deleuze.

Ansell-Pearson (1999, 185–8), in a section of *Germinal Life* titled 'On the Advantages and Disadvantages of Deleuze's Reading of Uexküll,' has also drawn attention to Deleuze's 'formalism,' in which all becomings appear to be the same. In a manner strikingly reminiscent of Ávila and Crocco, he contends (ibid., 186) that Deleuze and Guattari are 'blind to the specific ethology of the animal'; he goes so far as to write (ibid., 185) that their work 'comes perilously close to philosophical idealism.' In the Deleuzian scenario, 'the entire world is an egg'[8] – but the egg is a 'staged theatre' dominated by Ideas or 'themes' (DR, 216) indicating *un jeu plus profond* (a more profound game) of pre-existing constitutive principles. The problem with such approaches is that they tend to be 'blind to *cadacualtez*' – that is, blind to the incongruity of positing a 'standardized' logical uniqueness that does not distinguish between being one and being not another. This approach may be adequate for particles or quantum field events, but not for semovient 'persons,' be they human or non-human, whose non-systemic uniqueness cannot be exhaustively accounted for in this way. How *cadacualtez*, or non-standard uniqueness, would differ from 'a more profound game' of difference and repetition in which identities are 'only simulated, produced as an optical "effect"' (DR, preface), is of course a story yet to be told, one in which the actual circumstances of circumstantiation become constitutive: 'Yet, since in persons contingencies become ontically constitutive and, so, finite existentialities lack essence, for persons in no way the "différance sans concept" is "l'essence de la répétition," a mistake in which all those who grasp being as predication, in this case of a concept in particular, do fall along with those who inscribed the difference "dans le concept en géneral"' (Ávila and Crocco 1996, 506).

What is being argued is that Deleuze's ontology does not distinguish between an electron and a person (or existential finitude), largely because his ontology (with due reference to Sartre) is so impersonal. You are just 'any-body' and interchangeable with your neighbours. All electrons are the same, regardless of the time and place of their appearance, whereas for persons the time and place of their embodiment or circumstantiation becomes constitutive of their onticity. Persons, unlike sand or cement, are not interchangeable – they are cadacualtic.

Does the A in Deleuze's 'Immanence: A Life' really do justice to a non-standardized singularity or uniqueness? He seems to always emphasize a pre-personal force when he claims that little children all resemble one another and have barely any 'individuality.' They are traversed by a singular, neutral essence: a life – 'pure power.' But what actually makes one life not another life? Clearly not a standardized, systemic, or neutral process of individuation. Deleuze emphasizes processes of individuation, or 'deeper games' that do not presume already individuated conditions (like a mould explaining a statue). The common interests, convergence, and distinctions between pre-individual processes of individuation or theories of 'actualization' or 'emergence' and the *cadacualtez* of Argentinian neurobiology may, at the very least, be unsettling for our habits of thought. Self-movers all make use of the same physical forces, but they are all unique, or cadacualtic. Neutral essences do not make this distinction clear. Luce Irigaray (particularly in *to be two* [2000]) seems to be one of the few contemporary philosophers to engage with the question of 'irreducible alterity' in a manner that resonates with the Argentinian school of philosophy and neurobiology. However, Irigaray tends to base her ontology on sexual difference (male/female), which is still too generic.

Given that Deleuze (1988b, 117) encourages us to constitute a metaphysical image of thought corresponding to a contemporary molecular biology of the brain, we have here much material for further articulation within an ecology of practices that might allow for the emergence of *interesting* novelty in creation, and that might disturb thought and 'suit' no one, this being the risk of relations or risky practices – we do not always know what relations can do. We do not know what an ecology is capable of. We might just have to engage with concepts whose existence we do not even suspect, or which we have become blind towards. Thought might just have an interesting future creating and sustaining new relations – perhaps the most elemental philosophical act.

Notes

Introduction: The Drama of Relation and Its Characters

1 See Deely 1997.
2 Without wishing to enter at this point (or perhaps ever) into a complex discussion of Kant's position on relations, let me simply note that Kant's approach is distinct from a Cartesian one. As Deely has observed (1999, 66–7): 'With Kant knowledge is no longer the "simple possession of idea" it tended to be with Descartes and Locke. Knowledge, and with it experience, is made through and through relational, suprasubjective and not merely subjective in its terminus.' However, as will very slowly become more evident, Kant's relations do not have the peculiar, univocal ontological status that would allow them to have *intersubjectivity* among knowers, or between knowers and 'things' of nature. In 'critical' thought no representation could ever terminate in mind-independent being, or in something that is not changed by being known. For Kant, we find ourselves in the objects of our knowledge, and it is man himself (rather than God) who is the source of any order perceived in nature. One of the emerging themes of this work is the escape from the dualism of 'nature' and 'culture,' and from the scenario wherein phenomena are the meeting place between inaccessible things in themselves and the categories of the Ego.

This work will ultimately seek to articulate a position (à la Stengers and Latour) that does not claim a relation with Kantian 'things-in-themselves' but rather the discovery and emergence of relational events that have little to do with the imposition of *a priori* forms of understanding onto a silent world and much to do with a richly articulated collective of humans and non-humans in a process of conjoint becoming or copoiesis. To make this more than 'metaphorical gesturing' will require more than a few lines of text.

3 Two fine articles that emphasize the importance of external relations for Deleuze are Hayden (1995) and Baugh (1993).
4 Deely's English translation of this seminal work was published in 1985 by the University of California Press.
5 As Massumi notes (1992, 145), this is an 'antiphallic' image: 'Deleuze's image expresses a desire to *pervert* the phallic function, in the literal sense of "turning away from" (away from the "royal road" of the unconscious, as Freud dubbed the Oedipal complex).'
6 As Heidegger (1992, 162) phrases the matter: 'The contention that there is no longer a problem of knowledge, if it is maintained from the outset that Dasein is involved with its world, is not really a contention but only the restoration of a datum which any unbiased seeing sees as obvious. Moreover, it is nowhere prescribed that there must be a problem of knowledge. Perhaps it is precisely the task of a philosophical investigation ultimately to deprive many problems of their sham existence, to reduce the number of problems and to promote investigation which opens the way to the matters themselves.'

Deely often claims that the Heideggerian philosophy of being provides the best example of *an attempt* to approach the requirements of a semiotic account of experience. Deely also notes that Heidegger *fails* in this endeavour. One of the claims of this book is that an encounter between Deely's post-Peircian, Poinsot-inspired semiotic and Deleuze and Guattari's work provides useful tools for constructing existential territories that include non-humans. It does not appear that Deely is familiar with Deleuze and Guattari's texts, although he has written a book on Heidegger.
7 Deely will argue that Kant (a hypermodern Scotist?) does not have the notion of ontological relation. His relations are always mind-dependent; so, although he has an 'objective' world, it remains intramental or immanent to consciousness. We can *know* nothing apart from our representations, which are ideal. Kant does not have relations that can be simultaneously physical (extra-mental) *and* objective. If experience is a texture of relations indifferent or 'external' to their foundation, then appearances or consequent phenomena are not the meeting place between inaccessible 'things-in-themselves' and the categories of the Ego. We enter into a different, more 'realistic,' world where this distinction breaks down, and there arise things that are more and more in themselves the more they are for us. Appearances all the way down (or around), but they are not nothing but appearances – they participate in a collective that includes the knower. Not representations of an unknown cause but, to use Whitehead's (1978, 237) terminology, 'a cumulation of the universe and not a stage-play about it.' See also the conclusions of André de Muralt (1958, 193), in *La Conscience transcendentale dans*

le criticisme Kantien, essai sur l'unité d'aperception: 'Kant is realist if one considers that he admits the possibility of things in themselves. But this realism is a limit aspect of his philosophy. Kant is idealist because the only object of knowledge that he recognizes is representation, that is to say, the subject' (my translation). As Zourabichvili (1996, 44) notes, considered apart from signs, thought appears like a simple *faculty*. However, this is an abstract view in which thought only operates reflexively within the closed horizon of representation.

8 Others do this much better than I ever could – for example, Olivier Boulnois (1989, 1990) on Duns Scotus. Note that Boulnois does not mention Poinsot's 'synthesis of irreconcilibles.' The present work has no pretention to being an accomplished study in medieval thought. It simply plunders it. The bibliography gives references to some of the contemporary master medievalists, such as André de Muralt, Olivier Boulnois, and more recently Deleuze's student Eric Alliez, whose work draws significantly on the above-mentioned authors.

1: An Even Briefer History of Relations

1 See Constantine Cavarnos (1975) for a traditional academic presentation that has the merit of at least emphasizing that Aristotle did have a theory of relations, albeit an incomplete one: 'I do not see what Aristotle can be speaking about, when he seems to be speaking about relations, except about relations. What are these strange entities?' (1975, 65). Cavarnos does not engage with Poinsot's work and move from an ontology of relations to a semiotic.
2 Aristotle, *Categories*, 6a36–39. In Aristotle (1941, 17).
3 *Categories*, 8a28–34 in ibid., 22.
4 See Aertsen (1996) for a book-length treatment of the medieval notion of transcendental. Particularly note the distinction between the medieval notion of transcendentality – that which transcends the Aristotelian doctrine of the categories – and the Kantian transcendental, which is concerned with the categories of reason. The medieval transcendentals transcend the Aristotelian categories of mind-independent being by belonging to all of them, but not in the sense that they refer to a separate reality 'beyond' the categories (ibid., 93). Deely (1990, 39) notes that the medieval transcendentals were sometimes called *ens vagans* – the vagrant aspects of being.
5 I am not attempting to give an account of Ockham's approach, which is widely available. I am simply indicating it as the polar opposite of Poinsot.
6 Poinsot's ontology of relations makes the two categories of relation – transcendental and ontological (i.e., relative beings and their relations) – prior

to the division of being into substance and accident, which are themselves subordinate to this analysis. More importantly, both these categories can be experienced directly. All accidents (or attributes) can be experienced; and since accidents are either transcendental or ontological relations, both can be experienced: 'Experience gives these categories only in what *will be called accidents* once substance has been rationally distinguished as a distinct category or reality. Experience itself gives only, e.g., this white object, that sound, etc' (TDS 469, EA III. C.2 19).

This ontology of relations is strikingly reminiscent of Latour's (1999a, 151) observation that 'substances' are substantiated. We move from attributes to substances. Pasteur's ferment began as attributes and *ended up being a substance* – that is, a stable *assemblage* gathering together a multiplicity of agents; or a concrescence.

7 That is to say (à la Poinsot and Deely), by understanding colours, sounds, and so on, as *signs* bringing into awareness something other than themselves, such as position, shape, movement ... 'Sense data' are *already relational* prior to habit and species variations.

8 Raymond Ruyer (1950, 15), whom Deleuze and Guattari draw on especially in their final work *What Is Philosophy?* also criticizes James's 'neutral monism' or 'double context' theory, which Ruyer claims can be summarized as follows: 'There's nothing to seek beyond sensation or pure experience. There is nothing to seek either "in front" or "behind." Neither "in front": consciousness designates a simple function, a group of relations established between the different parts of experience. Neither "behind": the object is only a state of consciousness; and between the colour as a psychological state and the colour as worldly object there is only a difference of function. Concerning this double thesis, we reject the second part, we think that "behind" the object there is a being.' Deely also sees James as tied to the paradigm of modernity in which what the mind knows is its own constructs.

9 As Hayden (1995, 300) notes in his fine essay, 'the most obvious adversary for Deleuze on this issue is Hegel, although his critique is also directed to Plato, Aristotle, and Descartes.' Russell, in emphasizing external relations, was reacting largely against the British Hegelians (e.g., Bradley). James (and Peirce) also takes up arms against Hegel (with whom, I might add, I am totally unfamiliar). Deely has a more sympathetic approach to Hegel (claiming that at least Hegel accepted the mind-independent reality of relations), but affirms that nowhere does Hegel develop the ontological rationale of relation as 'external' to its terms or, in other words, the peculiar indifference of relation to its foundation – the fact that whether mind-dependent or mind-independent, a relation is a relation.

10 Without wishing to overburden the text at this juncture, it is worth noting that at a relatively early research stage, Deely (1972, 229) suspected 'that the philosophical doctrine that all relations are internal is the result of taking the transcendental relation as paradigmatic, while the doctrine that all relations are external admits only the *secundum esse* [ontological relation] paradigm.' The slow elaboration of these terms will take some time, but a hint is in order: remember the difference between relative terms and the actual 'ontological' relations they are involved in. 'Transcendental relations' are *not* relations, they are *relative terms*. This is a pluralistic 'radical empiricism' that allows for independence and relation.
11 For more on which, see Latour (1999a, 5–9).

2. Deleuze and External (or Ontological) Relations

1 As Hayden notes in his fine essay 'From Relations to Practice in the Empiricism of Gilles Deleuze,' (1995, 301n11), similar arguments were given by Bertrand Russell when he contested the British Hegelians. Hayden cites as an example Bertrand Russell, *Our Knowledge of the External World*.
2 See Hume, *Treatise on Human Nature*, Book 1, Part 2, sec. 4 (Everyman's Library edition [London, 1911], 1, 52). Deleuze (1991, 99) cites this passage as the proof that every relation is external to its terms.
3 Jean Wahl, who influenced Deleuze's reading of the British empiricists, had made this observation (see 1948, 236).
4 *Dialogues* (first French publication 1972) was a series of essays written with Claire Parnet. It provides one of the best introductions to Deleuze and Guattari's work.
5 It is one aspect of Poinsot's genius that he reduced the Aristotelian categorial schema to these two senses of relative being: (1) the fact that all beings require for their intelligibility that they be considered in relation to things other than themselves – that is, as transcendentally relative; and (2) the actual relations or field of intersubjectivity – that is, the external or ontological relations. It is Deely who must be credited for reintroducing (with some difficulty) this forgotten distinction in the late twentieth century.
6 I am only trying to focus on *one* important aspect of a lengthy work.
7 See Lecercle (1985, 92).
8 See Eco (1984, 214–15); and Deely (2001, 96–112).
9 See Deely (1994a, 209); and Gasché (1999).
10 Drawn from Brehier's account of Stoic philosophy (1970).
11 Gregory of Rimini earned the nickname 'infant torturer' for his assumption that children who died without baptism would suffer eternal damnation.

150   Notes to pages 33–40

12 This involves an incredibly complex set of issues that I am only beginning to appreciate.
13 Muralt (1991), in what may currently be the finest study of Gregory of Rimini, *L'Enjeu de la philosophie médiévale*, suggests that it would be interesting to compare Gregory with the Stoics! He does not appear to be familiar with Deleuze's *The Logic of Sense* (1990), although he also refers to Elie's *Le Complexe signifiable* as providing a link between Gregory and phenomenology.
14 Deely's fine expression (1993, 264) in 'Reading the Signs: Some Basics of Semiotics.'
15 Heidegger also clearly attempts such a reconfiguration with an approach to Being that is neither 'subjective' nor 'objective' in the classical modern sense. However, his phenomenology does not appear to have the necessary semiotic awareness that would allow for Being not to be subordinated to representation. (This concurs with Deleuze's criticism of Heidegger [see DR, 64–6.]) Deely makes a similar claim in his fine book on Heidegger, *The Tradition via Heidegger* (1972).
16 For Deleuze (DR, 35), 'there has only ever been one ontology, that of Duns Scotus, which gave being a single voice.'
17 Deleuze will go on to argue that Scotus only *thought* univocal being, whereas Spinoza affirmed univocity and Nietzsche realized it (DR, ch. 1).
18 This formal distinction is one of the most difficult subjects to write about, and these tentative lines merely seek to indicate the barest outlines of what is one of the most important steps in the development of modern philosophy. For further analysis, consult Alliez (1999) and especially Wolter (1965).
19 I am basing this account on Muralt's commentary on Gregory of Rimini, (1991, 127–67).
20 Muralt (ibid., 130) quoting Ockam: 'soalae propositiones sciuntur.'
21 My translation.

3. Poinsot and Deely on Relations and Signs

1 It is impossible to discuss Poinsot without Deely, in that Deely has both translated Poinsot's *Tractatus de Signis* and been one of the very few contemporary scholars to have extensively engaged with that work for a period of over thirty years.
2 Augustine, *De Doctrina Christiana*, Bk II, ch. 1, n1.
3 'De Signis,' being chapter 1 of their commentary on Aristotle's *De Interpretatione*, in *Commentarii Collegii Conimbricensis et Societatis Jesu: In Universam Dialecticam Aristotelis Stagiritae. Secunda Pars.* Lyon: Sumptibus Horatii Cardon, pp. 4–67. An earlier edition minus the Greek text of Aristotle was pub-

lished at Coimbra itself in 1606. The English version used here is Doyle (2001).
4 Pedro de Fonseca, *Institutionum dialecticarum libri octo*, 1564: lib. 1, cap. V111. Translated and quoted by Deely (1986a, 10).
5 Deleuze refers specifically to this aspect of Peirce's thought in *Cinema 1* (1996, 197).
6 It is interesting that Florent Gaboriau (1970, 131, translator's note), the translator of the French edition of Heidegger's book on Duns Scotus and signification, draws attention to the importance of a study of *relation* as consecutive to a study of *action*, and remarks that without this preliminary, words like sense, or order, remain vague.

See also Heidegger's comment (1970, 125, author's translation): 'First of all it is a matter of clarifying the notion of "sign." *Significare extensive sumitur pro dare itelligere* [quoting Scotus]. Through the sign something becomes objective to consciousness. In the notion of the sign there is thus something relational ... The relational character and the being-foundation are the constitutive coefficients of the sign, and according to which the different kinds of signs are also specified.' Note here the idea of objective being/ *esse objectivum*.
7 This appreciation of the univocal ontology of relations as external to their terms is why Deleuze *would* have appreciated Poinsot.
8 As this analysis of intentionality progresses, it will become apparent (as it did for Deely in reading and translating Poinsot) that the concept of intentionality is derivative from the more fundamental concept of relation as 'external' or indifferent to its subjective ground, be it posited as mind-independent or mind-dependent. It is relation that allows for 'intentional' existence.
9 See Jean-Luc Solère (1989, 36). This article gives a good account of traditional Thomism. The form itself of intelligence is the thing as cognized. It is not a representation.
10 Solère notes that for Thomism this mystery finds a parallel in the Incarnation, since in Christ there is a union in one person without mixture of two natures, the divine and human. Peiffer even takes this notion of 'mystery' as the very title for his 1952 work on the subject.
11 Soheil M. Afnan (1958, 276) claims that the influence of Avicenna on Aquinas 'could be considered the most serious and prolonged encounter of Christianity with Islamic philosophy in Europe.' This is not without interest when we realize the importance of Avicenna for Deleuze, Duns Scotus, and Deely. It is Avicenna who initiates Duns Scotus' univocal conception of being with the concept of 'being-as-first-known.' 'Neither private nor public, neither collective nor individual ... it is more terrible and powerful in

this neutrality, to the extent that it is all of these things at once?' (Deleuze LS, 35).

12 This account of species is based principally on Deely (1994a, 123–43) and secondarily on Maritain (1959, 115–19). Deely's account of the notion of species remains the most succint. He appears to be one of the very few contemporary semioticians (if not the only one) capable of understanding the move from early Thomism to Poinsot's semiotic interpretation of the species. The links to Alliez's comments on Duns Scotus and Maritain remain my contribution. Deely does not refer to Deleuze and Guattari, nor should he have to! One of the refrains of this book is that it can be interesting to read them together.

13 For a complex historical account see Leen Spruit (1994, 1995). Although a scholarly tour de force, Spruit's two-volume *Species Intelligibilis* does not mention Poinsot. It is a brilliant example of a scholarly academic production that almost drowns the reader in meticulous historical detail.

14 Without wishing to overburden the text, note that there were, for example, Euclidean 'extramission' theories of vision in which 'visible rays' emanated from the eye and illuminated the object. These extramission theories were shown to be untenable principally by Avicenna, Averroes, and Alhazen. Here again we note the enormous impact of Islamic thought on medieval Europe. In fact, as Spruit (1994, 84) emphasizes, Alhazen's influence on the medieval doctrine of species cannot be overestimated. For a useful account of the revival of a modified Aristotelian theory of vision, see David C. Lindberg's remarkable study *Theories of Vision from Al-Kindi to Kepler* (1976).

15 I claim no originality here and encourage the reader to refer to Deely's text. No plagiarism is intended. I will try to make it clear when I am supplementing his account rather than merely paraphrasing. One point I will develop is the great affinity between Duns Scotus and Poinsot. In fact, in the account Deely (1994a) gives in *New Beginnings*, he places Scotus in the *same* position as Poinsot in their understanding of the species. He does not elaborate on this equivalence.

16 In *Chaosmosis* (1995, 22), Guattari's approach to 'subjectivity' emphasizes the '*founding instance of intentionality. This involves taking the relation between subject and object by the middle and foregrounding the expressive instance (or the interpretant of the Peircean triad)*' (my italics).

17 See J. Cronin (1966) for a treatment of Descartes's scholastic sources in the Suarezian tradition, which Poinsot would have opposed.

18 Levinas, (1973, 41) understands Husserl's theory of intentionality in a way that mirrors the Thomist approach; Husserl's idealism shares little with Thomist intentionality other than the name.

19 Deely (1997, 80) uses the fine term 'Cyclopean Thomism' for a traditional realist Thomism that has not grasped that the semiotic notion of 'objective being' allows for realism but is not reducible to it. Muralt (1991) presents the most sophisticated attempt to distinguish traditional Thomism from Scotism. Muralt is one of the few scholars other than Maritain (partially) and Deely (fully) to grasp the importance of Poinsot's semiotic synthesis, which includes aspects of Scotism.

20 It will become apparent that this 'being of the between' is univocal and grounded in the concept of 'being-as-first-known' developed by Scotus from Avicenna. It is ultimately not between things already known (like a line between already known subjects and objects), but between that which allows for things to come to be known and that which allows for the question 'what is?' Deleuze (DR. 65) claims that Heidegger 'gives renewed splendour to the Univocity of Being.' I will not attempt to pursue the differences between Heidegger and Deleuze in this footnote, except to say that Deleuze claims that Heidegger does not go far enough in assuming the consequences of the univocity of being. Deleuze also claims that Scotus only *thought* univocal being, whereas Spinoza *affirmed* it and Nietzsche *realized* it. The point here is that the questions we are examing were central for Deleuze and that Poinsot's semiotic is based on the univocity of relations. Mind-dependent and mind-independent coincide univocally in 'objective being' because relations are indifferent to the nature of their terms. They are 'external' or 'ontological' relations. Nature and 'culture' interpenetrate in semiosis. *This is not a theory but a natural phenomenon.* Scotism does not grasp the full importance of signs as relations. It takes time for a semiotic to coalesce, and it would be Peirce who ultimately achieved this coalescence in moving from the 'being' of signs to their 'becoming': Autosemiopoiesis.

21 It is strange to see Scotus qualified as a nominalist, but as Peirce remarked, the Scotist theory of formalities was 'separated from nominalism only by the division of a hair' (Peirce, 8.11). Peirce, like Deleuze, was inspired by Scotus: 'There has only ever been one ontology, that of Duns Scotus, which gave being a single voice. We say Duns Scotus, because he was the one who elevated univocal being to the highest point of subtlety, albeit at the price of abstraction' (DR, 35).

22 *Capital Times* (1996) is the published version of Alliez's doctoral thesis. Deleuze was his thesis director, and, according to Alliez, Guattari was involved throughout the production of the book. I note this because it shows the *relevance* of these issues.

23 Alliez does not explain these terms in *Capital Times*, but he notes that Solère, basing his analysis of intentionality on Aquinas, 'has no trouble showing that

species escapes the orbit of classical *representation* and its aporias' (1996, 288). Following a conversation with Alliez (Paris, 1997), it seems that he was aware of the existence of Poinsot's work but not of the details of Poinsot's 'strange synthesis.'

24 Maritain (1930) also develops these arguments in *Reflexions sur l'intelligence et sur sa vie propre*. 'With Kant the beautiful monster born from this seed achieves its full development' (ibid., 34); 'The Kantian revolution was an historic catastrophe for Western civilization' (ibid., 36). He cites Poinsot's expression for these scholastic deviations (Suaréz, Vasquez): 'a strange aberration – *magna hallucinatio*' (ibid., 67). As long as we don't recognize the distinction between entitative being and intentional being, we will be subsumed by Konigsberg. Maritain always affirms realism against idealism. He never fully masters the realization that Poinsot's semiotic is prior to these distinctions, with the notion of ontological relation capable of signifying 'non-being' just as easily as 'being.' The sign as a relation, be it 'mind-dependent' or 'mind-independent,' is indifferent to its foundation. Realism as the possible coincidence between thought and thing is an insufficient image of thought. 'Being-in-a-world' is more than this!

25 Muralt translates Poinsot directly from the Latin into French.

26 Gregory of Rimini took the object of knowledge to be a state of affairs, *complexe significabile* (tantum) – that is something that can only be expressed in a complex way, for example, by a proposition, not by a term. This is opposed to the significates of each of its ingredient terms. Gregory denied that the tantum was either mental or extra-mental. Deleuze (LS, 19) claims that Gregory was the second discoverer, after the Stoics, of 'sense as the fourth dimension of the proposition' (in this Deleuzian scenario, Meinong was the third discoverer). A 'sense' or 'event' that merges neither with the proposition nor the object: this is a Scotist treatment of the propositional logic that I find isomorphic to Poinsot's specification of relations as univocal. Relations have one 'sense': as relations they are indifferent or neutral with respect to their foundation in mind or matter. Sense as a pure event ... neither private nor public, 'it is more terrible in this neutrality' (LS, 35). Deely, following Poinsot, will demonstrate, like Meinong and Frege, how the object qua object 'is distinct in principle from physical things and psychological conditions alike ... But [in difference from Meinong or Frege, who seem to place objectivity in an unqualified Platonic 'third realm'] the object qua object is fully separable existentially only from physical things; it is existentially inseparable, though analytically and really distinct from the psychological conditions sufficient for its existence – in the same way that concepts (ideas or images) are inseparable from, though intrinsically other than, the neurolog-

ical states sufficient to generate them' (Deely 1972b, 232). For Deleuze, this is the brain become metaphysical surface. Deleuze's 'sense' is also not a Platonic Idea. Through his use of Stoic logic, sense becomes a 'surface effect' that is irreducible to physics without being abstract: 'Only empiricism knows how to transcend the experiential dimensions of the visible without falling into Ideas' (LS, 20); 'Univocal Being inheres in language and happens to things' (LS, 180). Deleuze's 'sense' arises from the univocity of being-as-first-known: 'Sense ... is a pure sign' (LS, 176). Deleuze is particularly inspired by the work of Pierre Klossowski, who in developing his own semiotic 'borrows from scholastic philosophy as much as Husserl did, but which traces its own paths.' (LS, 298).

27 This 'subtle' doctrine is inspired by Avicenna's notion of a 'common nature' that is neither universal nor particular. Horseness is just horseness, neither in things nor in thought. Like 'sense.' Scotus' doctrine of univocity, as well as that of Poinsot, is inspired by Avicenna. As we shall see, the docrine of 'being-as-first-known' is also derived from Avicenna.

4. *Umwelten*

1 It seems that Sebeok was unaware of the attention given by Heidegger and Merleau-Ponty to von Uexküll's work.
2 In *Pandora's Hope: Essays on the Reality of Science Studies*, Latour (1999a, 21), sets up an opposition between the postmodern, which seek, 'more absence, more debunking, more negation, more deconstruction,' and the nonmodern, which seeks 'proof of presence, deployment, affirmation, and construction.'
3 The turn 'non-languaging' will be developed throughout this chapter. At issue is the extent to which animals other than human animals grasp the *relation* of signifaction as such. The argument to be presented here is that non-human animals communicate but do not 'live in' language. They use signs without knowing they are using signs.
4 In the following chapter we shall see that this is a critical issue for Maturana. The frog does not 'aim' at anything: 'What the frog's eye tells the frog's brain.'
5 Clearly, some will see this as a gross caricature of Kant. Nevertheless, it is unclear how the Kantian subject learns about something other than itself and how it escapes from a deep 'psychologism.' When a fly is trapped in a bottle I do not create its prison, or the nature of its space, by being aware of it (Ruyer).
6 There is a website dedicated to von Uexküll's work: http://www.zbi.ee/~uexkull.

7 In the following chapter on autopoiesis, we shall see that this autonomy corresponds to Maturana's concept of 'structure determinism.' A living being does not have 'inputs' but responds to a triggering effect (or perturbation) in a manner determined by its own structure.

8 Deleuze often refers to von Uexküll's tick. Heidegger seems more fascinated (or benumbed) by von Uexküll's description of the being of the bee 'Beeing.'

9 Here 'meaning' is like Peirce's 'thirdness' – mediation or relation as an interpretive process over and above dyadic physical interaction or 'secondness': the connecting link of relations that are necessarily 'external' to their terms.

10 Gregory Bateson (1977, 241) affirms this in claiming that 'mental process' (immanent to 'mind' and 'nature') is triggered by 'news of difference,' *not* by energy. It is news of difference that is circulating – 'the pattern that connects.' Bateson illustrates this with von Uexküll's tick (although he does not actually mention von Uexküll): 'A tick on the twig of a tree waits for the smell of butyric acid that would mean "mammal in the neighbourhood." When he smells the butyric acid, he will fall from the tree. But if he stays long enough on the tree and there is no butyric acid, he will fall from the tree anyway and go to climb up another one. He can respond to the "fact" that something does not happen.'

11 Deleuze and Guattari often refer to von Uexküll's work. The following passage from Deleuze's *The Fold* (1993, 92–3) is worthy of an extended quotation; it beautifully expresses the material we are engaging with and suggests that the human monad can sink to a level lower than that of the tick:

> The tiniest of all animals has glimmers that cause it to recognize its food, its enemies, and sometimes its partner. If life implies a soul, it is because proteins already attest to an activity of perception, discrimination, and distinction – in short, a 'primary force' that physical impulsions and chemical affinities cannot explain ... If life has a soul, it is because it perceives, distinguishes, or discriminates, and all animal psychology is first of all a psychology of perception. In most cases, the soul gets along quite well with a very few clear or distinguished perceptions: the soul of the tick has three, including a perception of light, an olfactory perception of its prey, and a tactile perception of the best place to burrow, while everything else in the great expanse of Nature, which the tick nevertheless conveys, is only a numbness, a dust of tiny dark and scattered perceptions.
> But if an animal scale exists, or an 'evolution' in the animal series, it is insofar as increasingly numerous differential relations or a deepening order are determining a zone of clear expression that is both more extensive and increasingly hermetic. Each of the conscious perceptions that

comprise the zone is associated with others in the infinite process of reciprocal determination ... Few monads fail to believe themselves damned at certain moments of their existence. When their clear perceptions are now and again extinguished, when they recede into the night – in relation to this the tick's life appears to be singularly rich. But with freedom there also comes the moment when a soul is won over to itself and can whisper a convalescent's astonishment, 'My God, what did I do in all of these years?'

12 This is the title of an unpublished article by Keith Ansell-Pearson (as well as a term in Deleuze and Guattari's ATP, 314, which refers to von Uexküll). I have appropriated parts of Ansell-Pearson's succinct account of the relation between von Uexküll's ethology and Deleuze and Guattari's work.

13 Maturana will call this mutual specification or contrapuntal relation 'structural coupling.' He once told me that von Uexküll had everything except the notion of structural coupling, which is a more analytical and less musical account of nature's 'harmony.' Varela's 'enaction' or 'embodied action' is a version of von Uexküll's *Umwelt* theory. Cognition depends on various linked sensorimotor capacities (perceptors and effectors – a double articulation). The organism 'enacts' or '*brings forth*' (taking up the Heideggerian *Hervorbringen*) a world.

Varela (in a personal correspondence) saw von Uexküll as having had a 'good intuition,' but dismissed his semiotic approach as inadequate in accounting for the generative mechanisms of meaning that Varela, Thompson, and Rosch try to engage with in *The Embodied Mind* (1991). In that book, they quote Merleau-Ponty referring specifically to the concept of *Umwelt* (174).

14 This seminar (dated 14 January 1974) is online at http://www.webdeleuze.com/php/sommaire.html (accessed 24 October 2005). Kindly translated by Timothy S. Murphy.

15 Consult DR, ch. 1, 'Difference in Itself,' for Deleuze's complex and original propositions on the univocity of being. Deleuze traces a complex path through Duns Scotus (thinking univocity), Spinoza (affirming), and Nietzsche (realizing), which I will not attempt to engage with here. The emphasis here is on the relevance of univocity to relation as such. Deleuze likes grouping thinkers in threesomes. For a logic of the event it is the Stoics, Leibniz, and Whitehead. For the logic of sense it is the Stoics, Gregory of Rimini, and Meinong. Ultimately, in WIP, it will be Spinoza who constructs 'the best' plane of immanence – that is, one which does not give in to any transcendent plane. A univocal plane – an abstract machine or rhizosphere.

16 For the 'serious' student, Alliez engages with Duns Scotus and the univocity of being in his *Capital Times* (1996). I make no attempt to emulate his mas-

terful account, which also refers to a fine article by Olivier Boulnois, 'Analogie et univocité selon Duns Scot: la double destruction' (1989). The new *Routledge Encyclopaedia of Philosophy* has a valuable entry on Duns Scotus written by Barry Taylor.
17 Deely's classic account of ontological and transcendental relatives – that is, the two kinds of relative being – can be found in Appendix 1 of his *New Beginnings*, 'Contrasting Ontological and Transcendental Relatives' (1994a). I base my account on his singular efforts. In chapter 6 we shall come to see that this distinction is similar to Maturana's distinction between the 'relational domain' and the domain of anatomy or physiology.
18 See, in particular, Deely (1988a).
19 See Deleuze (1990, 34–5), for his reference to Avicenna.
20 See the afterword to TDS for Deely's brief discussion of Hegel.
21 My translation. Ruyer was aware of Jakob von Uexküll's work, which he sought to free from its Kantian heritage. See also Ruyer's *Néo-finalisme* (1952, 217), a work that significantly influenced Deleuze and Guattari's final work WIP: 'Note that von Uexküll, in his general philosophy (cf. *Theoretical Biology*, Preface), is Kantian and confuses, as does Merleau-Ponty, comprehensive biology and critical biology. For example: "All reality is subjective appearance. This must constitute the one great, fundamental admission, even of biology" (Preface). We take his "word" in itself, without reference to his general doctrine.'
22 Karl von Frisch, *Bees, Their Vision, Chemical Senses, and Language* (Ithaca, NY: Cornell University Press, 1950).
23 See Maritain (1957).
24 It is important to understand that an animal can be aware of 'absent signifieds' (although it cannot pass on this awareness). The critical distinction is that a non-languaging animal is not aware of what are in principle imperceptible objects, such as relations or linguistic objects.
25 I am encouraged to see that my interest in Deely's semiotic has infected/affected Keith Ansell-Pearson's thoughts.
26 This univocal 'truth of the relative' rather than the intrinsically negative 'relativity of truth' (tied to a subject) will be engaged with in a later chapter. It is the approach taken by thinkers such as Deleuze and Guattari, Bruno Latour, and Isabelle Stengers, and in the actual practice of science.
27 This, of course, begs the question of whether robots or computers *in their currently purely reactive form* have *Umwelten*. We will get to this ...
28 Heidegger wanted FCM to be the first lecture series published in the *Gesamtausgabe* (Collected Works). It was first published in German in 1983 and published in English in 1995. Nowhere else in his work does Heidegger

engage so extensively with experimental science, in particular with the *Umwelt* theory of Jakob von Uexküll.

29 The most forceful criticism of Heidegger's biology lectures comes from Krell in *Daimon Life* (1992). It is certain that Heidegger's approach is awkward, and I am not seeking to defend his understanding. However, it remains a remarkable attempt that cannot be dismissed out of hand. A semiotic approach along the lines of Peirce and Deely offers a perhaps more nuanced avenue.

30 Deleuze and Guattari also significantly return to von Uexküll's work in WIP (183–6), suggesting that art begins with the animal, 'at least with the animal that carves out a territory and constructs a house (both are correlative, or even one and the same, in what is called a habitat).' This is a contrapuntal theory of nature where nature and art become indistinguishable. The bowerbird is a 'complete artist' (ibid., 184). *Scenopoetes dentirostris.* Alliez (1993, 94) will seek to distinguish Deleuze and Guattari's approach to ethology from Heidegger's phenomenology of behaviour and 'word-poverty' of the animal by commencing with refrains, counterpoints, and expressive qualities; assemblages and becomings rather than behaviour – 'becoming-colours, becoming-sounds.' A superior ethology ...

31 The following chapter on Autopoiesis or self-production will take up this question using the theory of the biologist Humberto Maturana, whose work has a similar Kantian framework to that of von Uexküll and who, like von Uexküll, sheds light on a new paradigm in spite of his epistemology.

32 Michel Haar (1993, 160n8) notes (without any development of the relation) that this proper peculiarity of self-production or autopoiesis 'would come close to the notion of the "unified field" or "absolute domain" of individuality or presence, which according to R. Ruyer (*La Conscience et le corps*) would characterize life.' This is a truly interesting conceptual relationship, as Deleuze and Guattari draw significantly on Ruyer's work, especially in WIP and *The Fold*. For Deleuze and Guattari, following Ruyer, the organism has an 'absolute interiority' and the brain is 'a primary true form' or 'absolute domain' in 'self-survey.'

33 In personal correspondence Deely makes the following observation: 'Remember that "relatio secundum esse," unlike "relatio secundum dici" which has already the Latin one-word synonym "transcendentalis," never acquired a one-word counterpart among the Latins. So my "ontological" relation is a neologism for the purpose. The term occurs in Heidegger, but not the concept, i.e., not the notion of the "relatio secundum esse" indifferent to the otherwise contrasting orders of what is and is not independent of cognition. I have since wondered if there might not have been a better choice; but what might it be still eludes me.'

34 See Corrington (1994, 188) for further discussion of the difference between human and animal *Umwelten* undertaken within a generalized Peirce/Deely perspective: 'Human meaning horizons are not simply augmented versions of animal *Umwelten*, but have distinctive features that radically alter the semiotic structures of the world.'

35 As Corrington notes (ibid., 188-9) traces of alterity/otherness within zoosemiosis do not always constitute or generate apprehension of their source, or involve conscious awareness of *otherness*. This requires an awareness of relations. This is not in itself a judgment but a distinction.

36 Claus Emmeche (2001) provides the most comprehensive discussion of this question in 'Does a Robot Have an *Umwelt?*' The answer, for Emmeche, is no: 'Thus only genuine living beings (organisms and especially animals [as active subjects]) can be said to live experientially an *Umwelt*.' The Argentinian school of neurobiology (referred to in the conclusion to this book) will take a different approach. There can be artificial substrates for 'persons,' or active self-moving subjects, but purely reactive 'robots' will never, by definition, have experience. These observations require 'development' that will not be undertaken here.

37 As Deleuze notes in *The Fold* (1993, 104), following Ruyer (and Whitehead): 'A great line of difference does not separate the organic from the inorganic, but crosses the one like the other by distinguishing what is individual from what is a collective or mass phenomenon, what is an absolute form and what are massive, molar figures or structures.' Remember also that Haar (1993, 160) sees a relation between Heidegger's 'proper peculiarity' of the organism and Ruyer's 'absolute domains,' which Deleuze and Guattari draw on particularly in their final work, WIP.

38 CP is the standard abbreviaton for *The Collected Works of Charles Sanders Peirce*.

39 This is one of the central claims of François Zourabichvili (1996) in *Deleuze: Une Philosophie de L'Evenement*.

5. Autopoiesis and Languaging

1 This finite research project does not allow me to give Varela's current 'solo' career as director of research in neuroscience at the CNRS, Paris, the attention it certainly merits. He has undoubtedly moved beyond Maturana's observer-dependent approach with his project of developing a 'naturalized phenomenology.'

2 Reprinted in McCulloch (1988). Included in that volume is McCulloch's own essay 'What's in the Brain That Ink May Character,' in which he discusses Stoic logic and the *lekton* – 'something in the head like a fist in the

hand'– a subject Deleuze takes up in the *Logic of Sense* (1990). Mary Catherine Bateson notes that Bateson refers to McCulloch more 'than any other modern scientist' (see Bateson and Bateson 1987, 186).

3 Poster, in a recent commentary on Deleuze and Guattari, describes their view in these terms: 'It is as if the earth itself were to describe the changes on its surface in the course of human history, a vantage point quite remote from the ego of the individual.' (1990, 137).

4 I am not presuming to give an outline of Leibniz's 'monadology' but simply to explain briefly the relationship between Maturana and Varela's 'self-contained' entities and Leibniz's 'windowless monads.'

5 Kant moves from a pre-critical position in which relations are *ens reale* (e.g., in his first published work *Living Forces* [1747] and in the important dissertation *Monadologia physica*, [1756]) to the critical position where all relations, be they spatial, temporal, or causal, are *ens rationis* or mind-dependent. Kant does not grasp the univocal being of relations, which may be *ens reale* or *ens rationis* depending on the circumstances.

6 The problem with Leibniz's monads is that relations cannot be *ens reale*; they are reduced to a phenomenon, an appearance, or 'a mere ideal thing which is nevertheless useful.' 'Thus Leibniz is forced, in order to maintain the subject-predicate doctrine, to the Kantian theory that relations, though veritable, are the work of the mind' (Russell 1964, 14). Deleuze is aware of this when he writes that for Leibniz, all relations are internal (WIP, 54). Deely (1972b, 227) argues that the philosophical doctrine that all relations are internal is 'the result of taking the transcendental relation (relation *secundum dici*) as paradigmatic, while the doctrine that all relations are external admits only the *secundum esse* paradigm.'

7 Two useful introductions are Winograd and Flores (1988, ch. 4); and Dell (1985). See also Mingers (1995), for a book-length treatment of autopoietic theory.

8 In the ensuing presentation I will make use of substantial extracts from Maturana and Varela's writings. It seems useful to give a feel for their manner of expression, which will be unfamiliar to most readers and without which this commentary would be difficult to evaluate.

9 Varela and von Glasersfeld (1987) have noted that although the literature on perception was limited during Socrates' lifetime, he was nevertheless able to demonstrate the subjective relativity of sensory perception with no difficulty.

10 Quoted by T. Sebeok (1979, 198).

11 Science as community-dependent concurs with Kuhn's (1970) 'paradigms': 'Scientific knowledge, like language, is intrinsically, the common property of a group or else nothing at all.'

12 Deleuze and Guattari (in a related context) characterize this change from chemical trophallaxis to linguallaxis: 'What a curious deterritorialization, filling one's mouth with words instead of food and noises' (ATP, 62).
13 Does Derrida's 'textualism' have ontological relations or only transcendental relations? But if ontological relations, does he realize the difference in status between one and the same relation when it belongs to the order of *ens reale* rather than to the order of *ens rationis* alone?
14 See Deleuze (1988, introduction), for a brief but admirable linking between Bateson and Deleuze.
15 See Jacob (1973, 278, 289–90).
16 'Languaging' is a neologism of Maturana's invention meant to refer to the act of being in language without necessarily associating such an act with speaking.
17 See Maturana (1988) for his most detailed treatment of language.
18 Lecercle wrote one of the first books in English on Deleuze and Guattari: *Philosophy through the Looking Glass* (1985).
19 Winograd and Flores (1987) have drawn parallels between the speech act theories of Austin and Searle and Maturana's 'biology of cognition.'
20 Compare this perspective with that of Nietzsche (1968, §480): 'There exists neither "spirit, nor reason, nor thinking, nor consciousness, nor soul, nor will, nor truth: all are fictions ..." There is no question of "subject and object" but of a particular species of animal that can prosper only through a certain relative rightness; above all regularity of its perception.'
21 To foreshadow Deleuze and Guattari's approach and indicate their unique 'style,' I have included some extended quotations in this text, especially as the reader may be unfamiliar with their work: 'Once again, a whole intensive map must be accounted for: the mouth as a deterritorialization of the snout (the whole "conflict between the mouth and the brain," as Perrier called it); the lips as a deterritorialization of the mouth (only humans have lips, in other words, an outward curling of the interior mucous membranes; only human females have breasts, in other words, deterritorialized mammary glands: the extended nursing period advantageous for language learning is accompanied by a complementary reterritorialization of the lips on the breasts, and the breasts on the lips). What a curious deterritorialization, filling one's mouth with words instead of food and noises' (ATP, 61–2).
22 'For the operation of a living system, there is no inside or outside, and it cannot make a representation of what *an observer* sees as exterior to it' (Maturana 1988, 57). Self-conscious imagery arises with descriptions an *observer* makes of his or her changes of state.
23 Roger Sperry is a Nobel laureate in medicine. For an account of his work on

epilepsy and 'split-brain' experiments see Maturana and Varela (1987, 225–31).
24 See Sperry, 'Restoration of Vision' (1945), for the original experiment.
25 This essay, 'Biology of Self-Consciousness' (1995), is one of Maturana's more recent published works and gives a condensed and fascinating account of his approach.
26 Dissensus as opposed to consensus is a neologism of Guattari's invention. He uses it particularly with respect to the domain of social ecology.
27 See particularly Dupuy and Varela (1992) for a discussion of the Derridian logic of the supplement in relation to the self-referential nature of autopoiesis.
28 Their essay 'Brain, Language and the Origin of Human Mental Functions,' is a condensed account of the approach of the Santiago School of Cognition. The abstract deserves citing in full: 'We propose that to understand the biological and neurophysiological processes that give rise to human mental phenomena it is necessary to consider them as behavioural relational phenomena. In particular, we propose that: a) these phenomena take place in the relational manner of living that human language constitutes, and b) that they arise as recursive operations in such behavioural domain. Accordingly we maintain that these phenomena do not take place in the brain, nor are they a result of the unique operation of the brain, but arise with the participation of the brain as it generates the behavioural relational domain.' Varela (1999, 73) would refer to this brain as 'Dasein's brain.' The mind is not a brain-encased self or 'skin-encapsulated' ego; 'it is in this no-place of the co-determination of inner and outer, so that one cannot say that it is inside or outside.' Varela (ibid., 77) uses language strikingly similar to Guattari's in *Chaosmosis* (1995), especially when he claims that 'the mind is not about representing some kind of state of affairs. The mind is about constantly secreting this coherent reality that constitutes a world.' Also like Guattari, he refers to Daniel Stern's studies of infant life: 'Being a "me" and constituting a "you" are concomitant events' (ibid., 80). Guattari writes in terms of the chaosmotic interface of subjectivity, secreting interiority and exteriority. Deely also uses the term 'labile interface' in his semiotic analysis of the mind-dependent, mind-independent relation that occurs within an expanded conception of experience that includes an interpenetration of material and ideal elements. The 'mind' becomes a relational dynamics of a body enfolded with the world rather than an entity with a location, the folding of an inside beyond any internal world with an outside beyond any external world. Or the non-place where the world is not outside and the mind is not inside (as in a vat).

29 Quoted in Candrakirti (1979, 233): 'Neither self or non-self exist.'
30 This would be in accord with Peirce's contention that '"the question of the origin of language" is one "which must be settled before linguistics takes its final form," as against the Linguistic Society of Paris, which adopted as the second article of its founding Statutes (1868.3) that no communication concerning the origin of language be admitted into discussions of linguistic science' (Deely 1990, 61).
31 See Austin (1962).
32 Carl Jung (1963, 4) seems to be one of the few thinkers to have made use of this image, outside its technical botanical sense: 'Life has always seemed to me like a plant that lives on its rhizome. Its true life is invisible, hidden in the rhizome. The part that appears above ground lasts only a single summer. Then it withers away – an ephemeral apparition. When we think of the unending growth and decay of life and civilizations, we cannot escape the impression of absolute nullity. Yet I have never lost a sense of something that lives and endures underneath the eternal flux. What we see is the blossom, which passes. The rhizome remains.'
33 This example is drawn from Massumi(1992, 24–6).
34 In his later work Foucault (1988, 19) remarked that 'perhaps I've insisted too much on the technology of domination and power.' Foucault was ultimately interested in how we constitute our identities through ethical techniques: The Care of the Self.
35 See Eco (1988, 197–212) for a useful discussion of the historical change in the meaning of denotation, which prior to Bacon was intensional rather than extensional. Only in Anglo-Saxon philosophy since Bacon has denotation been tied to external reference.
36 Deleuze and Guattari also speak of a 'body without organs,' that is, 'an abstract machine.'
37 Fuzzy logic in advanced mathematics refers to a form of set theory in which there is a gradual transition from membership of one set (collection of 'objects') to another. Both/and rather than either/or. Auto-focusing systems in video cameras now incorporate elements of 'fuzzy logic,' which compensate for a subject located off-centre.

Conclusion

1 *Multitudes* can be located at http://www.samizdat.net/multitudes
2 Gasché (1999, 11) gives the following examples of relation: 'Encounter, arrival, address, contact, touch, belonging, distance, accord, agreement, determination, measuring, translation and communication ...'

3 *'What is "old" (the sign) is still so new (as a relation secundum esse) that Jacques Derrida does not yet seem to have heard about it'*; see Guagliardo, cited in Deely (1994a, 150). The issue is whether Derrida has a notion of semiotic relations as relations that are indifferent to their status as physical as well as objective, or objective only. Does the Derridean 'unmotivated trace' achieve this indifference? Given Derrida's acknowledgment of Peirce's seminal influence, there is certainly a 'family resemblance' that Guagliardo (1994; 393n84) seems also to acknowledge. Others with the required bent (of) mind might seek to explore further this vein of inquiry.

4 Another useful relation is to Ferré's *Being and Value* (1996), in which he seeks to 'understand' relations within an 'ecological world model,' and to his *Knowing and Value* (1998), in which he seeks to develop a 'Scotistic' and Whiteheadian theory of knowledge. Robert Cummings Neville, who reviewed this latter book in *Process Studies* (28[3/4][1999]), argues that while this is a remarkable work, Ferré has rather neglected Peirce's late-modern 'Scotist' semiotic, and as a consequence has not produced the 'gap closing' epistemology he wants.

5 See Ávila and Crocco (1996). A limited edition of this work exists in Argentina. This school is based at the Centre for Neurobiological Studies, the Laboratory of Electroneurobiological Research, and the Neuropsychiatric Hospital 'Dr Jose Tirburcio Borda' in Buenos Aires. Its website is http://electroneubio.secyt.gov.ar/index2.htm. A valuable essay by Mariela Szirko that gives an overview of this tradition is *'Effects of Relativistic Motions in the Brain and Their Physiological Bearing*,' available at that address. That essay will be published in a forthcoming anthology, *Ontology of Consciousness: Percipient Agency*, ed. Helmut Wautischer (MIT Press, 2006). The same anthology will include an essay by Mario Crocco: 'A Palindrome: Mindful Living Creatures as Instruments of Nature; Nature as an Instrument of Mindful Living Creatures.'

6 'Persons' in this work are self-movers, or psychisms capable of initiating causal series rather than simply continuing previous ones reactively. Persons display 'semovience' and 'cadacualtez,' and have the capacity to co-create a reality not bounded by fate or necessity. Ávila and Crocco note that 'Semovience' is the Spanish term for the low Latin 'se movere,' self-moving. It appears in the Romance languages c. 1100 and is used in the mercantile trade to distinguish self-moving goods from movable and unmovable goods. Monopsychisms and theories of emergence are 'blind to *cadacaultez*.' Alliez (1993; 68) seems to hint at a medieval monopsychism in Deleuze and Guattari's work that would be at variance with the pluralist approach of *Sensing* which specifically denies any monopsychism as a 'myth' denying the

finite reality of semovience and *cadacaultez*. To deny the plurality and finitude of psychisms is a political act. The Argentinian school would see Deleuze and Guattari's 'pure contemplation without knowledge' as non-semovient, epiphenomenal, and passive.
7 Szirko, 'Effects of Relativistic Motions in the Brain and Their Physiological Bearing,' see note 5.
8 Professor Mariela Szirko (electroneurobiologist and philosopher, Buenos Aires) notes in a personal correspondence that this is a key monopsychical Orphic formulation.

Bibliography

Aertsen, Jan A. 1996. *Medieval Philosophy and the Transcendentals: The Case of Thomas Aquinas.* Leiden and New York: E.J. Brill.
Afnan, Soheil. 1958. *Avicenna: His Life and Works.* London: Allen and Unwin.
Agamben, Giorgio. 1993. *The Coming Community.* Trans. Michael Hardt. Minneapolis: University of Minnesota Press.
– 1999. *Potentialities: Collected Essays in Philosophy.* Stanford, CA: Stanford University Press.
Alliez, Éric. 1999. *Les temps capitaux.* Tome II. *La capitale du temps, I, L'état des choses.* Paris: CERF.
– 1996. *Capital Times: Tales from the Conquest of Time.* Foreword by Gilles Deleuze. Trans. Georges Van Den Abbeele. Minneapolis and London: University of Minnesota Press.
– 1993. *La signature du monde: ou qu'est-ce que la philosophie de Deleuze et Guattari?* Paris: CERF.
Ansell-Pearson, Keith. 1999. *Germinal Life: The Difference and Repetition of Deleuze.* London: Routledge.
– n.d. 'Nature as Music.' Unpublished essay.
Aristotle. 1941. 'Categories.' *The Basic Works of Aristotle.* Trans. E.M. Edghill, ed. Richard Mckeon. New York: Random House.
Austin, John L. 1962. *How to Do Things with Words.* Cambridge, MA: Harvard University Press.
Ávila, Alicia, and Mario-Fernandez Crocco. 1996. *Sensing: A New Fundamental Action of Nature.* Buenos Aires: Institute for Advanced Studies.
Baer, Eugen. 1992. 'Via Semiotica.' *Semiotica* 92(3/4): 351–7.
Bains, Paul. 2001. '*Umwelten.*' *Semiotica* 134(1/4): 1–31. Special issue on Jacob von Uexküll.
– 1997. 'Subjectless Subjectivities.' *Canadian Review of Comparative Literature*

24(3): 511–28. Special Issue, *Deleuze/Guattari and the Philosophy of Expression*. Reprinted in Gary Genosko, ed. 2000. *Critical Assessments: Deleuze and Guattari in Three Volumes*. London: Routledge. Reprinted in Brian Massumi, ed. 2002. *A Shock to Thought: Expression after Deleuze and Guattari*. London: Routledge.

Bateson, Gregory. 1977. 'Afterword.' In J. Brockman, ed. *About Bateson*. New York: Dutton.

Bateson, Gregory, and Mary Catherine Bateson. 1987. *Angels Fear: Towards an Epistemology of the Sacred*. New York: Macmillan.

Baugh, Bruce. 1993. 'Deleuze and Empiricism.' *Journal for the British Society for Phenomenology* 24(1).

Bergson, Henri. 1975. *Creative Evolution*. Trans. Arthur Mitchell. Westport, CT: Greenwood Press.

Beuchot, Mauricio. 1994. 'Intentionality in John Poinsot.' *American Catholic Philosophical Quarterly* 68(3): 279–96. Special Issue on Poinsot.

Boulnois, Olivier. 1990. 'Être, luire et concevoir: note sur la genèsese et la structure de la conception Scotiste de l'esse objective. *Collectanea Franciscana* 60(1/2): 117–35.

– 1989. 'Analogie et univocité selon Duns Scot: la double destruction.' *Les etudes philosophiques* 3/4.

Bréhier, Emile. 1970. *La théorie des incorporels dans l'ancien stoïcisme*. Paris: Vrin.

Candrakirti. 1980. *Lucid Exposition of the Middle Way*. Boulder, CO: Prajna Press.

Cavarnos, Constantine. 1975. *The Classical Theory of Relations: A Study in the Metaphysics of Plato, Aristotle, and Thomism*. Belmont, MA: Institute for Byzantine and Modern Greek Studies.

Conimbricenses. 1607. '"De Signis," being chapter 1 of their commentary on Aristotle's *De Interpretation*.' Pp. 4–67 in *Commentarii Collegii Conimbricensis et Societatis Jesu. In Universam Dialecticam Aristotelis Stagiritae. Secunda Pars*. Lyon: Sumptibus Horatii Cardon.

Corrington, Robert S. 1994. *Ecstatic Naturalism: Signs of the World*. Indianapolis: Indiana University Press.

Cronin, Timothy, J. 1966. *Objective Being in Descartes and Suárez*. Rome: Gregorian University Press.

Deely, John. 2001. *Four Ages of Understanding: The First Postmodern Survey of Philosophy from Ancient Times to the Turn of the Twenty-First Century*. Toronto: University of Toronto Press.

– 1999. *The Best of Times ... The Worst of Times: The Way of Ideas and Where It Led: A Pamphlet on Modernity*. Houston, TX: University of St Thomas, Modern Philosophy, Department of Philosophy.

– 1998. The Ethics of Terminology. *American Catholic Philosophical Quarterly* 72(2): 197–243.

- 1997. 'Quid Sit Postmodernismus?' In Roman T. Ciapalo, ed. *Postmodernism and Christian Philosophy*. Washington, DC: Catholic University of America Press.
- 1994a. *New Beginnings: Early Modern Philosophy and Postmodern Thought*. Toronto: University of Toronto Press.
- 1994b. 'A Morning and Evening Star: Editor's Introduction.' *American Catholic Philosophical Philosophical Quarterly* 68(3): 255–77. Special Issue on Poinsot.
- 1994c. *The Human Use of Signs or Elements of Anthroposemiosis*. London and Lanham, MD: Rowman and Littlefield.
- 1993. 'Reading the Signs: Some Basics of Semiotics.' *Semiotica* 97(3/4): 247–66.
- 1992. 'Philosophy and Experience.' *American Catholic Philosophical Quarterly* 66(3): 299–319.
- 1990. *Basics of Semiotics*. Bloomington: Indiana University Press.
- 1988a. 'The Problem of Interpreting the Term "First" in the Expression "First Philosophy."' In John Deely, ed. *Semiotics 1987*. New York and London: University Press of America.
- 1988b. 'The Semiotic of John Poinsot: Yesterday and Tomorrow.' *Semiotica* 69(1/2): 31–127.
- 1986a. 'The Coalescence of Semiotic Consciousness.' In John Deely, Brooke Williams, and Felicia E. Kruse, eds. *Frontiers in Semiotics*. Bloomington: Indiana University Press.
- 1986b. 'Semiotic as Framework and Direction.' In John Deely, Brooke Williams, and Felicia E. Kruse, eds. *Frontiers in Semiotics*. Bloomington: Indiana University Press.
- 1986c. 'Idolum: Archeology and Ontology of the Iconic Sign.' In Paul Bouissac, ed. *Iconicity: Essays on the Nature of Culture*. Tübingen: Stauffenberg Verlag, 29–49.
- 1982. *Introducing Semiotic: Its History and Doctrine*. Bloomington: Indiana University Press.
- 1978. 'Toward the Origin of Semiotic.' In Thomas A. Sebeok, ed. *Sight, Sound, and Sense*. Bloomington and London: Indiana University Press.
- 1975. 'Reference to the Non-Existent.' *The Thomist* 39(2): 253–308.
- 1974. 'The Two Approaches to Language: Philosophical and Historical Reflections on the Point of Departure of Jean Poinsot's Semiotic.' *The Thomist* 39(4): 856–907.
- 1972a. *The Tradition via Heidegger*. The Hague: Matinus Nijhoff.
- 1972b. 'The Ontological Status of Intentionality.' *New Scholasticism* 46: 220–33.

Deleuze, Gilles. 1997. 'Immanence: A Life ...' *Theory, Culture and Society* 14(2): 3–7.

- 1996. *Cinema 1: The Movement Image.* Trans. Hugh Tomlinson and Barbara Habberjam. Minneapolis: University of Minnesota Press.
- 1995. *Negociations: 1972–1990.* Trans. Martin Joughin. New York: Columbia University Press.
- 1994. *Difference and Repetition.* Trans. Paul Patton. New York and London: Columbia University Press/The Athlone Press.
- 1993. *The Fold: Leibniz and the Baroque.* Foreword and trans. by Tom Conley. London: Athlone Press.
- 1991. *Empiricism and Subjectivity: An Essay on Hume's Theory of Human Nature.* Trans. and with an introduction by Constantin Boundas. New York: Columbia University Press.
- 1990. *The Logic of Sense.* Trans. Mark Lester with Charles Stivale. Ed. Constantin V. Boundas. New York: Columbia University Press.
- 1988a. *Spinoza: Practical Philosophy.* Trans. Robert Hurley. San Francisco: City Light Books.
- 1988b. *Bergsonism.* Trans. Hugh Tomlinson and Barbara Habberjam. New York: Zone Books.
- 1972. 'Hume.' In François Châtelet, ed. *Histoire de la philosophie.* Tome 4. *Les lumières.* Paris: Hachette.

Deleuze, Gilles, and Félix Guattari. 1994. *What Is Philosophy?* Trans. Graham Burchell and Hugh Tomlinson. London: Verso.
- 1988. *A Thousand Plateaus: Capitalism and Schizophrenia.* Trans. Brian Massumi. London: Athlone Press.
- 1983. *Anti-Oedipus: Capitalism and Schizophrenia.* Trans. R. Hurley, M. Seem, and H.R. Lane. Minneapolis: University of Minnesota Press.

Deleuze, Gilles, and Claire Parnet. 1987. *Dialogues.* Trans. Hugh Tomlinson and Barbara Habberjam. New York: Columbia University Press.

Dell, Paul. 'Understanding Bateson and Maturana: Toward a Biological Foundation for the Social Sciences.' *Journal of Marital and Family Therapy* 11: 1–20.

Derrida, Jacques. 1999. 'L'animal que donc je suis.' In *L'animal autobiographique: autour de Jacques Derrida.* Paris: Éditions Galilée.
- 1991. '"Eating Well," or the Calculation of the Subject: An Interview with Jacques Derrida.' In E. Cadavar, P. Connor, and J.-L. Nancy, eds. *Who Comes After the Subject?* New York and London: Routledge.
- 1989. *Of Spirit: Heidegger and The Question.* Trans. Geoffrey Bennington and Rachel Bowlby. Chicago and London: University of Chicago Press.
- 1974. *Of Grammatology.* Trans. Gayatri Chakravorty Spivak. Baltimore and London: Johns Hopkins University Press.

Doyle, John P., ed. and trans. 2001. *The Conimbricenses: Some Questions on Signs.*

Milwaukee, WI: Marquette University Press. (Bilingual critical edition of *Conimbricenses* 1607.)
Dupréel, Eugène. 1968. *Similitude et dépassement.* Brussels: Presse Universitaire de Brussels.
Dupuy, Jean-Pierre, and Francisco Varela. 1992. 'Understanding Origins: An Introduction.' In J. Dupuy and F. Varela, eds. *Understanding Origins: Contemporary Views on the Origin of Life, Mind, and Society.* Dordrecht: Kluwer.
Eco, Umberto. 1988. 'Whodunit? The Case of Denotation and/or Signification.' Pp. 197–212 in *Semiotic Theory and Practice.* Vol. 1. Berlin: Mouton de Gruyter.
– 1984. *Semiotics and the Philosophy of Language.* Bloomington: Indiana University Press.
Elie, Hubert. 1936. *Le complexe significabile.* Paris: Vrin.
Emmeche, Claus. 2001. 'Does a Robot Have an *Umwelt*? Reflections on the Qualitative Biosemiotics of Jacob von Uexküll.' *Semiotica* 134(1/4): 653–93.
Ferré, Frederick. 1998. *Knowing and Value: Toward a Constructive Postmodern Epistemology.* Albany: SUNY Press.
– 1996. *Being and Value: Toward a Constructive Postmodern Metaphysics.* Albany: SUNY Press.
Foucault, Michel. 1988. *Technologies of the Self: A Seminar with Michel Foucault.* Ed. Luther H. Martin, Huck Gutman, Patrick H. Hutton. London: Tavistock Press.
Gasché, Rodolphe. 1999. *Of Minimal Things: Studies on the Notion of Relation.* Stanford: Stanford University Press.
Goodchild, Philip. 1996. *Gilles Deleuze and the Question of Philosophy.* London: Associated University Presses.
Guagliardo, Vincent. 1994. 'Being-as-First-Known in Poinsot: A-Priori or Aporia?' *American Catholic Philosophical Quarterly* 68(3): 363–93.
Guattari, Félix. 1996. *The Guattari Reader.* Ed. Gary Genosko. Oxford: Blackwell.
– 1995. *Chaosmosis: An Ethico-Aesthetic Paradigm.* Trans. Paul Bains and Julian Pefanis. Indianapolis and Sydney: Indiana University Press and Power Publications.
– 1979. *L'inconscient machinique.* Paris: Editions Recherches.
Haar, Michel. 1993. *The Song of the Earth: Heidegger and the Grounds of the History of Being.* Trans. Reginald Lilly. Foreword by John Sallis. Indianapolis: Indiana University Press.
Hayden, Patrick. 1995. 'From Relations to Practice in the Empiricism of Gilles Deleuze.' *Man and World* 28: 283–302.
Heidegger, Martin. 1995. *The Fundamental Concepts of Metaphysics: World, Finitude, Solitude.* Indianapolis: Indiana University Press.
– 1992. *History of the Concept of Time: Prolegomena.* Trans. Theodore Kisiel. Bloomington: Indiana University Press.

- 1970. *Traité des categories et de la signification chez Duns Scot.* Trans. and introduced by F. Gaboriau. Paris: Gallimard.
- 1962. *Being and Time.* Trans. John Macquarrie and Edward Robinson. London: Basil Blackwell.

Hjelmslev, Louis. 1961. *Prolegomena to a Theory of Language.* Trans. Francis J. Whitfield. Madison: University of Wisconsin Press.

Hoffmeyer, Jesper. 1996. *Signs of Meaning in the Universe.* Trans. Barbara J. Haveland. Indianapolis: Indiana University Press.

Irigaray, Luce. 2000. *to be two.* Trans. Monique M. Rhodes and Marco F. Cocito-Monoc. London: Athlone Press.

Jacob, François. 1973. *The Logic of Life: A History of Heredity.* Trans. Betty E. Spillman. New York: Pantheon Books.

James, William. 1977. *A Pluralistic Universe.* Cambridge, MA: Harvard University Press.

Jonas, Hans. 1965. 'Spinoza and the Theory of Organism.' *Journal of the History of Philosophy* 3: 43–74.

Jung, Carl G. 1963. *Memories, Dreams, Reflections.* New York: Vintage Books.

Kant, Immanuel. 1992a. *Inaugural Dissertation: On Form and Principles of the Sensible and Intelligible World.* In Cambridge Edition 1, *Theoretical Philosophy, 1755–1770.* Trans. and ed. David Walford in collaboration with Ralf Neerbote. Cambridge: Cambridge University Press.
- 1992b. *The Jäsche Logic.* In Cambridge Edition 9, *Lectures on Logic.* Trans. and ed. J. Michael Young. Cambridge: Cambridge University Press.
- 1985. *Prologemena to Any Future Metaphysics that will be able to come forward as a Science.* In *Immmanuel Kant: Philosophy of Material Nature.* Trans. James W. Eddington. Indianapolis: Hackett.
- 1978a. *Critique of Pure Reason.* Trans. Norman Kemp Smith. London: Macmillan.
- 1978b. *Anthropology from a Pragmatic Point of View.* Trans. Victor Lyle Dowdell. Carbondale and Edwardsville: Southern Illinois University Press.
- 1967. *Kant: Philosophical Correspondence, 1759–99.* Ed. and trans. Arnulf Zweig. Chicago: Universtity of Chicago Press.

Klossowski, Pierre. 1998. *Nietzsche and the Vicious Circle.* Trans. Daniel W. Smith. Chicago: University of Chicago Press.

Krell, David, Farrell. 1992. *Daimon Life: Heidegger and Life-Philosophy.* Indianapolis: Indiana University Press.

Kuhn, Thomas S. 1970. *The Structure of Scientific Revolutions.* Chicago: University of Chicago Press.

Latour, Bruno. 1999a. *Pandora's Hope: Essays on the Reality of Science Studies.* Cambridge and London: Harvard University Press.

- 1999b. *Politiques de la nature: comment faire entrer les sciences en démocratie.* Paris: La Découverte.
Lecercle, Jean-Jacques. 1985. *Philosophy through the Looking Glass: Language, Nonsense, Desire.* La Salle, IL: Open Court.
Leclerc, Ivor. 1972. *The Nature of Physical Existence.* London: Allen and Unwin.
Levinas, Emmanuel. 1973. *The Theory of Intuition in Husserl's Phenomenology.* Evanston, IL: Northwestern University Press.
Lindberg, David C. 1976. *Theories of Vision from Al-Kindi to Kepler.* Chicago and London: University of Chicago Press.
Locke, John. 1690. *An Essay Concerning Human Understanding.* London: Thomas Bassett.
Maclean, C. 1977. *The Wolf Children.* New York: Penguin Books.
Maritain, Jacques. 1959. *Distinguish to Unite, or The Degrees of Knowledge.* New York: Scribner's.
- 1957. 'Language and the Theory of Sign.' In *Language: An Enquiry into Its Meaning and Function.* New York and London: Kennikat Press.
- 1930. *Réflexions sur l'intelligence et sur sa vie propre.* Paris: Desclée de Brouwer.
Massumi, Brian. 2000. 'Too-Blue: Colour Patch for an Expanded Empiricism.' *Cultural Studies* 14(2): 177–226.
- 1992. *A User's Guide to Capitalism and Schizophrenia: Deviations from Deleuze and Guattari.* Cambridge, MA, and London: MIT Press.
Maturana, Humberto. 1995. 'Biology of Self-Consciousness.' In Giuseppe Trautteur, ed. *Consciousness: Distinction and Reflection.* Naples: Bibliopolis.
- 1990. *Ontology of Observing. The Biological Foundations of Self-Consciousness and the Physical Domain of Existence.* Available at http://www.inteco.cl/biology/ontology/.
- 1988. 'Reality: The Search for a Compelling Argument.' *Irish Journal of Psychology* 9(1): 25–82.
- 1983. 'On the Misuse of the Notion of Information in Biology. Comments on "All things are full of Gods."' *Journal of Social and Biological Structures* 6: 155–8.
- 1980. 'Biology of Cognition.' In H. Maturana and F. Varela, eds. *Autopoiesis and Cognition: The Realization of the Living.* Dordrecht: Reidel.
- 1978. 'Biology of Language: The Epistemology of Reality.' In G. Miller and E. Lenneberg, eds. *Psychology and Biology of Language and Thought.* New York: Academic Press.
Maturana, Humberto, Jorge Mpodozis, and Juan-Carlos Letelier. 1995. 'Brain, Language, and the Origin of Human Mental Functions.' *Biological Research* 28: 15–26.
Maturana, Humberto, and Francisco Varela. 1987. *The Tree of Knowledge: The Bio-*

logical Roots of Understanding. Foreword by J.Z. Young. Boston: New Science Library.
- 1980. *Autopoiesis and Cognition: The Realization of the Living.* Dordrecht: D. Reidel.

McCulloch, Warren. 1988. *Embodiments of Mind.* Cambridge, MA: MIT Press.

Mingers, John. 1995. *Self-Producing Systems: Implications and Applications of Autopoiesis.* New York and London: Plenum Press.

Monod, Jacques. 1971. *Chance and Necessity: An Essay on the Natural History of Modern Biology.* Trans. Austryn Wainhouse. New York: Knopf.

Muralt, André de. 1991. *L'enjeu de la philosophie médiévale: études thomistes, scotistes, occamiennes et grégoriennes.* Leiden: E.J. Brill.
- 1985. 'Adéquations et intentions secondes. Essai de confrontation de la phénoménologie husserlienne et de la philosophie thomiste sur le point du jugement.' In *La métaphysique du phénomène. Les origines médiévales et l'élaboration de la pensée phénoménologique.* Paris: Vrin.
- 1958. *La conscience transcendantale dans le criticisme Kantien: essai sur l'unité d'apperception.* Paris: Aubier.

Nietzsche, Friedrich. 1968. *The Will to Power.* Trans. Walter Kaufmann and R.J. Hollindale. New York: Vintage Press.
- 1962. *Philosophy in the Tragic Age of the Greeks.* Trans. Marianne Cowan. Washington, DC: Henry Regnery.

Paterson, F., and E. Linden. 1981. *The Education of Koko.* New York: Holt, Rinehart and Winston.

Peiffer, John. 1952. *The Mystery of Knowledge.* Albany, NY: Magi Books.

Peirce, Charles Sanders. 1866–1913. *The Collected Papers of Charles Sanders Peirce.* Vols. 1–6, ed. Charles Hartshorne and Paul Weiss. Cambridge: Harvard University Press, 1931–5. Vols. 7-8, ed. Arthur W. Burks (Cambridge: Harvard University Press, 1958).

Perler, Dominik. 1993. 'Duns Scotus on Signification.' *Medieval Philosophy and Theology,* vol. 3. Notre Dame and London: University of Notre Dame Press.

Poinsot, John. *Tractatus de Signis.* 1985. Arranged in bilingual format by John Deely in consultation with Ralph A. Powell. Berkeley: University of California Press.

Poster, Mark. 1990. *The Mode of Information: Poststructuralism and Social Context.* London: Polity Press.

Russell, Bertrand. 1964. *A Critical Exposition of the Philosophy of Leibniz.* London: Allen and Unwin.

Ruyer, Raymond. 1964. *L'animal, l'homme, la fonction symbolique.* Paris: Gallimard.
- 1952. *Néo-finalisme.* Paris: PUF.
- 1950. *La conscience et le corps.* Paris: PUF.

Sebeok, Thomas. 1979. *The Sign and Its Masters.* Austin: University of Texas Press.
- 1976. *Contributions to the Doctrine of Signs.* Bloomington and Lisse: Indiana University Press and Peter De Ridder Press.
Serres, Michel, with Bruno Latour. 1995. *Conversations on Science, Culture, and Time.* Trans. Roxanne Lapidus. Ann Arbor: University of Michigan Press.
Solère, Jean-Luc. 1989. 'La notion d'intentionnalité chez Thomas Aquinas.' *Philosophie* 24: 13–36.
Sperry, R.W. 1945. 'Restoration of Vision after Crossing of Optic Nerves and after Contralateral Transplantation of Eye.' *Journal of Neurophysiology* 8: 15–28.
Spruit, Leen. 1995. Volume 2. *Species Intelligibilis: From Perception to Knowledge. Renaissance Controversies, Later Scholasticism, and the Elimination of the Intelligible Species in Modern Philosophy.* Leiden: E.J. Brill.
- 1994. *Species Intelligibilis: From Perception to Knowledge.* Volume 1: *Classical Roots and Medieval Discussions.* Leiden: E.J. Brill.
Stengers, Isabelle. 2002. *Penser avec Whitehead.* Paris: Seuil.
- 1997. *Power and Invention: Situating Science.* Trans. Paul Bains. Minneapolis: University of Minnesota Press.
- 1996. *Cosmopolitiques.* Tome 1. *La guerre des sciences.* Paris: La Découverte/Les empecheurs de penser en rond.
Stern, Daniel. 1985. *The Interpersonal World of the Infant.* New York: Basic Books.
Varela, Francisco. 1999a. 'Steps to a Science of Inter-Being: Unfolding the Dharma Implicit in Modern Cognitive Science.' In Gay Watson, Stephen Batchelor, and Guy Claxton, eds. *The Psychology of Awakening: Buddhism, Science and Our Day-to-Day Lives.* London: Rider Books.
- 1999b. 'The Naturalization of Phenomenology as the Transcendence of Nature: Searching for Generative Mutual Constraints. *Alter: Revue de Phenomenologie* 5: 355–81.
- 1996. 'The Early Days of Autopoiesis: Heinz and Chile.' *Systems Research* 13(3): 407–16.
- 1987. 'Cognitive Science and the Logic of Mirrors.' *International Synergy Journal* 2(2).
- 1979. *Principles of Biological Autonomy.* New York: Elsevier–North Holland.
Varela, Francisco, and Ernst von Glasersfeld. 1987. 'Problems of Knowledge and Cognizing Organisms.' *Methodologia* 1: 29–45.
Varela, Francisco, Evan Thompson, and Eleanor Rosch. 1991. *The Embodied Mind: Cognitive Science and Human Experience.* Cambridge, MA: MIT Press.
von Uexküll, Jacob. 1982. 'The Theory of Meaning.' *Semiotica* 42(1): 25–87. Special Issue: Jakob von Uexküll's 'The Theory of Meaning.'
- 1957. 'A Stroll through the Worlds of Animals and Men.' In Claire Schiller, trans. and ed. *Instinctive Behaviour: The Development of a Modern Concept.* Intro-

duction by Karl S. Lashley. New York: International Universities Press. Reprinted in *Semiotica* 89(4): 279–315 (1992).
- 1926. *Theoretical Biology*. London: Kegan Paul.
von Uexküll, Thure. 1989. 'Jakob von Uexküll's *Umwelt*-Theory.' In Thomas A. Sebeok and Jean Umiker-Sebeok, eds. *The Semiotic Web 1988*. Berlin and New York: Mouton de Gruyter.
- 1982. 'Introduction: Meaning and Science in Jakob von Uexküll's Concept of Biology.' *Semiotica* 42(1): 1–23.
Wahl, Jean. 1948. *The Philosopher's Way.* New York: Oxford University Press.
- 1932. *Vers Le Concret*. Paris: Vrin.
Weinberg, Julien. 1965. 'The Concept of Relation: Some Observations on Its History.' In *Abstraction, Relation, and Induction. Three Essays in the History of Thought*. Madison and Milwaukee: University of Wisconsin Press.
Whitehead, Alfred North. 1978. *Process and Reality: An Essay in Cosmology.* Corrected edition. Ed. David Ray Griffin and Donald W. Sherbourne. New York: Free Press.
Winograd, Terry, and Fernando Flores. 1988. *Understanding Computers and Cognition*. New York: Addison-Wesley.
Wittgenstein, Ludwig. 1967. *Philosophical Investigations*. Ed. G.E.M. Anscombe and R. Rhees, trans. G.E.M. Ascombe. Oxford: Blackwell.
Wolter, Allan B. 1965. 'The Formal Distinction.' In J.K. Ryan and B.M. Bonansea, eds. *John Duns Scotus, 1265–1965*. Washington, DC: Catholic University of America Press.
Zourabichvili, François. 1996. *Deleuze: une philosophie de l'evenement*. Paris: PUF.

Index

accident, 16, 56, 67, 147–8n6
Aertsen, Jan A., 147n4
Agamben, Giorgio, 136–7, 138–9
Alhazen, 152n4
Alliez, Éric, 52, 147n8, 152n12, 153–4nn22, 23, 157–8n16; on ethology, 159n30
allopoietic systems, 88, 89
alterity. *See* otherness
animals, non-languaging, 69, 70–1, 73, 82, 140–1, 155n3; affective ability, 113–14, 115; apprehension of world, 60, 69; awareness of absence of object, 82, 158n24; awareness of otherness, 82, 84, 160n35; awareness of relations, 114; behaviour, 80–1, 159n30; communication between, 106–8; Heidegger on, 79–80; as interpretants, 63; participation in languaging, 109, 119–20; response to signs, 61–2, 62–3, 71, 72, 158n24; sensory-motor determination, 113–14, 115, 116; suffering, 60, 140; world of. *See Umwelt*
Ansell-Pearson, Keith, 71, 73, 141, 157n12
apprehension, human, 70, 78, 83, 84

Aquinas. *See* Thomas, Aquinas, St; Thomism
Argentinian school of neurobiology, 139, 142, 160n36, 165n5
Aristotle: on cognition, 44; realist categories, 16, 17, 69; on relation, 15–16, 17–18, 10, 25–6, 138, 147n1; on unity of being, 3, 39; on vision, 152n14
assemblages, 8, 73, 87, 127–9
Augustine, on signs, 40, 41, 49–50
autopoiesis, 12, 80–1, 86, 93, 94, 156n7, 159nn31, 32; at cellular level, 105; as cognition, 92; and communication, 107; and generation of language, 93; and *Umwelt*, 85; Varela's description, 90–1
autopoietic systems, 88–9, 94–5, 99, 128–30; and autonomy, 129, 130; organization in, 88, 129
Avicenna, 9, 39; on being, 66, 68–9, 83; influence, 44, 151–2n11, 152n14, 153n20, 155n27
Ávila, Alicia, and Mario-Fernando Crocco, 139–41, 142, 165–6nn5, 6

Baer, Eugen, 71

178 Index

Bains, Paul, ix, 4, 5, 6, 8–9; book, ix–x, 4–5; research potential, x, 5, 13, 138, 139, 143
Bakhtin, Mikhail, 104
Bateson, Gregory, 38, 73, 160–1n2; triggers to mental process, 156n10
behaviour, 12, 97–8; animal. *See under* animals, non-languaging; and structure, 97; unconscious, 114
being, 7, 133; analogical, 65–6; awareness of, 35; categorial differences, 66; equivocal, 65, 66; mind dependent, ix, 7, 9, 39, 69; mind independent, ix, 7, 9, 69; minimal, 31; objective. *See* objective being; prederivative sense of, 68, 141, 142; primary focus of intellect, 66; univocal. *See* univocal being
being-as-first-known, 66, 68, 83
being of the between, 51, 153n20. *See also* univocal being
being-toward. *See under* relations
Bergson, Henri, 71–2, 115
Beuchot, Mauricio, 43, 46
Boulnois, Olivier, 147n8
Brentano, Franz, 43

cadacualtez, 139–40, 141, 142, 165–6n6
Carroll, Lewis, 29
Cavarnos, Constantine, 147n1
Chatton, Walter, 36
Chomsky, Noam, 122, 128
cognition, ix, 11, 12, 35, 39, 44, 50; Kant on, 25, 61, 155n5; Maturano's definition, 92–4, 101. *See also* species
colour vision, 95–6, 97, 100, 101. *See also* sensory perception
communication, as social interaction, 107

concepts, 11, 49, 154–5n26; Kant on, 23; and language, 56; as representation, 54; as signs, 5, 9, 10, 39, 40, 50, 52, 54, 55, 140; subjectivity of, 5; as univocal relation, 10. *See also* ideas
Conimbricenses, 42; *De Signis*, 40–1, 150–1n3
consciousness, mystery of, 44
Corrington, Robert S., 160nn34, 35

DNA. *See* genetics, molecular
Deely, John, ix, 4, 55, 76, 78; compatibility with Deleuze and Guattari, 12–13; epigram, 133; *Four Ages of Understanding*, 138; on Hegel, 70, 148n9; on Heidegger, 84, 146n6, 150n15; on James, 148n8; on Kant, 22, 145n2, 146–7n7; *Lebenswelt*. *See Lebenswelt*; on Locke, 46–7; objective world, 60, 76–7, 78; on Peirce, 70, 83–4; on Poinsot, 6, 42, 47–8, 150n1; on reality, 7–8, 9, 20, 21; relations, ontological, 159n33; relation defined, 149n10; relative being, 75, 158n17; on Russell, 20; semiotic consciousness, 11, 20, 32, 67, 69, 75, 119, 163n28; sense, logic of, 30; on species, 46, 47–9, 152n12; transcendentality, 147n4; on *Umwelten*, 60, 75–6, 82, 83–4; on von Uexküll, 57–8, 60–1, 74
Deleuze, Gilles, ix, 4; assemblages. *See* assemblages; *Difference and Repetition*, 3, 34, 36, 73, 135, 141, 153nn20, 21, 157n15; on Duns Scotus, 150nn16, 17, 153nn20, 21; epigrams, 3, 15, 59; on events, 31–2; on external relation, 5–7, 8, 9, 20, 21, 25, 27, 42; *The Fold*, 160n37; on

Gregory, 32, 33, 36–7; on Heidegger, 153n20; on history of philosophy, 6; on Hume, 25–6; on identity, 141–2; on Leibniz, 161n6; *Logic of Sense*, 29, 84, 154–5n26, 160–1n2; and multiplicity, 28, 73; on perception, 120–1, 156–7n11; phallic imagery, 6, 146n5; relations define being, 73; on sense, 29, 30–2, 33, 83, 134, 154–5n26; and social processes, 117; Spinoza, 73, 113; on the Stoics, 31; on univocal being, 7, 9, 64, 68, 73; on von Uexküll, 64, 156–7n11

Deleuze, Gilles, and Félix Guattari, 4, 165–6n6; on art, 159n30; content and expression, 123–5, 127; epigram, 85; event-centred ontology, 16, 73; language, superlinearity of, 111, 124, 125, 162n21; on linguistics, 104, 121, 122–3; machine concepts, 95, 97, 127, 128–9; order words, 127; on organisms, 159n32; relations, ecology of, 37–8, 73; signifying systems, 104, 127; strata of the organic body, 122–3, 124, 127–9; thought, 37; *A Thousand Plateaus*, 6, 29, 72, 73, 79, 105, 110, 122–4, 126–7, 157n12 162n21; *What is Philosophy?* 4, 38, 45, 57, 138–9, 158n21, 159n30, 160n37

Deleuze, Gilles, and Claire Parnet, *Dialogues*, 21, 26–7, 28, 29, 149n4; on Stoics, 31

denotation of language, 121, 128, 164n34

Derrida, Jacques: on animals, 140–1; on Heidegger, 70; on relations, 138, 162n13, 165n3; terminology of, 137

Descartes, René: on ideas, 40, 47; on objective being, 51; on representation in the mind, 43

dreams, 119

Duns Scotus, John, 4, 9, 10, 33–4; being, 65–6; being of known in the knower, 37, 153n20; concepts as signs, 39, 52, 55; and nominalism, 51–2, 153n21; objective being, 35, 37, 42, 50, 53, 56; on signs, 39, 151n6; on species, 152n15; univocity of being, 34–5, 64, 65, 157–8n16. *See also* Scotism

Dupréel, Eugene, 129

Eco, Umberto, 164n35
ecology: generalized, 135; political, 135–6; of relations, 37–8
Elie, Hubert, 33
Emmeche, Claus, 160n36
empiricism, 25, 26, 27; and multiplicity, 28
ens rationis. *See* mind-dependent *under* being
ens reale. *See* mind-independent *under* being
esse objectivum. *See* objective being
ethical issues, 12, 13, 118, 133–4, 136–7; arising from mutual acceptance, 125; and languaging, 125–6
ethology. *See* behaviour *under* animals, non-languaging
event, philosophy of, 16, 31–2, 73
experiential worlds, 7, 22, 74; Deely's model, 76–7; semiotic account of, 146n6; trichotomous, 7, 70; univocal web of sign relations, 42, 57, 69, 75

Ferré, Frederick, 165n4
firstness. *See* apprehension, human

Fonseca, Pedro de, 40–2
Foucault, Michel, 104, 117, 126, 164n34
Frege, Gottlob, 37
frog's eye experiment, 113–14; fly catching, 114–15
fuzzy logic, 130, 164n37

Gaboriau, Florent, 151n6
Gasché, Rodolphe, 138, 164n2
genetics, molecular, 105, 111, 124, 129
Gregory, of Rimini, 32–3, 149n11; comparison with Stoics, 32, 150n13; *complexe significabile*, 33, 35, 39, 55, 137, 154–5n26; object of proposition, 36; on sense, 30, 35–6
Guagliardo, Vincent, 165n3
Guattari, Félix, 4, 13; and autopoiesis, 12, 86; *Chaosmosis*, 7, 11, 12, 32, 78, 86, 152n16, 163n28; epigram, 85, 133; ethical issues, 134; on identity, 13; on manner of being, 82–3; on relation, 5, 12, 152n16; on subjectivity, 78, 134. *See also* Deleuze, Gilles; Deleuze, Gilles, and Félix Guattari

Haar, Michel, 159n32, 160n37
Hayden, Patrick, 148n9; on Russell, 149n1
Hegel, Georg: on relation, 70, 148n8; systems, enclosed, 8
Heidegger, Martin, 3, 4, 91; on being, 35, 67, 80, 83, 150n15, 153n20; on biology, 79, 158–9n28, 159n29; epigram, 59; *Fundamental Concepts of Metaphysics*, 70, 78–82, 158–9n28; on knowledge, 145n6; phenomenology, 75; on signs, 151n6; on worlds, 60, 79–81

Hjelmslev, Louis, 123
Hume, David, 5–6, 20; on externality of relation, 25, 26, 149n2
human beings: ethical issues, 118, 125–6, 133–4; infancy and language, 124–5; mental functions, 118–19, 163n28; as networks of conversations, 112, 117–18, 118–19; and social systems, 117; structural change to bodyhoods, 111–12, 124–5, 162nn12, 21
human societies, 125; change in, 117, 127; communication without physical interaction, 111; culture, 126; development of language. *See under* language; multiplicity of domains of existence. *See* multiplicity; mutual acceptance in, 125
Husserl, Edmund, 30, 37, 43, 152n18

ideas, 40, 48, 49, 51, 53; Locke's definition, 46–7. *See also* concepts
identity, 13, 16, 112, 129, 141–2; and difference, 135
information, 105–6, 108, 128
intentionality, 43, 44, 57, 137, 151n8, 152n18, 153–4n23; species as medium for, 45
interest, 3
interpretants, 11, 50, 63, 78, 152n16
ipseity, 140–1
Irigaray, Luce, 142–3
Islamic thought, influence of, 151–2n11, 152n14. *See also* Avicenna

Jacob, François, 105
James, William, 4, 19, 20, 148nn8, 9; pluralism, 21, 27–8; *A Pluralistic Universe*, 21
John, of St Thomas. *See* Poinsot, John

Jonas, Hans, 21–2
Jung, Carl, 164n32

Kant, Immanuel, 4, 7, 145n2, 146–7n7; categories, 16, 69–70; on cognition, 25, 61, 155n5; on experience, 22; on ideas, 53, 154n24; on relation, 16, 19, 161n5; on sense, 22–3; transcendental, 147n4
Klossowski, Pierre, 154–5n26
knowledge, 8, 12, 93, 146n6, 146–7n7
known in the knower. *See* objective being

Labov, William, 104
language, ix, 32, 37, 84; and apprehension of *Umwelt*, 60, 69, 75; autonomy of, 111, 124–5, 130; as consensual, 102, 104, 110, 115, 130; content and expression, 123–4; as coordination of acts, 104, 111, 115, 128; and creativity, 130–1; denotation of, 121, 128, 164n34; generation of, 99, 104–5, 108, 110–11; and internal dialogue, 118–19, 120; in isolation, 120; and observation, 113; order words, 127; origins of, 121, 125, 164n30; and recursive acts, 121, 122, 125; as relation, 12, 82, 102, 122, 127; and self-consciousness, 12, 102, 108–9, 113, 115, 116, 118–19; as semiotic, 12; and social forces, 104–5; as social phenomenon, 115, 117, 122–3, 125; and the speech act. *See* speech act; from structural coupling, 102; transferability, 71, 72–3, 124, 130. *See also under names of philosophers*
languaging, ix, 12
languaging acts: ethical meaning of, 125–6; social character of, 126–7. *See also* speech act
languaging entity, 108–9, 162n16
Latour, Bruno, x, 4, 60, 155n2; political ecology, 135–6; realism, 9, 21; substance, 147–8n6
Lebenswelt, 13, 71, 75, 82, 83. *See also Umwelten*
Lecercle, Jean-Jacques, 29–30, 110, 162n18
Leclerc, Ivor, 136
Leibniz, Gottfried Wilhelm von: monad theory, 89–90, 161nn4, 6; relations internal, 161n6
lekton, 30, 33, 36, 137. *See also* sense
life, 138, 140
linguistic domain, 108–9; communication between animals, 107; participation in, 116–17
Linguistic Society of Paris, 164n30
linguistics, 30, 104, 107, 121, 122–3
Locke, John, 46–7

Magnus, Albert, 41
Maritain, Jacques, 43, 52–3, 73, 152n12, 153n19; on Kant, 53, 154n24
Massumi, Brian, 123–4; epigram, 133
Maturana, Humberto, 4, 7, 155n4, 156n2, 157n13, 159n31; animals and language, 82; on cognition, 12, 92–3; on consensual coordination, 109, 116, 117; on culture, 126; on Heidegger, 91; on information, 105–6; on language, ix, 102–3, 122; on objectivity, 103; on reality, 90; on self-consciousness, 114, 163n25; on social systems, 117
Maturana, Humberto and Francisco

182 Index

Varela: *Autopoiesis and Cognition*, 86, 89; autopoietic machines, 94–5, 99, 129; biology and cognition of language, 85; cognition, 92–4, 101, 110, 118; communication, 107–8; generative mechanisms, 99; language generation, 87, 89, 99, 100, 102, 106, 110–11, 121, 125; and Leibniz, 89, 90; on linguistics, 107; living systems, operationally defined, 86–8, 93, 95–7, 100, 161n3, 162n22; living systems, organization of components, 88, 89, 97–9; objectivity, 94; observer description, 86–7, 90, 109, 116, 118; scientific hypothesis, 99; self-consciousness, 87, 98, 102; sensory perception, 95–6; signs as exterior to organism, 105; structural coupling 100, 101–2, 106; structural determinism, 97–8, 100, 128
Maturana, Humberto, Jorge Mpodozis, and Juan Carlos Letelier, 119, 163n28
McCulloch, Warren
Meinong, Alexius, 30, 33, 36; extra being, 32
metaphysics, 34, 66
mind, 119, 163n28
monism, 21, 148n8
Monod, Jacques, 129
Multitudes (journal), 136
multiplicity, 8, 9, 28, 73, 104, 112, 115
Muralt, André de, 146–7n7, 147n8, 153n19; on Duns Scotus, 55; on Gregory, 36–7, 150n13; on objective being, 52; on Poinsot, 51–2, 53–4, 55

nature/culture dualism, x, 50, 67, 70, 75, 103, 145n2, 153n20; and signs, 103
nervous system, 85–6, 93, 95, 97; closed system, 100, 113–14, 115, 116; and language, 111, 118–19; relations not perceived, 119; submarine navigator analogy, 86–7. *See also* sensory perception
Neville, Robert Cumming, 165n4
Nietzsche, Friedrich, 6, 137, 162n20; idea of the world, 90; social processes, 117; on univocal being, 150n17, 153n20, 157n15
nominalism, 7, 19, 26, 31, 52, 153n21
non-languaging. *See* animals, non-languaging

objective, 60
objective being, 10, 35, 39–40, 50–1, 52–3, 77–8; intentional existence in knower, 44, 52; as relation or event, 37; understanding of, 36, 42–3, 153n20. *See also* being
objective worlds, 70–1, 74, 75; Deely's model, 60, 76–7, 78; threshold to, 82, 83. *See also Umwelten*
objectivity, 50–1, 94, 103; biological impossibility, 96–7, 102; expressed and signified, 37. *See also* truth of the relative
objects, 10, 11, 35, 36, 45; in language, 112; linguistic distinctions, 109–10; and relations, 28–9, 42, 134, 154–5n26
observation, 115; and language, 113
observers, 118, 122; descriptions by, 86–7, 90, 118; and imagination, 130; and information, 128; and sign production, 121
ontogeny, 129–30

ontology, 34
otherness, 84; awareness in animals, 82, 84, 160n35

Peiffer, John, 151n10
Peirce, Charles Sanders, 4, 5, 19, 32, 33; autosemiopoiesis, 153n20; Firstness, 83, 84; interpretants, 11, 50, 78, 152n16; Scotist influences, 55, 153n21; semiotic categorial schemes, 70, 78
Perler, Dominik, 55–6
phenomenology, 33, 43, 75
philosophy (western), 13, 51; history of, 4, 6, 32, 33–4, 36; realist/idealist oscillations, 4; on relation, 25–6
Piaget, Jean: brain and mind, 100; on structure, 99–100
'plane of consistency.' *See* relations; relations *under* language
pluralism, 21; and externality, 28
Poinsot, John, ix, 4, 5, 9–10; at Coimbra, 42; Deely as translator, ix, 6, 9; objective being, 37, 42, 78, 154n24; ontological relations, 6–7, 9, 10, 17–19, 26, 134, 147–8n6, 149n5; relation and intentionality of thought, 43; on Scotism, 51, 153n19; semiotics based on univocity of relations, 38, 56, 153n20; signs and relations, 9, 33, 42, 53–4, 55, 67, 68; on species, 48, 152n15; *Tractus de Signis*, 6, 8, 18, 19, 33, 54–5, 147–8n6
Poster, Mark, 161n3
postmodernism, 4, 6, 60, 118, 140, 155n2
propositions: neutrality of, 37; relation with the physical, 37, 39; understanding of, 36–7

rationalism, 25, 28
realism, 4, 9, 21, 154n24
reality, 7–8, 9, 20, 21, 57, 90, 91–2; consensual, 99; Kant on, 23; Maturana on, 90, 118; mind-dependent, 118, 163n28; mind-independent, 35, 69; semiotic, 21
relatio secundum dici. See relations, transcendental
relatio secundum esse. See relations, ontological
relations, 11–12, 66–7, 133, 138, 164n2; and being, 11, 57; being-toward another, 11, 138; and categories, 69; event centred, 7; dependence on mind, ix, 19, 20; dependence on subject, 15–16; externality of, ix, 3, 4–5, 28, 66–7; human recognition of, 82; between knower and known, 12, 50; responsibility for, 12, 13, 133–4; and self, 11; signs as, 9; suprasubjectivity of, 11; triadic, 50, 70, 75; as web-like, 76–7; Whitehead on, 135–6
relations, concept of, 9, 20, 21, 35; history, 7, 17–18, 19–23
relations, ontological, ix, 3, 4–5, 17, 18, 19, 28, 147–8n6, 159n33; and categories of being, 67, 69; ecology of, 37–8; and minimal being, 31; and semiotics, 32; univocity of, ix, 7, 32, 66–7
relations, transcendental, 17, 18–19, 28, 67–8, 149nn5, 10
relative being, 57; and relations, 73; transcendental, 67–8
relative terms, 17–19
representations, 10, 146–7n7; of being, 35; and signification, 47, 54–5; and thought, 35

184 Index

rhizome metaphor, 122–3, 164n32
Robinson Crusoe, 120
robots and *Umwelt*, 83, 158n27, 160n36
Russell, Bertrand, 4, 19; on relation, 20, 136, 148n9
Ruyer, Raymond, 4, 71, 83, 139, 158n21, 159n32; on Helen Keller, 72; on James, 148n8

Santiago School of Cognition, 163n28
scholastic period, 39, 40–4, 50–1, 141. *See also* Scotism; Thomism
science, 158–9n28; as consensual reality, 99, 161n11; as explanation of human experience, 90; objectivity, 57; structural determinism, 98; truth of the relative, 74, 158n26
Scotism, 3, 10, 25–6, 34; on cognition, 50; on external relation, 26; on objective being, 35, 51, 153n19. *See also* Duns Scotus, John; scholastic period
Sebeok, Thomas, 61, 75, 76; epigram, 59
self, 11, 108–9; generated from language, 109; and internal dialogues, 120
self-consciousness, 87, 98, 102, 114; arising from language, 12, 102, 108–9, 113, 115, 116, 118–19; as social phenomenon, 115–16
self-production. *See* autopoiesis
self-relation, 141
semiosis, 5, 17; anthroposemiosis, 67, 69, 71, 76, 82; and categorial schema, 67, 68; and language, 70–1; as process in nature, 60–1, 63; zoosemiosis, 60, 140

semiotic consciousness, 11, 20, 32, 67, 75, 119, 163n28
semiotic reality, 8, 9, 21, 57, 77; limitless, 68, 71; univocal, 68
semiotics, 31–2, 57, 71, 84; based in univocal relation, 32, 69, 153n20; of concepts, 5; of Duns Scotus and Poinsot, 55; and experience, 69, 75; nature and culture in, 67, 70, 153n20; postmodern, 140; terminology, history of, 40–1
semovience, 142, 165–6n6
sensation, 48
sense, theory of, 29, 30–2, 154–5n26; Kant on, 22–3. *See also* lekton
sense data: as semiotic, 20; as relational, 20, 148n7
sensory perception, 95–6, 97, 161n9
Serres, Michel, 9
signs, 9, 39, 40, 50, 53, 55, 75; debate about, 40–1; defined by Augustine, 40, 41, 49–50; as exterior, 105; language prerequisite, 121, 130; as relations, 7, 9, 42, 49, 57, 67, 91, 134, 151n6, 165n3; and signification, 104, 114, 122, 137; in thought, 135; transferability of, 71–2; triggers for animals, 61–2; as univocal, 67, 68, 103
signs, formal, 10, 41, 49–50, 53; and psychological states, 140; as subjective, 40, 42, 74. *See also* concepts
signs, instrumental, 41, 52, 53
social insects: structural coupling, 106–7; trophallaxis, 111
solipsism, 102
species, 10, 41, 44–6, 47–8, 56, 73–4, 152nn12, 13; *expressae*, 49; *impressae*, 46, 48–9, 50; as signs, 47, 56
species-specific worlds. *See Umwelt*

speech act, 110, 121–2, 127, 162n19
Sperry, Roger, 113, 162–3n23
Spinoza, Benedictus de, 6, 38; on univocal being, 64, 73, 150n17, 153n20, 157n15
Spruit, Leen, 45, 152nn13, 14
Stengers, Isabelle, 4, 135–6; epigram, 3
Stern, Daniel, 163n28
Stoic philosophy, 6–7, 29, 31, 137, 160–1n2; object of proposition, 36; semiotic, 30; sense, 30–1
structural coupling, 100, 101–2, 106
structure: and behaviour, 97–8; generative, 98–9; of Piaget, 99–100
Suárez, Francisco, 47
subjectivity, 11, 50–1, 77–8
subject relation as attribute, 25–6
substance, 147–8n6
Szirko, Mariela, 139–40, 165n5, 166n8

text, 71
textualism, 161n13
thirdness, 42, 156n9
Thomas, Aquinas, St; on cognition, 44; on intentionality, 153n23
Thomism, 3, 10, 25–6, 151nn9, 10; cognition and intentionality, 42, 43–4, 50; concept as formal sign, 52; objective being, 50–1, 153n19; realism, 10, 43; relation, 20, 26, 43; on signs, 53, 54. *See also* scholastic period; Thomas, Aquinas St
thought, 8, 37, 38, 134, 143, 146–7n7; and being, 35, 69; categorial, 65; image of, 8, 51; intentionality of, 43; and realism, 154n24; and relations, 4, 8, 9, 143; as representation, 35; and signs, 135; as subjective, 29

ticks, 62–3, 73, 113, 156–7nn10, 11
Tournier, Michel, 120
transcendental relations. *See* relations, transcendental
transcendentality, 33–4
triad. *See under* relation
truth of the relative, 74, 103, 158n26

Umwelt sign theory, ix, 7, 11. *See also* semiotics
Umwelten, 7, 11, 60–1, 64, 70, 72, 73, 75–6, 77, 81, 114, 137; human/animal threshold, 82, 160n34; objective being, 60, 64, 74; reality, 91–2
univocal being, 3, 7, 9, 34–5, 36, 39, 64, 65, 68, 73, 153n20; apprehension of, 69; linguistic expression of, 69; pre-categorical, 67, 69. *See also* being
univocity, 34–5, 37; of being. *See* univocal being; of experience, 74; of relation, ix, 9

Varela, Francisco, 7, 12, 157n13, 160n1; animal communication, 108; on autopoiesis, 90–1; language as emergent property, 104; mind/brain, 163n28. *See also* Maturana, Humberto; Maturana, Humberto, and Francisco Varela
vitalism. *See* life
von Frisch, Karl, 72–3, 77
von Uexküll, Jakob, ix, 7, 11, 32, 38, 57–8, 61, 75–8, 157n13; influence of Kant, 11, 64, 77, 96, 158n21; and perception, 96; signs as triggers, 62–3
von Uexküll, Thure, 61, 63; reference to Leibniz, 89, 91–2

Wahl, Jean, 149n3
Weinberg, Julius R., 7, 15; *Concept of Relation*, 7; on relation, 16, 19, 20
Whitehead, Alfred North, 4, 16, 146–7n7; prehension, 43, 136; on relations, 135–6
William, of Ockham, 4, 7, 36; nominalism, 18, 19, 33; realism, 47; understanding of proposition, 36

Winograd, Terry, and Fernando Flores, 105, 162n19
Wittgenstein, Ludwig, on language, 60

Zourabichvili, François, 38, 134, 146–7n7, 160n30; epigram, 39

www.ingramcontent.com/pod-product-compliance
Lightning Source LLC
Chambersburg PA
CBHW030321080526
44584CB00012B/654